The Grand Design of Dreams

Contemplating Divine Revelation

by

Dr. Steven A. Ross, Ph.D.

with
Dr. Jeffrey P. Wincel, D.Min.

Theosis Press
5121 N. 71st Place
Paradise Valley, AZ 85253
© 2019 by Steven A. Ross & Jeffrey P. Wincel
No Claim to original U.S. Government works
Printed in the United States of America
International Standard Book Number- 978-0-9833257-7-2
(paperback)
Printed and bound by Lulu Publishing
Cover design by Emily Wincel

This book contains information obtained from authentic and highly regarded sources. Reprinted material is quoted with permission, and sources are listed. A wide variety of references are listed. Reasonable efforts have been made to publish reliable data and information, but the author and the publisher cannot assume responsibility for the validity of all material or the consequences of their use.

Library of Congress Control Number: 2019907814

Note on Websites: The publisher has used its best endeavors to ensure that the URLs for external website referred to in this book are correct and active at the time of going to press. However, the publisher has no responsibility for the websites and can make no guarantee that a site will remain live or that the content is or will remain appropriate.

The·oph·a·ny (THēˈäfənē)

from late Latin theophania and from late Greek theophaneia,
meaning "appearance of God"
(Theo-, God + phainein, to show)

A mystical manifestation or appearance of God, one that may
be visible, audible but not be material - reflects allusions to the
Divine.

Jacob's Dream at Bethel.
(Gen 28:12-16)

*Then he [Jacob] had a dream: a stairway rested on the ground, with its top
reaching to the heavens; and God's angels were going up and down on it.*

*And there was the LORD standing beside him and saying: I am the
LORD, the God of Abraham your father and the God of Isaac; the land
on which you are lying I will give to you and your descendants.*

*Your descendants will be like the dust of the earth, and through them you
will spread to the west and the east, to the north and the south. In you and
your descendants all the families of the earth will find blessing.*

*I am with you and will protect you wherever you go, and bring you back to
this land. I will never leave you until I have done what I promised you.*

*When Jacob awoke from his sleep, he said, "Truly, the LORD is in this
place and I did not know it!"*

New American Bible, revised edition

Table of Contents

Dedications

This book is dedicated to the True Higher Self of Life that dwells within each individual.

- Steven Ross

Within the complexities, discoveries, and challenges of life, being surrounded with those who love, cherish, honor and support you makes the journey a sweet one. It is to those who I dedicate this book.

- Jeffrey Wincel

Acknowledgements

I would like to acknowledge Deborah Cambio who has come into my life through time at this time. She has brought wisdom, beauty, integrity, love, laughter and fun into my life.

I would also like to honor my parents who were always supportive and provided a beautiful home of love that was filled with music and art.

To Edward A. Monroe and Jock McKinnetry who set my feet on the pathway of spirituality and philosophy.

I want to thank Jeff Wincel who volunteered to help me write this book and whose long hours of work have produced this beautifully written history of my life.

Finally, it is important for me to acknowledge the unseen spiritual entities that have provided me with support, guidance and encouragement throughout my life and without them I would have missed the true richness and beauty of the true underpinnings of this physical reality.

- Steven Ross

An endeavor like this takes time, time and more time away from those you love. This is especially true of your spouse and partner. In this I must again acknowledge with love and gratitude Heather, my spouse and partner in all things.

It is with great appreciation and humility that I thank and honor Steve Ross for asking me to join him on this project. To be asked to help voice the experiences and discoveries of someone's life is a great honor. His trust and confidence are more than I deserve.

Lastly, I want to acknowledge the special love that I have for my children and grand-children. There are not many ways we are able to leave the world in a better place than we found it; through them I have found a way. Take on the world with passion!

- JPW

Foreword

By Cyndi Dale, Author of *The Subtle Body Encyclopedia* and the related series. www.cyndidale.com

For thousands of years, the Australian Aboriginals have spoken about the Dreaming. At one level, the Dreaming marks the beginning of Creation, at which time the Original Ancestors broke through a cold and lifeless earth and then breathed life into rocks, plants, animals, and humans. Dreaming isn't only a time period, however.

More fundamentally, Dreaming is the state of our greatest awareness and power. While usually considered a temporary experience, in which we linger between wakefulness and sleeping, it is actually always available, a "somewhere" that isn't only accidently discovered when we're nodding off. Dreaming is a way of being and it lies inside of us.

It is in the Dreaming that we relate to God, the Holiest of Holies, the Oneness that wears many names and faces. It is also in the Dreaming that we allow God to see us. Stripped away are our cloaking devices, from make-up to make-believe. What remains is our essential self, God, and the communication between us.

We reach the Dreaming through our dreams, which serve as the portals into—and the extensions of—the greater Dreaming space. In our dreams, a special sort of alchemy occurs. Besides communing, we also dream the dreams that become our life, crafting the storylines we call "happenings." It stands to reason that the more time we consciously spend within the Dreaming, or within our dreams, the more playful, loving, and joyous our scripts will become.

Most of us haven't been raised to find or negotiate the Dreaming, much less remember, cultivate, or analyze our dreams. But across time, all known and unknown luminaries have employed their dreams to perform healing and manifesting, receiving inspiration and guidance in the process. How can you learn to do the same?

There is no better D/dreaming advisor than Dr. Steven Ross, whose brilliant teachings and tellings are assisted by Dr. Jeffrey Wincel in this amazing book, A Grand Design of Dreams, which reveals the means for receiving divine revelation through your dreams.

In his book, Steve so aptly points out that you don't need to bend and twist to relate to your dreams. Neither do you need to be an established guru, saint, or metaphysician. We all dream. We always dream. To assure that our dream interactions are fruitful, however, we must apply ourselves. Steve has been fostering and analyzing his own brilliant dreams for over 40 years and is standing ready, through this book, to light the way for you.

It takes courage to seek inside what we've been taught to find outside of ourselves. I know. I spent most of my life in an "external odyssey," traveling from here to there to discover the secrets to life. Namely, I was looking for my soul, which was hidden underneath a Norwegian-Protestant upbringing that left little room for color and shadow.

Journey I did, amongst shamans and healers along the winding Amazon, through the deserts of Morocco, atop the mountains of Venezuela, and within the temples of Kyoto. While pursuing certainty and truth in far-off places, I also attended a Christian seminary, attempted to teach myself Sanskrit, participated in Lakota sweat lodges, and studied psychic phenomenon. While I gained insight and education, my deeper self evaded me, as did an easy way to connect with God. I started to feel as if my searching was as evasive as that light seen in the periphery of the eye. Move your head and away it dashes.

As Steve explains, the ladder of enlightenment, the touch-stone of our own spirit, doesn't dwell in the external world. The center point is in our dreams, which occur inside of us. Ironically, this nail was hammered in because of the way in which I met Steve.

I've known Steve about twelve years. When I first contacted him, I was—and still am—an intuitive and energy healer. I was also an author.

One fateful day, I accepted a phenomenal assignment. A publishing company asked me to write a subtle body manual. I was honored but also completely overwhelmed. I had no idea where to start, how to gather all the research, and what theme I should adopt. All I knew was that the deadline was so tight that I would have to finish the project as soon as I started it.

Lying abed that night, I asked God to help. Then I went to sleep—and dreamed.

In my dream, angels ushered me into a room full of books. At a table sat a librarian, but what a librarian. He was wearing a hat made of stars and reading—and maybe writing—the grandest manuscript I'd ever seen. My feet made a tiny noise and he lifted his eyes from the work and gazed into me. Then the entire scene disappeared in a blaze of light.

I knew that I needed to meet that librarian!

The next morning, I received a call from a friend. He was super excited, having returned from Sedona the day before.

"Have you heard of the World Research Foundation?" my friend asked.

I hadn't, but ought to have. Apparently, the World Research Foundation (WRF) was THE global source of health information. Its founder, world-renown Dr. Steven Ross, had gathered into his library thousands of volumes of books, from ancient texts to modern research. Having traveled the world to discover—and sometimes rescue—these pieces, he was making the related knowledge available through newsletters, teachings, and the use of the library. Of course, he employed dream-guidance to figure out which people to contact in order to locate the manuscripts.

I called the WRF, expecting to be greeted by a receptionist. Instead, Steve answered the phone.

Within a few days, a box of WRF newsletters, as well as pages copied from one-of-a-kind documents, arrived at my doorstep. I could hardly lift the box. During our initial conversation, Steve had already pinpointed the exact theme of my book and the basic organizational structure. In short, his virtuosity created my book, which has since been reprinted over and over and has won several publisher's awards.

Since that initial connection, my awe of Steve and his vocation has only increased. I daresay that few have embodied the magic of the dream world as completely and thoroughly as has Steve, who could now be said to be walking and talking directly with the gods.

As is Steve, I'm aware that our inner world isn't the only world, but it is the connection point between our true self, our worldly self, God, Nature, and the countless spirits who seek to assist us. Steve makes this fact clear through his sharings in this book. After first offering instruction on cultivating your own dream-life, he next outlines dozens of his own dreams and their interpretations. He then features the many way-showers whose dreams and knowledge have lit our world with truth.

You'll meet Phineas Quimby, the founder of the New Thought movement, who revealed the Creator present in all Creation. In attendance will be J.R. Newton, whose connection to the Divine enabled the healing of over 200,000 individuals. You'll help Dr. Royal Rife rediscover an incredible and curative microscope and dine with German healers of all backgrounds, who have understood that manifesting and healing is actually quite simple, beginning with clean living and right diet.

In the end, the sum total of every analysis, story, and rendering will underscore the highest truth of all. Everything is made of the light of love. With the assistance of God and the divine helpers, always available through our dreams, we can clear our blocks and find our way; after all, our problems are nothing more than congested light. We can then set afire our own spirit. Aglow, you can join with the ranks of men like Steve and Jeff and make manifest the heaven already embedded in this earth.

Preface

By Jeffrey P. Wincel. D.Min.

During my career, I have had the opportunity to meet and work with amazing and interesting people. My definition of "amazing and interesting" typically has meant those who were able to inspire, encourage, challenge, and essentially leave me in some level of "awe". Steve Ross is exactly one of those people. To try to chronicle Steve's life and experiences is like trying to capture lightning in a bottle.

That however is exactly what we will try to capture here. A book dedicated to not just sharing an inspiring life story, but also one to provide a means for expanded personal discovery, inspiration, and spiritual guidance. A book dedicated to provide both practical practice and inspirational motivation. Practice and motivation, inspiration and lessons on the beauty and meaning of life. While you may encounter "religious" themes as we experience the unfolding of Steve's journey, this does not propose or advocate any specific religious practice. We leave the alignment of that to you and the tradition that calls to you.

It is easy to look at Steve's life experiences with admiration and wonder. His life seems to be one of miracles; from the daily miracles many of us miss or don't appreciate to the transcendent and divinely inspired miracles that profoundly change lives. Nearly every spiritual tradition shares a common theme – to live in the present moment…and to listen to inspiration (whether intuition or divine guidance). This has been the effortless reality of how Steve has journeyed through his life. Many of us struggle to find this peace and purpose, essentially "white knuckling" it through life. Steve's example can be one that encourages all of us that it can be far simpler and much more natural.

Steve has been a world class athlete, an exceedingly successful businessman, a health investigator and activist, a speaker and presenter, a researcher and academician, and a total body healer. He has worked with leaders in every one of these areas, has made discoveries and rediscoveries of new and ancient healing modalities, and has been the archivist and preserver of critical knowledge and inventions. This book will explore these experiences and show how to access inspiration and guidance through dream reflection, meditation and interpretation. This has been the means by which Steve's guidance has led to his actions.

As you progress through this book, we encourage you to approach the suggestions and dreams with an openness to the potential of your own inspirations. Those that you can begin to unlock. It's not necessary to try to imitate or emulate the examples shared with you. Simply endeavor to find a practice that opens you up to the possibility of your own theophany. See in Steve's examples and the recommended practices for your own future.

It is an honor to be working with Steve on this book, and it is my hope that you enjoy reading it as much as we have enjoyed writing it.

About the Author

The Author, The Librarian

Steven Ross is president and co-founder of the World Research Foundation. For nearly 40 years, he has been the librarian and caretaker for a 30,000-volume health and philosophical library. Steve has acted as an expert witness in health and environmental issues for government municipalities; been an invited guest on over a hundred radio programs; had two near-death experiences and had possession of one of the greatest scientific discoveries of the ages.

A Grand Design of Dreams is based on Steve's 45 years of literary, scientific and spiritual discoveries made throughout the world. However, it is more than just a story; it is intended to inspire people to pursue more within their own life. Steve examines the revelation, inspiration, and life lessons that are manifest in our dream state. He shows that these experiences are not distant, unattainable or clouded, but easily accessible.

Steve has traveled around the world investigating state-of-the-art health therapies as well as deciphering ancient alchemical books and scrolls to help learn and share secrets of the past. He has spent his adult life studying various philosophical regimes but has never joined any group or organization. He believes that we all possess a great internal guiding mechanism within us. This mechanism is our day and night dreams. We must have the trust to follow the gifts that come to us at these times.

Discovering a Loving Philosophy

In Steve's words, he was very reluctant to write this book. Not because he didn't feel that he had meaningful and unique information to share, but he felt there are more than enough books available to read about dreams, spirituality and personal discovery. In preparing for this journey of writing, Steve was reminded of the lyrics of a Dusty

Springfield song, 'what the world needs now, is love, sweet love, that's the only thing that there's far too little of...'

These lyrics meant to Steve that in our lives and discoveries, we need to demonstrate a *loving philosophy* as opposed to just talking a good story. His approach to this book then is to provide more than just added "noise" to spiritual discovery and self-exploration. It is a reminder that life can be magic.

The magic of our own lives sometimes escapes us, and it takes the observations of others to help us more clearly see our own alchemy. It was Steve's friends who finally convinced him that perhaps others might be interested in magic of this 40-year investigative journey. Those who had heard the mystery around these discovery experiences reminded Steve that his life is indeed magical and the wisdom and knowledge he gained needed to be shared. Steve didn't see this path as anything more than normal, it had just been his life not thinking that others might find it helpful. While he has never joined any groups or organizations, Steve none the less found a wonderful divine or spiritual influence overshadowing his journey.

Steve's *loving philosophy* can be summed up with the acronym LEFL. It stands for Laughter, Excitement, Fun and Love. This has been Steve's guiding principle throughout his life. After 40 years of counseling others, he discovered that if someone's "LEFL-ometer" is charged then health is present – physical, emotional, and spiritual. However, if any one of these aspects is lacking then they begin to lose life energy which leads to health and well-being challenges.

By sharing some of the experiences and discoveries of his life, Steve hopes that you will come to understand that the choices each of us make creates the pathway of our lives. The pathways can be meaningful, purposeful, and deliberate or they can be random, without meaning, and unconscious. How we recognize, respond, and react to the experiences and discoveries determine the ease, quality and joyfulness of the pathway.

Steve has discovered that sometimes those who seem to talk the most, often have the least to say. There are those who offer that they have discovered the secret of the ages but can't seem to find the secret to living well within their own life. It appears through Steve's observation that particularly those in the media who give advice to others, don't seem to be able to function in their own real world. There is often a tendency to over complicate; to act as if only a few possess the skill, enlightenment and intellect to access the truth. The discovery of the truth and the mystery in the spiritual life is its simplicity. The many and obvious ways in which we are spoken to. The plentiful signs, symbols and messages surround and are presented to us daily.

The Purpose of this Book

So, what is the purpose of this book? To inspire, encourage, empower and support YOU. To assist you in understanding that your journey through life is to be honored and respected. To believe in YOU. We don't have to be perfect to accomplish beauty in life because we ARE beautiful. Your life is your journey and your journey is the right path.

Often the challenge in traveling down a path of growth is seeing the simplicity that may be right in front of us. In this book, we explore how the simplicity of our dreams and understanding their message shapes who we are. We all dream, whether it occurs by day or night, but few of us dare to follow our dreams and visions or give them the importance that they deserve. Perhaps this book will encourage you to take the step and follow through with the gift of guidance that comes through these times of inspiration.

This book includes Steve's worldwide discoveries of important health techniques, perhaps rediscovering therapies and practices that you can use in your own life. Also included in the following pages, you will find scattered pearls of wisdom from ancient and modern teachers, without the unnecessary weight of social, scientific or theological orthodoxy.

The many interesting facts and informative ideas just might provide to you, greater happiness, fun, health and love in your life.

Join Steven Ross in exploring this journey and discover your own piece of divinity reveled to you in your dreams of theophany.

Part I – Theophany of the Spirit

Introduction

The spiritual masters throughout the ages have been called prophets, teachers, masters, gurus, messiahs and saviors. Their traditions believe them to be essence or founders or fulfillment of religious and spiritual destiny. For their followers they embody the fullness of the faith, the fullness of the truth, and the fullness of revelation.

Regardless of their tradition, all of these masters share as common trait, the ability to take the ethereal, the transcendent, and the divine and make them accessible, understandable, and relatable. These masters aren't sharing theologies or dogmas, they are sharing stories of revelation and purpose. They use story, whether it be parables, visions or myths, they make plain that which is transcendent; relatable that which is mystery; and clear that which is symbolic.

The voice of God, the Divine, the source continues to be heard, or better said, continues to be spoken. The journey of spiritual enlightenment and growth of the soul is the pursuit of hearing this voice, being enlivened to it and acting upon it. Those responding to the call of this journey can spend a lifetime seeking externally that which is already present internally.

As in the story of Jacob's ladder, revelation, truth and purpose can be made clear simply in a dream. The victory in Jacob's dream is not the gift offered by God, but Jacob's acceptance of the gift. Recognizing the dream is the offer to believe, to respond, and to act. *Jacob awoke from his sleep, he said, "Truly, the LORD is in this place and I did not know it!"*

The purpose of this book is to offer to you the reader, the simple idea that your purpose, the revelation meant for you, and the direction of your life is ready for you to access. This book offers an idea and a design of how to make sense of that which often seems beyond understanding. It offers to you the idea that your dreams are more than random neuro-connections processing your conscious day's events. It offers to you that within our dreams the voice of the Divine can be heard.

> *The dreams which reveal the supernatural are promises and messages that God sends us directly: they are nothing but His angels, His ministering spirits, who usually appear to us when we are in a great predicament.*
>
> Paracelsus, 15th/16th century Swiss Physician

The Energetic Journey

In almost every spiritual, religious or wisdom tradition, instructors, theologians and spiritual masters teach that "victory has already been written." In that, while we may struggle mightily in the earthly plain, that struggle may be unnecessary. What we see as darkness and negativity is a defeated enemy in its final death throes, grasping and clawing its last vestiges of power and control. But the authority to ascend to ones' divine nature has already been provided. The wisdom to journey a different path is ours to take.

Within ourselves we have the ingredients to ascend to a higher vibration, to experience wisdom and enlightenment. Ingredients that simply need to be energized and animated. We could be considered receivers of divine energy, so the power to animate may not originate from within us, but it flows to and through us and requires us to participate in the empowerment that has been written for each of us.

In the ancient Christian churches of the East, the Orthodox recognize the *Energeia of God* (the energies of God) as a reality and manifestation of God different than the Essence (*Ousia*) of God. This tradition considers God's Essence is ultimately unknowable, but the Energies of God fully realizable. It is these Energies which we arouse within ourselves, that lead to our divine being, and raise our own energies. THIS is the path that we are meant to travel.

But this is not typically the path that most of us travel. Our humanness, or perhaps our human frailty, creates the condition in which we are pulled back from the ascendance. How we see this opportunity is the result of our conditioning. Conditioning that can be both externally initiated or from our internal dialogue. This counter ascendant pull might be called low vibration, dark, evil or even demonic. Perhaps, yes, but equally as likely simply a loss of our humanity in our humanness. The transition from this lower journey to that of the higher Energeia is the proving ground of the soul and the path of the spirit.

The Gift of Guidance

Most spiritual pilgrims seem to look for their enlightenment outside of themselves, and to a source other than the Divine. External acts of piety or spirituality performance are substituted for authentic discovery and spiritual work. It almost seems as if we think there are barriers other than those we create for ourselves. But there are no barriers, only resistance to the delivery of the information we are meant to receive. We contend that we all have been given the gift of insight, recognition, and revelation – our dreams. There are no artificial barriers that stop us from dreaming. It requires no training, no guru, no effort. It simply happens.

> *There is a story about a man who lived in a town very much like your own hometown. He went by the name T.S. and he thought of himself as a true seeker of truth. T.S. was in his early 50s, he was a family man with two grown children and had been working at his current job for the last 15 years. He lived what to others seemed to be an ordinary life, one that anyone would gladly take as their own.*

T.S. had an interest in the spiritual wisdom known only to a few – in the esoteric subjects, but he never spent too much time studying any particular topic. Despite his seemingly "perfect" life. T.S. had become a bit restless and started to dwell upon the thought of what was the purpose of life. The more he thought about it the more confused he became. He had a wonderful partner, his children seemed well suited to make their own journey in life and he enjoyed his job. Yet, something deep inside seemed unfulfilled.

One morning upon waking T.S. felt the strongest urge that finally he must know the meaning of life – not just of life, but of his life. He had gazed at the stars the previous evening and the thought crossed his mind, how far does it all go? Why was he created and did he have some greater purpose to his life?

Like many true seekers and following a small voice from inside, T.S. decided to go to a spiritual/metaphysical bookstore that was just a few blocks from his home, where maybe he would find the answers that was seeking. He met a wonderful clerk who listened to all of his questions and she offered the following advice - "There are numerous books within our store that can provide answers to your questions. One book might not have all of your answers but each book might provide some answers to the questions that you have."

T.S. looked at the great number of books in the store and felt slightly overwhelmed. The woman in the store recognized the look of confusion and crushing feeling that the he was going through and offered the following suggestion... "You seem lost in your search, but perhaps this will help. Many seekers seem to agree that the place to receive the greatest enlightenment is in the East. The yogis in the Himalayas hold the secret of all things. Perhaps your answer could be found there."

T.S. felt a strong feeling coming from deep within himself and reasoned that this should be his course. He would go to the East and find the answer to the meaning of life. He told his very understanding life partner that he had to make this quest. In one-week T.S. was off and soon found himself at the Himalayan range.

Since he was driven in his quest to find the answer to the meaning of life, when he arrived at the foothills of the Himalayas T.S. discovered that he hadn't prepared very well for his journey. He was only thinking of reaching the people who could quench his thirst and calm this inner feeling that had continued to grow in intensity. Despite being unprepared, nothing was going to stop T.S.. Up he climbed, higher and higher, looking only to find the wise ones. Those with the answers who were said to live high on the mountains.

As he proceeded higher into the Himalayas he came into deep snow and finally began to realize that he was not dressed properly for this journey. After all, he was from a small US town, and he had never been to this altitude or experienced such extreme temperatures. Finally, his body weary from the journey and unprepared for the exhaustive travel T.S. became overwhelmed and he couldn't climb any further. It simply was too much for him to handle. T.S. just sank into the snow and slipped into unconsciousness.

Almost like waking from a dream T.S. slowly regained consciousness. His eyes glanced upon several people gathered around him. Nearby there was a fire, and T.S. felt warm and he began to regain his strength. Everything around him seemed surreal and T.S. wondered if he was still alive or had passed over in to some other dimension.

Even though only barely just conscious and still single-mindedly on his quest for the pursuit of truth, T.S. asked no one in particular if they were a yogi and if they had the answer to the secret of life. He was fortunate that one of the men spoke some English. The man answered that he was indeed a yogi but unfortunately, he did not have the secret of the man's life. The yogi asked, where he came from and why he is climbing these mountains? The man answered, I'm from the U.S.. I was told that if I climbed the mountains here in the East, I would find the people who could answer all of my questions.

Saddened but undeterred, T.S. asked the yogi, if you don't have my answers, where can I find the answer to the purpose of my life? The yogi then looked softly but deeply within T.S. and said, the location where you would find the answer is your home town, back in the U.S..

T.S. was completely dumbfounded and said, I just came from there and no one had the answer for me. The yogi said in reply, the truth, the meaning of your life was there in your city, now it is here. But the answers are not with us, not with the Yogis or enlightened one. The answer is always and only within you.

T.S. sat quietly and a bit perplexed. The answers always seemed to be "out there" …somewhere. It would be a while before he could wrap his mind around the Yogi's teaching that the meaning of T.S.'s life was found within him. He came to understand that this was the wisdom of the ages; the truth known only to a few but available to all.

Chronicling the Gift

What does take effort is capturing our dreams *and the details* that make them important. Our dreams are the sacred writings of our own lives, the biography of who we are and who we will become. The experiences we encounter, in this both the visible and invisible worlds. To discover the meaning dreams are meant to convey, we have to preserve the artifacts that make up our dreams. Capture the details, the feelings, and the senses of the experience.

Certainly, nearly everyone reading this book is undoubtedly aware of dream journaling and dream interpretation. Journaling dreams is not a new practice and seeking interpretation of those dreams is nothing new. In fact, there is a colorful story of a boy interpreting dreams about 4,000 years ago. His interpretations saved a country, but also ultimately enslaved a people. Many cultures throughout the world honor the interpretation of dreams, and often live their lives according to their dreams.

Then the LORD answered me and said: Write down the vision; Make it plain upon tablets, so that the one who reads it may run. For the vision is a witness for the appointed time, a testimony to the end; it will not disappoint. If it delays, wait for it, it will surely come, it will not be late.
Hab2:2-3

There are countless books and traditions that provide dream interpretation. These books however provide limited interpretation to individual symbols within dreams. These may or may not be accurate, as the same symbol or image has been interpreted in different ways by different cultures. We would also challenge you that individual symbol interpretation, while they may be helpful, in themselves do not provide interpretive direction.

So, if not using the many resources of tried and true sources of dream interpretation, then what? Once again, this goes back to the idea that we don't need to be searching externally for what has already been provided internally. Rooted deep within the nearly every spiritual tradition are practices of quieting, contemplation, and meditation. It is here where the interpretation of the dream can find context, translation, interpretation, expansion, and many other elements of a greater fullness.

Divine Sight, Divine Words, Divine Reading

If for a moment we could dare to believe that our dreams and the possibilities they portray are more, much more than just ordinary, then perhaps we would treat them with the reverence and honor they deserve. Our dreams are most certainly divine sight. They are images given to us from the Source, the Creator, the Divine about *our* divinity ever-present in our humanity. Signs, symbols, markers, codes, languages all pointing us toward our own divine nature lived out in this life and brought to perfection in the next. We are a fractal of that from which we emerge, a perfect image of the original.

Humankind is being led along an evolving course, through this migration of intelligences, and though we seem to be sleeping, there is an inner wakefulness that directs the dream, and that will eventually startle us back to the truth of who we are. - *Rumi from the Poem Inner Wakefulness*

Making sense of our divine sight through reflection and meditation allows us to capture the migration from and to the Source, from and to our divinity. In her book, *Dreaming on Both Sides of the Brain,* Dr. Doris Cohen, Ph.D. offers a method for chronicling dreams and their meaning. In her methodology she offers a practical path of capturing, titling, reading, prioritizing, describing, summarizing, and finding guidance in one's dream. She suggests aligning logic, emotion and creativity in interpreting dreams – her both sides of the brain approach. She moves readers further than dream interpretation had taken them before.

Our suggestion is to take the dream beyond that which Dr. Cohen suggests. Beyond the realm of rational or even creative thought and consider it an energetic and divine download – a theophany, emanating from what some call the 8th chakra – where time is transcended and the spirit is connected to higher truth[i]. This theophany joins our physical, emotional and intellectual body through the mind. This is more than just knowledge, but insight with what some call the 3rd eye. But it doesn't take new age mysticisms to find meaning in spiritual pursuit, it is the ancient practices that sustain us throughout time.

Reflecting on our dreams in the light of spiritual meditation provides the mechanism in which insight can be determined. This practice of reflection in meditation has many forms and many possibilities. The method we suggest comes to us from a 6th century monastic practice. The art of divine reading (or lectio divina) has for 15 centuries provided insight to the mind of God. Adopting this form of meditation create a unique approach to meditative dream journaling.

The steps of meditative journaling are:

1. <u>Recording the dream</u>. There is a point somewhere being asleep and being awake when dream and reality converge. It is here that the fullness of details, senses, feelings are the clearest. This is the time to capture what your dream has been. Don't wait until the morning, as you will undoubtedly forget the images, the story, the feelings, the colors, etc. and may even create other details that weren't part of the dream.

   You will likely be tempted to record only the story and the images of your dreams. But there is more to your dream than just the narrative. You should be sure to fully capture your senses as well. Dreams often have emotions (joy, freight, anger, sadness), feelings/sensations (hot, cold, wet, dry, pain, pleasure), smells, tastes, sounds, etc. Chronicling these details might be the difference in finding a shadowy illusion of your direction or purpose versus discovering clear insight that moves you and your spirit.

   Be willing to have your journal be messy since you can always refine it and make it look pretty later. Sleep with a legal pad and pen next to your bed. Write without looking at the page. Write in the dark. Write one line per page if that is what it takes. Flip the page as often as you need to. Your night writing will be messy. You will have written one line over another. The next day you may not be able to decipher what you have written. But over time your skills will be refined, your journaling more precise, and the time to refine compressed.

   In our era of modern technology, we are often asked why not just use your iPhone to make a recording? Seems simpler, more precise and less clumsy in the darkness of the night. On the face of it this seems to be logical and reasonable; however, the way in which our brain engages in its speech center is different than that of our writing center. While both are forms of human communication, they are processed in different parts of the brain with each having its own higher centers of processing.[ii] Our experience seems to suggest that voice recording of dreams shifts the experience from imaginative and affective to rational and logical. The act of transcribing the dream in writing seems to keep open the creative channels.

2. Dream Meditation. Meditation is more than simply "pondering" the meaning of something. Meditation is using prayerful practices to discern depth and meaning. It means separating the mind from the intellect, separating emotion from feeling, and instead letting meaning unfold in small and incremental ways.

    There may be times in which an interpretation of your dream will come to you in an immediate download. It could feel very much like a continuation of your dream while awake. The meanings of the feelings and images are abundantly and unmistakable clear. In those cases, capture the interpretation immediately, as you did with your dream journaling. Don't seek additional meaning not already present, just be your own scribe, your own chronicler. In those times where the interpretation is not apparent, which will unlikely be most cases, permit yourself to enter into the dream meditation sequence we'll now provide.

    As we said earlier, our dream journal is the sacred writings of our lives. Capturing the theophany from the Divine. So, treating them this way in meditation can be the sacred reading or the "*lectio divina*" of our own lives. This method is taken from an ancient 6th century meditation practice first used by monks in the mountains of central Italy.

    As with that ancient practice of meditation of sacred writings, we suggest you read your chronicled dreams in a 3-fold repetition. Your first reading should be one in which you simply ruminate with the words, images, senses, and feeling of the dream; but one in which you are not yet searching form meaning. Allow some time for these ruminations to set in. Allow for the power of the words and images simply to shower you. Allow yourself to feel the possible power within the vibrations of the words. Reading your dreams aloud begins the process of becoming immersed within the dream and its power.

Your second reading begins to explore the themes or meanings that might start to emerge. As you read your dream, pay attention to any words, phrases or images that resonate with you. Do they offer any meaning, or do they lead to other thoughts? Stay conscious that you are not beginning to daydream but remaining in meditation and reflection. See if there are any emotions or sensations in your body that occur. These could also be insights into meaning and direction.

Finally, in the third reading determine if you are being called into action or change based on your dream meditation. This is really, the big "so what." So, what does this mean? So, what am I supposed to do? So, what or where does this lead me? The inspirations may be clear and decisive or they may only point to some unknown something yet to be revealed. Typically, they are somewhere in between. A suggestion of a course of action. One that is just being planted and needs time to grow and finally flower.

3. Interpretation – With the chronicling and meditation now complete, your journal should capture the interpretation of your own dream. This might be more challenging than transcribing your dreams because you will be primarily engaging your left-brain logic and reason. You may be prone to second guessing or reinterpreting your dream as opposed to capturing the meditation revealed meaning.

    Typically, the initial interpretation is the most authentic, and likely to be the most accurate. But that doesn't mean that you can't discover more than a single interpretation. Follow your intuition. Capture one or two or even more interpretations. Your spirit will know what resonates with truth and what is being artificially "created". What we want the interpretations to be can be very different from what they ultimately are.

"Words that come with the dream"

Throughout the upcoming chapters following Steve's dream sequences you will typically see the phrase, "Words that come with the dream." It is important to set the context of what this means.

Often within Steve's dream experiences and when he had finished journaling his dream, Steve would remain with his eyes closed and within a quasi-dream state. In this transitional state, Steve would be given an initial interpretation of the dream as well as added philosophy or guidance to understand 'what more is possible.' The interpretation, philosophy and/or guidance were given to Steve without him *consciously thinking* of an interpretation at that moment.

For Steve, these mid-dream theophanies came very early in his journey when he asked in sincere faith if he could be given further explanation of the meaning of his dreams. He asked this not for himself but how might he be in service of mankind with all of his love and energy, and that he dream true. Steve recalled the admonition, "if you ask for bread you are not given a stone."

Steve explains this simply by recognizing that it is possible for anyone to receive additional guidance and understanding if they but ask - recognizing that this is indeed possible. The interpretation and guidance come directly from the same source of the dream experience. What one can do, others are also able to do - Now!

The substance behind the form

Revisiting your dream journal and examining them and the interpretations on regular intervals will allow you to see the ways in which the theophanies may have played out in your life. You may begin to see that you are not alone on this journey. That your angels or guides or even the Divine has been with you throughout.   The randomness by which you might have seen your life events may readily get replaced with an understanding and sense of purpose and guidance. There may have been multiple lessons embedded within your dreams and interpretations, and the outcomes become manifest in many ways and at many times.

The energies of the spirit are not a metaphor for some remote or external unattainable mystical realities, but that which points to real, near, and attainable physical and transcendent experiences.   The vibrations of the body, spirit and soul are raised and become more harmonious with one another. To imagine these energies to be something else, or something less, removes the immediate personal connectedness with the divine. It lessens the importance, and maybe more importantly the responsibility, one plays in collaborating in their own life's journey (both physical and spiritual).

Discernment of Dreams

Nearly everyone invariably asks if all dreams should be considered inspiration, or direction, or enlightenment. Our answer would be simply, no. Sometimes dreams are just dreams, and sometimes they are not. They can reflect a multitude of experiences, from our wishes and worries, to our hidden desires or undealt with traumas. Dreams may even be nothing more than the neurological processing of the day's inputs – the mind categorizing and filing the sensory and extra-sensory. Sometimes they are more; experiences beyond dreams, beyond the physical, cognitive, emotional and spiritual.

There are many traditions which teach various categories of dreams. For instance, in Islam there are three categories of dreams.[iii]   The highest of these are called Ru'ya or "true dreams." Ru'ya dreams those that we have been describing here; dreams inspired by the divine, dreams that provide inspiration and guidance. These are the Islamic theophany where the dreams are communication with God (Allah), the Prophet Muhammad or the Muslim saints. Hulm, or "bad dreams," are the next type of dream. These are essentially "evil theophany." These are believed to be dreams sent by the devil or evil spirits. They may be dreams to create chaos in our lives, to attempt to drive toward evil actions, or create harm not good. Finally, in Islam there are dreams called hadith nafsi, or "talk of the self." These are dreams that come from within one's self and reflect or are a manifestation of the dreamer. They reflect the desires, concerns, hopes and ambitions of the dreamer.

Visions within the sleep state may be more than differing dream types. They may actually be different types of experiences. Here we offer an idea for consideration; a threefold experience of vision states. The first is the dream, the true dream. A processing of visions, feeling, thoughts, guidance, possibility, history, future, etc. while asleep, fully asleep. The dreamer must be asleep to experience a dream; unconscious, released from the limitations of the conscious mind. These will be the experiences we explore within this book. To help discern those that are theophany and guidance in contrast to those that may be something else. The emergence from the sleep state, to semiconscious to fully awake can be seen as the continuation and finalization of the dream. In the "in between state" the dreamer may find themselves in the closest state of unitive communion we have with the divine as we simultaneously exist within our human and divine natures – having just be in dialogue with our divine source. Pay particular attention to the visions that emerge during this consciousness progression.

The second vision encounter that we may experience is the "out of body" experiences called astral-travel. The recollection of the experience may seem to be nearly identical to that within the dream state, but the cause and source of them differ greatly. Within the dream state, the revelatory or theophany experiences originate from outside of one's self. The source of the information is from the divine with the dreamer as the receiver from the source. In contrast, the source of the astral-travel experience is the traveler themselves and that which they encounter. The traveler is not dreaming, but conscious within another plane of existence. While their body is unconscious within a sleep state, their soul/spirit has essentially left the body to experience within its own reality experiences from which to grow and learn. The traveler is the main participant in the travel, the architect of the journey, and the beneficiary of the travel. We do not intend to support or reject, prove or disprove here the reality of astral-travel other than to say there is sufficient investigation and conclusions in this space to offer support for its existence.

Finally, the third dream-like state is semiconscious fantasy. This is the state between asleep and awake were the mind is being freed of limitations and free thinking is able to occur. This is where day dreaming happens (even if it is at night). The "dreamer" tends to shape and reshape the narrative of the daydream, molding to that which aligns most effectively with the needed or desired outcome at the moment of the fantasy. This could be an idyllic fantasy of success, power, fame, fortune, etc.; one of wisdom, guidance, insight; or even one of despair, depression, hopelessness. It is one founded to satisfy primarily the mental and emotional needs of the dreamer. While guidance may find its way into a day dream, the divine is typically a secondary player in this movement.

Sacred Sleep – Higher Octane Dreaming

Dreaming can often seem to be arbitrary, with strange and unintelligible symbols, odd transitions from one scene to another, and disconnected people and events. Yet we all have dreams that repeat time after time, or dreams that are right on target to something that is happening in our lives. In these cases, we seem to dream with purpose; when our dreams speak to us the most. Have you ever asked yourself whether it is possible to dream like this every night?

The answer is a definitive…. maybe. However, with purpose and consciousness, dreaming can be "shaped" to respond to your needs and questions. This is called "dream incubation." Dream incubation is an ancient practice from cultures including Greece, Egypt, Israel, and in early Christianity. In this practice the dreamer would enter a sacred place with the desire to experience a theophany (a divinely inspired dream), which most often was used in seeking out a cure for some physical illness or affliction. But there was also the practice of dream incubation for the purpose of spiritual growth. In the story of the kings of ancient Israel, it is written that the wisdom given to Solomon was given to him in a dream following Solomon's offering at the "great high place" of Gibeon.[iv] Solomon entered the sacred place of Gibeon, made his offerings to the Divine, and then received the theophany he was seeking.

Since there are many books already written on dream incubation, we will not explore it in depth here, other than to say entering sleep with "intention" provides you the opportunity to experience dream revelations with purpose. When your dreams become a direct response to the intention you set, you are entering sacred sleep – where your sleep is the sacred temple. We call this practice high octane dreaming. Setting an intention however is not being prescriptive of what the outcome of the dream will be; it is opening one's self to receive the sacred inspiration with the hope that it addresses the need that was the basis of the intention.

Genius or Good Dreamers/Listeners?

Sacred sleep and high octane dreaming through dream incubation may seem like just another idea that new age practitioners have in their mystical practices, but it more than that – much more. History, both ancient and more recent is replete with examples of philosophers, artists, inventors, scientists and many others whose "genius" had come to them (in part) in and through their dreams. In fact, as you explore the lives and biographies of the men and women that the world would call the greatest of geniuses, you find a very interesting dynamic. Many of these individuals credited their amazing discoveries, inventions, poetry, music and ideas to either an inner guide or to their dreams. For them, creative inspiration truly meant in-spirit, with dreams being the means by which their creations were revealed to them. Following are just a few examples.

Robert Louis Stevenson, the 19th century Scottish novelist and author of *Treasure Island*, and the *Strange Case of Dr. Jekyll and Mr. Hyde* described his inner guides saying, "…and for the Little People, what shall I say they are but just my Brownies, God bless them! Who do one-half my work for me *while I am fast asleep*, and in all human likelihood, do the rest for me as well, when I am wide awake and fondly suppose I do it for myself[v]."

The great Italian opera composer Giacomo Puccini stated, "…the music of Madam Butterfly was dictated to me by God; I was merely instrumental in putting it on paper and communicating it to the public."[vi]

J.W. von Goethe described the writing of the novel, Werther, "I wrote the book almost unconsciously, *like a somnambulist [sleep walker]*, and was amazed when I realized what I had done."[vii] William Blake said of his work, Milton, that "I have written this poem from immediate dictation, twelve or sometimes twenty or thirty lines at a time, without premeditation, and even against my will."[viii]

Richard Strauss, said, "While the ideas were flowing in upon me, the entire musical, measure by measure, it seemed to me that I was dictated to by two wholly different Omnipotent Entities…I was definitely conscious of being aided by more than an earthy Power, and it was responsive to my determined suggestions."[ix]

Just three weeks before he died, Johannes Brahms said of the source of inspiration of his works, "When I feel the urge I begin by appealing directly to my maker"…"These are the Spirit illuminating the soul-power within and I realize at such moments the tremendous significance of Jesus' supreme revelation, 'I and the Father are one'"…"I have to be in a semi-trance condition to get such results – *a condition when the conscious mind is in temporary abeyance, and the subconscious is in control*."[x]

"The English poet Shelley declared that 'One after another the greatest writers, poets and artists confirm the fact that their work comes to them from beyond the threshold of consciousness.'"[xi]

The 1936 Nobel Prize in Physiology and Medicine was awarded to Otto Loewi, who discovered and demonstrated that nerve impulses are both chemical and electrical in nature. The experimental procedure to prove his theory came to him in a dream. Rudyard Kipling stated that he had an 'inner helper' who he could get into contact with if he did not think consciously about reaching him but rather drifted toward him.

The Russian chemist and inventor Dmitri Mendeleev said of his creation of the periodic table in 1869 that he had gone to bed exhausted after struggling to conceptualize a way to categorize the elements of nature based upon their atomic weights. He later said, *"I saw in a dream a table where all the elements fell into place as required. Awakening, I immediately wrote it down on a piece of paper."*[xii]

Elias Howe worked for years to invent a lockstitch sewing machine. For years his attempts were futile. Due to a 'nightmare,' as he defined it, he was shown exactly how to build the device that he sought for so long. "He dreamed he was captured by a tribe of savages who took him prisoner before their king. 'Elias Howe, 'roared the monarch, I command you on pain of death to finish this machine at once."[xiii] *Within the dream he was given the answer that he needed.*

Undoubtedly, the names mentioned have been recognized as great innovators, trail blazers and individuals of great genius. They are recognized as great due to their contributions in their various fields. But what is the nature of their genius? Where does their genius come from? Would they still have been considered great if they had not made their discoveries, composed their music or written their books?

We could have shared similar stories of hundreds if not thousands of artists, inventors and innovators throughout history who perceived through dreams, visions and help from within, information that has thrust them into the category of genius. Each of them would likely share a similar belief that the inspiration that led them to discover began from a place beyond them; revealed to them through dreams, vision, insights or in some way through Divine communication. We are proposing that many, if not most, of these creators were geniuses because they were great listeners.

Very few of us are bold enough to consider ourselves as geniuses or anything close to genius. In fact, not many of us would even consider ourselves as creative or inspired; but how much of this is simply not having mastered the skill or art of listening? Even the geniuses we looked at, while some of them certainly were seeking the answer to some question others stated that they weren't particularly searching for anything. Even those who were seeking nothing at all still received inspiration. So, if those not seeking but still willing to listen climbed the heights, what about you? Why not you?

Why not YOU! We believe, although biased, that our readers are very spiritual, loving, beautiful and talented and that with you all things are possible. All things are possible and you don't need gurus, special courses or secret symbols to achieve wonderful results. So, we come to you with an easy approach…how about just listening.

If you realize that this is possible then it will manifest for you. You can place your question in your mind and now you know you will get the answer if you believe and just listen. Perhaps we are here to awaken this concept in YOU. Yes, your guides and dreams will work with you. In fact, they have always been working with you but you may not have been listening. Now is the time to listen.

Dreaming through the Fruits of the Spirit

In drawing this introduction to a close, we'd like to take you into dream interpretation prepared in every possible way. The final preparation is discovering a way in which to capture and categorize your dreams, for you will find your own set of "themes". Our structure for Part I of this book will be to use the *Fruits of the Holy Spirit* as the organizing themes to categorize Steve's dream sequences. The Fruits of the Spirit aligns well within the structure of theophany and Divine inspiration. Traditionally, the fruits of the Holy Spirit are passed down as *Love, Joy, Peace, Patience, Kindness, Goodness, Faithfulness, Gentleness, and Self-Control.* There are many ways and interpretations to define each of these, and as we progress through each of the chapters, we will define each in our understanding. We diverge from the traditional list by adding *Wisdom* and *Knowledge* (traditionally 2 of the <u>Gifts</u> of the Holy Spirit) and also *Empowerment.* We do this not to redefine religious tradition but to make these gifts our own. They serve as the framework or the window through which we view the world as revealed through dreams and theophany.

One of Steve's earliest theophanies was on "Gifts of the spirit".

It now appears that your interest has been quickened. The truth you are looking for is that activities which transcend the physical being and the activities of materiality are a presentation from the Deity. Now you may find this sort of presentation from the Deity being very effective for the activities of Christ and the Disciples, you can find that in the New Testament. Near every one of the miraculous activities that you find in the New Testament, we find in the Old Testament. Now likely there would not have been the piecing together of the philosophies of the books that went to make up the orthodoxy that Christendom grew out of, were it not for those individuals who had Spiritual Gifts, nor would it have been possible for there to have been the activities of the Man who came to be an example for others, and those individuals who followed Him had it not been for "Gifts of the Spirit." There would not have been the effectiveness of His ministry without them. If we move into the Hindu, we would find the activities of Buddha in the revolution that he fostered in that faith, were supported and carried along by "Gifts of the Spirit."

The true concepts of spirituality are guidance from the Deity as presented to the individual self and if that guidance is followed, and followed rather religiously, individuals would develop something that would transcend their physical self. Now those individuals that have activities which are transcendent of the physical self should rather consider that they have a gift from the Creator, and they best have care how they use it.

October 30, 1975

Chapter One – *Beautiful Mind, Open Heart, Humble Spirit*

"I don't know where dreams come from. Sometimes I wonder if they're genetic memories, or messages from something divine. Warnings perhaps. Maybe we do come with an instruction booklet but we're too dense to read it, because we've dismissed it as the irrational waste product of the 'rational' mind. Sometimes I think all the answers we need are buried in our slumbering subconscious, in the dreaming. The booklet right there, and every night when we lay our heads down on the pillow it flips open. The wise read it, heed it. The rest of us try as hard as we can upon awakening to forget any disturbing revelations we might have found there."

Karen Marie Moning

Every journey has a beginning, but not every beginning starts from a single point. Such is the journey of spiritual awareness. Although there may be discreet and indeed memorable "ah-ha" moments, most journeys are the confluence of many paths of exploration and from a multitude of experiences. The alchemy of discovery derives gold from seemingly benign ingredients.

Within this alchemy the seeker begins to discover a divinity within themselves and sense the need, and even the longing, to follow this inescapable course. When one looks forward to the path they are traveling, the way forward may seem obscured or barely discernable. That is simply because one can't perceive that which they do not yet know. But out of the misty uncertainties, the clearness of one's path can be seen in the path already traveled. By reflecting on the path already traveled, the journey ahead becomes increasingly clear.

The following dream sequences are those which Steve believes to be among the most profound and meaningful theophanies in his life. He shares them with you to get a glimpse into his experience and the importance of listening to ones' dreams. To help frame the process, we will present the dream as Steve journaled them, followed by "words that came with the dream." These words may have come in the dream, following the dream while journaling, or even in poems. They are shared just as Steve journaled them, without editing or modification.

March 1977 – First Dream

The Dream: I was standing in front of a large book. The book suddenly opened and I could see that it was a book filled with pictures of all types of animals. I then heard a voice say, "What type of animal is Steve!" (I recognized the voice as belonging to a friend and former teammate when I played six-man volleyball some three years earlier.) Back in the dream I saw the pages flip by and then stop and I saw just a finger outstretched from a hand touch the animal picture of a hog. I then awoke.

Words that came with the dream: Upon awakening I felt very unnerved, surprised and confused since all of my conversations and experiences with my friend had never shown that this might be something I would connect with his thoughts. Although we had not spoken for about six months, I decided to telephone him. After exchanging pleasantries, I asked him, "is there anything bothering you about me?" He stated, 'what are you talking about?" I asked a second time, "Is there anything bothering you about me?" He responded, "I don't know what you are asking or what you mean." I asked again and his response was, "Are you sick, what is your problem, why do you continue to ask me?"
I am not sure why I said my next words but they just came forth, "I want to be a better person and if there is something bothering you, I would like to know." He responded, "Yes, there is something that has been on my mind for some time." My heart sank, I became slightly agitated and waited for this comment. "Steve, do you remember when we played on our six-man volleyball team how you treated our other teammate X?" I said, "I don't remember treating him badly." "Steve, you were one of the leaders of our team and everybody looked up to you and wanted to win your approval. Teammate X was our 7th player that would occasionally substitute into the game. He was not one of our best players but when he would make a mistake, you did not say

anything but you glared at him and made him even more nervous which led to him making more errors."

My friend continued, "When I would go out with teammate X after the game for pizza he would sometimes throw-up and state that it was upsetting that he could not win your approval. I thought you were such a hog without any feelings." [What is striking about this is that for whatever reason in his mind he used the word hog.] After this experience for the following two months I would have four to six dreams per night having me look at every aspect of my personality, likes and dislikes and the image of myself that I was projecting to others.

Heavenly Vision

Even though it was the end of the year I had spent the last several days working with people who had various health and physical problems. I was having a strong internal debate with myself regarding how the people were being healed. I knew that I could not be the source of their healing but was having difficulty sharing with people it was anything else other than their healing was a result of only mentalism and belief. Upon going to bed early on December 31 I asked from deep within my Being, what was happening and since I was in the middle of a divorce, was I hurting whatever ability I had by not having a wife and a stable marriage or relationship?

The Dream - I saw myself speaking, lecturing and healing around the world. The following words came as I was writing the dream on paper with my eyes closed...

> Miles and miles to travel, along the road of life,
> It is done in many ways, single or with a wife,
> Clasp upon those who love you, depend upon their love,
> They are there through thick and thin, and with guidance
> from above.

<u>The Divine Apparition</u>: I awoke to glance at the above poem and a brilliant light appeared before me at the foot of my bed. Although it was a bright as anything I have ever seen, I was not able to see within it but it did not hurt my eyes. Then the following words came from out of the light:

"Your healing ministry is to begin on all levels. Whether they believe in Jesus, Buddha, the Oracles of Enlightenment at Delphi or any others, you will assist them. Let It Be Done and Know That I Am God. Go forth and heal by your hands, voice and look. None truly know Me, but all live because of Me. Before Adam was I. Before the formation of the worlds was I. From the tumultuous world of matter, I formed flesh. I heal the body, mind and spirit. I Am that I Am. Go forth and know.

Why such little faith in healing Steve? I am He who built the mountains. He who makes the rivers flow. He who placed the stars in the firmament. Let all insects, animals, the people and worlds in all existences know who I Am. My angels Gabriel and Raphael protect you, Michael always leads the way. I come upon you as the rolling mist. I Am the sunrise, I can be the sunset. I Am the Knower of the Knower, the Father of all gods. I am the Mother of Invention and the Chief of all created worlds. I Am the spark of all that lives and the glue of all forms. I Am the Sower of all states, times and realities. The voice crying in the wilderness is the intellect perceiving the spirit of truth.

Come forth soul of Steve. Back to the forge and Blacksmith who forged your heart and spirit. Obtain the hands of light and the voice and tongue of truth. The Cayce group, the Betty group and others all related many things. But you will teach with fire; you will teach with lightning bolts upon the hearts of men and women. Let fly your courage and take hold of the staff to part the Red Sea of ignorance. Behold the miracles of God! You mentioned to someone [I spoke on the 31st with someone about healing) that you would feel strange and perhaps make them feel uncomfortable telling people that you heal with the power of God. IT IS IN THE NAME OF THE HOLY

SPIRIT THAT YOU HEAL. Come forth you child of God. Rise O Lazarus."

I can never express the feeling, emotions, awe, warmth and love coming from the light. As I watched it dissipate a second brilliant light appeared in my room. The following words came from this second light

"This is Jesus speaking, I baptize you with the spiritual awareness of our Father in the Great Heaven of Being. Love all people as I love you. Protect them as I protect you. Seek ye the kingdom and all is added unto you. More than thought…more than life…have faith my little one. Live, love and carry the truth with you."

A Beautiful Heart and Open Mind and a Humble Spirit

<u>The Dream</u>: I was walking on the shore at the ocean. Walking with me were all the spiritual seekers of the world. The ocean was on our left side and in front of us I could see a woman dressed in blue holding a microphone. To our right and in front of the woman in blue were horseshoe shaped stands that were filled with people. The woman was hard to see because there was so much smoke and clouds coming from out of the people in the stands. As we got closer, I saw that the woman was very beautiful and it was the Goddess Sophia. The goddess of Wisdom. In the stands I saw that they were all the people who have written spiritual books, offer spiritual classes, provide seminars and have religious movements.

The people in the stands were obliterating the Goddess of Wisdom so that she could not be heard and hardly seen. I looked up to the sky and said, if these people are covering the truth, what are people supposed to do to find greater wisdom and enlightenment? At that moment a big wind came from the ocean and blew away the smoke and fog. I heard the following words from the heavens…

"All that is needed and has ever been needed is **a beautiful heart, an open mind and a humble spirit.**"

Chapter Two - Wisdom

"Before all other things wisdom was created; and prudent understanding, from eternity. The root of wisdom—to whom has it been revealed? Her subtleties—who knows them? There is but one, wise and truly awesome, seated upon his throne—the Lord. It is he who created her, saw her and measured her. Poured her forth upon all his works, upon every living thing according to his bounty, lavished her upon those who love him."

– Ben Sira, 2nd Century B.C.[xiv]

From antiquity, Wisdom has always been embodied as a person. More than simply acquiring knowledge, Wisdom is the divine light shed on knowledge that reveals to each of us. Sophia (wisdom) is she that joins us to the divine knowledge; she that brings us to awareness; she that reveals to us the secrets of the truth – "Happy is the person who meditates on Sophia, who reflects in one's heart on Sophia's ways and ponders her secrets, pursuing her like a hunter, and lying in wait on her paths."[xv]

The dreams of theophany can be the visitations from Sophia bringing the knowledge meant for you. Knowledge, which in the reflection of the divine, illuminates truth. In this chapter we will chronicle for you Steve's dreams that were best understood as theophanies of wisdom.

Snakes Dancing

<u>The Dream</u>: Snakes were dancing in the air. Their lower part was connected to the ground but they were fully extended and swaying as if in trance. I was cautious as I explained their story to the listeners. I joked and explained how I watched them very carefully. These snakes could be tricky I told the listeners. Then one of the snakes came crawling toward me. I tried to use a long stick (staff) to beat on it. I then wedged a stick under its body and launched it into the street. It did not fly very far. It approached me again so I threw it out again. It

was very close to my feet and I expected it to strike at any time, although it was not angry and I did not see any fangs.

Words that came with the dream: "Hold the snakes head, it won't bite. The snakes of wisdom wind their way and the truth is always available. Use your staff to move them along. Final glory is yours as you shepherd along the wisdom of the past. 'Wise as serpents.' Pride and ambition have stopped many activities in their tracks. Humble dedicated service will help insure the successful joining of the seen and unseen."

Lighting the Way

The Dream: I was walking at night through a forest. I turned on a flashlight I had in my hand and many pathways became illuminated and I realized I was with many people.

Words that came with the dream: I heard from the starry night sky, "Steve, you are not the source, you illuminate the pathways that others traverse toward the Source."

The Spiritual Ocean

The Dream: I was observing an old man sitting upon a cliff overlooking the ocean. I knew that the man was wondering about his life. What meaning has it had and what does it matter in the great sea of eternity that rolls never ending in constant rhythm upon the shore?

Words that came with the dream: Then the following words came from out of the ocean… "Each wave is pushed by the unseen hand and plays its role upon the sand. Each life, like a wave, rolls on its way to be a part, of creation each day. Driven by, the Invisible Force, the wave of life, fulfils its course. Seek ye the kingdom and it will be given unto you. As the ocean laps upon the sand, your spiritual self is forever lapping upon your physical body."

The Angel and the Pillar of Fire

<u>The Dream</u>: I was with two women and was showing them my ring and trying to explain what it was. [I have a ring with the symbol of Raphael healing a child.] No matter how I explained the ring, the women couldn't visualize it. Then I tried to show them the picture of Raphael that I always carry in my wallet. Although, I knew it was in my wallet I couldn't find it.

<u>Words that came with the dream</u>: "The time for pictures and rings is over. Not by symbols or pictures will you heal but by living example. Raphael loves you. Thou shalt have no images before Me. I Am that I Am. Your symbol is the pillar of fire and light...the light of the ages."

<u>The Dream continued</u>: I then saw and heard…Steve worked in the water with a spiraling Pillar of Fire underneath him and it was connecting him to the Truth. A person was sent to find this in Steve while Steve was standing in the lake. Discover the fire within the form. The essence within all substance, people, animals and minerals.

<u>More Words</u>: "Many are called but few are ready at the time they are called. From Everlasting to Everlasting. There are no games in your life now, no other direction but forward. For this you have come to earth. Your physical will always be present. It is about the eminence that shines forth from within it. The Light of Light, the Light from within the darkness. I and the Holy Breath are One. Have faith and allow pictures to come to you within your consciousness. Words will flow to you and directions will be given."

Life even in the Darkness

The Dream: As I was sitting with a woman who was in charge of supplying products, a woman came up to us and was looking to make a special deal to distribute the products. She wanted to distribute in her own special way, but her proposal was refused and she left. I spoke with the woman next to me and asked if she would let me distribute to people. She just smiled. We then left together to find the first woman who had come to us. As we walked, two women and two men were walking next to us. We seemed to be walking into a forest, and the forest became darker with each step. I could feel the darkness surround us. I could hear the words, 'each center is a consciousness.' I turned to the woman next to me and said, 'I am out of here.' She had already turned around and was saying the same thing.

Words that came with the dream: "Even in the darkness there is still life. Feel the consciousness that is present. Being in the now means to feel the atmosphere, temperature, wind, light and the presence of life. In the course of this manufactured time (this living) which is a transitional reality, spiritual units have the opportunity to change. Each person is a point of radiating consciousness. Your goal in this life is to bring these points of random radiation to their highest and best state and have them vibrating as one. When enough of these points are radiating to the same potential then there will be a shift or flip of space time to a higher function unveiling a new possibility of expression upon your earth plane."

Standing above time

The Dream: I was flying in an airplane with many other people when something happened and it was announced that the plane was going to crash. The people around me were all frightened and screaming. I knew that if I held the concept of my Self and Total Being that even though the plane would crash, I would be standing up tall and completely unharmed. So, I calmed the other passengers and told them that those who saw themselves as a complete energy pattern that could not be harmed would survive. The plane crashed and I was standing amongst the wreckage unharmed in any way.

<u>Words that came with the dream</u>: "You have had several dreams which showed you the future. The point is to demonstrate that time is a continuum which slides both forward and backward. Events are seen by the pre-consciousness as they might happen. Time is at past, present and future during any moment. The reason you blend activities during your time jumping dreams is that you have not been shown how to stand above time. It is possible to place yourself at any given time in the continuum and to achieve awareness of a particular time period it is a matter of practice to hold the self at a particular vibration. You will not be going down in an airplane but the point was to 'place' yourself in a particular state of awareness.

Manifest your presence by duplicating the feeling of freezing yourself as you did on the airplane and become an observer viewing the activity without emotion, feeling or attempting to manipulate the outcome."

xvi

Wisdom exceeds the bounds of knowledge, the limitations of experience, and the restraints of human doctrine. Wisdom is the melding of the spiritual, the mental, the emotional and the physical – the experienced and the revealed. Wisdom is the incorporation of these realities into a perichoretic[xvii] relationship in which the bonds that restrain or deter us "gives way" or "makes room" for the fullness of truth. Wisdom increases and enhances each of the realities of our being, while magnifying the whole. In Wisdom we become more fully integrated in who we are, and also more fully integrated into the Divine. We gain a greater interpenetration of aspects of ourselves and with the Divine yet remain wholly who we were are in our creation and divinity.

Chapter Three - Knowledge

Knowledge is power and it can command obedience. A man of knowledge during his lifetime can make people obey and follow him and he is praised and venerated after his death. Remember that knowledge is a ruler and wealth is its subject.

- Imam Ali, Nahj Al-Balagha

The greatest minds from antiquity to modernity have long recognized the importance of knowledge in the human experience. Imam Ali, the Prophet Muhammad's, son-in-law, and successor [according to the Shia tradition] posited this in the early 7th century. In his book Meditationes Sacre (Sacred Meditations) in 1597, Sir Francis Bacon commenting on mans' place in divine creation wrote "knowledge itself is power". Thomas Jefferson, arguably one of America's greatest statesmen and orators, repeatedly writes that "knowledge is power" in many of his communications regarding the establishment of the University of Virginia. The great civil rights abolitionist Frederick Douglas wrote that knowledge is "the pathway from slavery to freedom." Knowledge is not just a piece of the human experience, it often takes a role front and center, essential to the success and order of society.

It leads us to wonder, what kind of power comes with knowledge? Is it the shadow power of a malevolent ruler under which people are oppressed? Is it the gracious power of a benevolent ruler who serves her people? Perhaps it is something much more profound. If we think only temporally, then the simple calculation provides that temporal knowledge derives temporal power.

But the calculus of life, of existence itself, is far beyond simple calculations. According to tradition, the Temple of Apollo at Delphi had the inscription "Know Thyself" on its entryway. But what does "know thyself" mean? Is this just a temporal question? Clearly, to be inscribed on the temple of the Greek god himself, this charge must be more than simply the acquisition of academic or even philosophical knowledge. The ancients, through their goals, challenge humanity to know the physical, the emotional, the moral, and the spiritual self – the "totus" of human experience.

More than temporal knowledge, knowing thyself means knowing all of one's self; knowing the complete self; or completely knowing the self. In this, the calculus becomes more complicated yet more important, more meaningful. In the architecture of the self, the keystone that locks all the other stone of our being into place is the spirit. Strength of spirit means strength of self. So, where spiritual knowledge precedes spiritual power, it is in this power which the fullness of self is established.

Lift your thoughts, lift your knowledge

<u>The Dream</u>: I was traveling along a road. I stopped at a light trying to get my car into the proper lane. Finally, the stick shift was put into gear and I made the proper lane. Up on the sign I could see the arrows pointing in the four cardinal points. The light had turned green and when I finally noticed it, I began to drive. The road narrowed as I went around a curve and I found a construction barrier which was damming back some water. Then the roadway turned into a mountain trail and I had to walk the car. A woman walked toward me and then by me as I started down a steep grade that wound down to the bottom. I was then in a room with a star athlete who has lost her confidence and was in a corner crying. [I recognized it was Monica Seles, the athlete who was stabbed on the tennis court during a tennis match.] I passed by her and went on my way.

<u>Words that came with the dream</u>: "It is important to have confidence in your activities and actions. You must believe that your abilities and our assistance will always carry you through. Allow the image of your desire to permeate your thoughts. When you hold your thought, you will become what you imagine. Lift your thoughts always to a level of perfection. Be what you want to be.

Cross the river,
You don't need a boat,
Work on yourself,
You'll be able to float,
Currents are present,
But all is not lost,
With Spiritual Guidance,
There isn't a cost,
Your body must follow,
The words from Up High,
So, keep on the pathway,
you'll arrive by and by.

What the eagle sees

The Dream: I was traveling to get to the final destination. I finally came to a point where I was driving over a barren field with small rocks and I began sliding off the cart which I was on as it scraped the ground. I found myself at a friend's house trying to discover the correct road to take. Time was getting late. I then was joking with a small boy while making play on words. I knew I had to get along since the time was 9:45. I had to be on my way. Finally, I took to the streets and knew I was once again on the right direction.

Words that came with the dream: "You must condition yourself to wake up more often during the night to record all the dreams and information that is sent. The crossing point of the real/unreal is the focus of mental perception. The soaring eagle gets a higher look at the whole field of action.

Keep clear your destination for the pathway of life is fraught with many roads, which do not lead directly to the goal but bring one to other experiences. It is not necessary to have these other experiences unless this is your choice. The call of the wild spurs you onward. New discoveries are re-awakening your dormant faculties of higher perception. Life experiences activate inherent forces that are a part of your original creation."

You walk the land,
To try to see,
If you can arrive,
At what God intended you to be,
The trials and worries,
Which surrounded your walk,
Have largely been caused,
By your erroneous thoughts,
So, elevate your thinking,
And you will see,
How easy it is
To receive guidance from Me.

"The activation of your talents and spiritual abilities is done through desire and the will. Be aware of the subtler movements of energy currents. The gross of materiality takes up your field of vision. Look beyond, around, behind to see a different movement. Take time to learn to see with your spiritual vision."

The hall of fame

The Dream: A baseball player who had been away in spirit returned to see himself enshrined at the stadium in front of his fans. I cried strongly in the dream as I saw the man glance up at the scoreboard and see his name and accomplishments.

Words that came with the dream: "The assumption of an identity, the alignment of energetic vibrations of one to another. The forces within the self are aligned to the vibrational characteristics of another. This is attested by those who are examples and have attained to their gifts by emulating another person. Carrying on within the mentals of that image you are reflecting into this reality, those qualities or attributes you wish to attain. The One, the Good and the Beautiful. The pool of mind reflects the image. If the pool, yourself in the mind, is moved by distractions the reflection becomes unclear and rippled. Keeping your surface clear and calm allows you to project the image upon yourself and you become it."

> Rivers flowing, toward the Source,
> A journey home, upon the course,
> A new beginning, a body you see,
> A continuation, of your destiny,
> Choices in spirit, a definite plan,
> The life to be lived, as either woman or man,
> Each has lessons, which are to be gained,
> The growth of the soul, is what is obtained,
> Round after round, your soul does make,
> Throughout eternity, your travels take,
> So does the river, flow back to its source,
> Back to the Creator, more perfected of course.

The light of knowledge

The Dream: Why do we talk in rhymes and symbols? Communication within yourself and between other people at a psychic level is accomplished with symbols. These are what are passed between sender and receiver. It is the easiest mechanism of communication between your various states of awareness. Also, the rhymes we give you stimulate you to keep listening to the transmission rather than hearing a monotony of words. Symbols stimulate various areas of the brain. You can't be emotionally attached to anything. You must be very matter-of-fact in your passing through of information and energy. The direction that things take should not be your concern. You are a conduit. The results of your actions will be what has been determined, but not determined by you. You do the laying on of hands, God does the healing.

<u>Words that came with the dream</u>: "The sun makes its arc across the sky. Things are affected by the sun based on their own status. Are they shaded or covered? Are they low on moisture, are they overheated to begin with? The sun shines regardless, giving off its rays and energy. In the same manner you must also move through your life giving off the same continuous light. The sun is consistent in its action as you must be. Those who want to receive will receive to the extent they make themselves available to the light."

Fulfilled in abundance

<u>The Dream</u>: A lady was walking over to a table to refill a glass of orange juice that a man was holding. I noticed that the pitcher she was carrying barely had any orange juice in it. Then as she went to pour, the pitcher was full with an unending supply of orange juice.

<u>Words that came with the dream</u>: "Prayerful thanks must be given before for the unlimited supply. You must condition your mind toward the concept of unlimited supply. You must learn that you have what you want or need and not accept just what you think you see. You receive what you see, you have access to all that you want. You must see your desire fulfilled and not see only what appears to you. It is about expectation. You must always visualize plenty. Look at the example of Jesus with the fish multiplying."

The 3rd substance

<u>The Dream</u>: I was in an area of consciousness working on my spiritual awareness. I was there with another man and I was checking/learning greater awareness. He was after me to learn how to work consciously and unconsciously. I was looking at something on the ground as he pushed a wall on top of me. He was laughing with a crazy type of laugh thinking I was underneath the wall. Then I was huddled in a ball and actually in some type of lighted space within the wall structure. I could see and turned to my left and right to see how much operating room I had. I knew if I raised my head through the wall I would go right

through the matter. I felt a little resistance as I pushed up. I only needed to rise up and through the material of the wall. As I awoke, I realized I was dreaming and knew it was an educational process for me to learn how to go through matter.

Words that came with the dream: "You are in the 3rd type of substance. All you have to do was nod your head and rise above and through it. You were dreaming but you must learn to relax and take breaths to rise up through matter as if it is just a cloud."

Claiming the prize

The Dream: I was about to receive a prize for a picture I had created and done. A painting of the future activities to be accomplished. We were sitting in rows and another man of our Order (the order of the day), who sat opposite to me, claimed his way was the right way and direction. He put in his claim of authenticity. The Master of the Order read a passage from an old book and then the man opposite me realized that he had not interpreted things correctly. He had not understood the picture of Ezekiel correctly and its relationship to something else. He then said, 'It's over!' He hoped that it was over but it really wasn't quite over until the other people said that my picture was the correct one. A woman next to me, she was also a part of our Order, went over to console the man. He was full of pride and ego. I just watched the action between them in quiet confidence.

Words that came with the dream: "All would now go forth. His vision was not correct or based on reality. So, hold fast Steve while others might say something different, hold fast and follow the guidance. Listen to us and speak to us. Always share with loving intent and know what you can share and what not to share. Watch for signs and go with the flow and current."

A matter of perspective

<u>The Dream</u>: I was sitting on a sofa in a room. Then there were spirits that came into the room and sat on the sofa. They looked exactly like people but they were in spiritual form. There was a bug flying around that kept coming into my face and I would swat at it. It was a wasp or hornet. Then I realized that it wouldn't touch the spirits because it couldn't see them.

<u>Words that came with the dream</u>: "Try to look at all things in a different manner than before. It takes practice but you will see it differently. Don't listen to what other people think or say about what you see. Look to your inner voice for guidance. All objects are not solid, you only believe they are. Objects are made up of light that is caught in the material vibration or level of frequency that holds the light together. It is a single purpose, a single point of accumulation. The right frequency can combine or hold the light into a form or release the forces that are held. Relax and learn to see differently but don't strain to see it."

Choices beyond the physical

<u>The Dream</u>: I belonged to a group of grifters or hustlers. We would do what people wanted done but leave before it was really finished. Someone was checking up on me but I was not there when they figured out what group I belonged to.

<u>Words that came with the dream</u>: "The activities of the day are coming into view. You can be a man or a woman and you will review a living based on your actions and reactions to the activities within the life. Choices are not just made through physical actions but by one's thoughts during the action. Each activity allows growth for the consciousness of the physical conveyance. In the life, the spiritual being within learns through this visitation in this plane of reality. Bringing oneself to the center of the action allows for the greater activation of changes throughout the activity. The closer you come to understanding the heart of the lesson brings about ripples throughout the activity as you change your thoughts which in turn modify the

action. To get a grasp on the situation you must still the picture or scene."

Know thyself

The Dream: I was watching as a long line of horses, people and animals moved along the pathway of life. They just were repeating the same actions over and over. I went up and asked somebody about the order they were in and he said the horses always stay in their same order and positions unless they are nudged. I looked for my Mom and saw her riding on top of some small animal and at first, I was concerned about her safety but nothing would go past or over her because all things repeat. Some people were on horses and their hands were tied behind their backs as if they were captives to the repeated action.

Words that came with the dream: "You slide up and down through time and space. Weep not for your fellows they are never hurt by their repeated actions. Actions are repeated until there is a phase shift that takes place when one feels emotion during their involvement with the action or their 'witness self,' nudges them."

To know yourself is to know God, and to know God is to know yourself. Knowledge is a manifestation of a circularity of the eternal. Through Divine revelation the mind becomes enlivened and illuminated. Illuminating the mind illuminates and enlivens the spirit. Illuminating the spirit restores our divine nature – the circle complete. In knowledge there lies beauty, because we discover ourselves in knowledge. We learn who we are, who we've been and who we will become. Knowledge shapes us for the greater self that we are, but yet may not realize. Knowledge quenches our innate thirst for growth and discovery. When we learn, when we gain knowledge, we share a glimpse of the deific vision – and the more we espouse celestial knowledge with temporal knowledge, the more we discover our eternal essence.

> *"Never regard study as a duty but as an enviable opportunity to learn to know the liberating influence of beauty in the realm of the spirit for your own personal joy and to the profit of the community to which your later works belong."*
>
> Albert Einstein

Chapter Four - Empowerment

*The happiness of your life depends upon the quality of your thoughts:
therefore, guard accordingly, and take care that you entertain no notions
unsuitable to virtue and reasonable nature.*

- Marcus Aurelius

In our contemporary spiritual movements there are few things as misunderstood as empowerment. We live in a self-help world in which many feel powerless, and often hopeless. In this type of world, there is little wonder that empowerment has been reshaped as self-empowerment, and why not? If we are unable to earn our empowerment through our works or character, then we will claim it for ourselves. The challenge with self-empowerment is that it can often be baseless, or hollow, having no substance or support. This kind of empowerment is fragile and can easily collapse under the pressure of the world.

Now don't be confused or judge our statements too soon or too harshly. We believe that empowerment does require an immediate and direct participation of self, and from that perspective is self-empowerment. Yes, empowerment is the authority given to us to act; and yes, empowerment means we own that which we do, that which we are. But we cannot confuse our desire to be empowered with actually being empowered. Like much of what we've been examining in this book, empowerment and self-empowerment is an age-old debate. It is a modern Pelagian idea debated through the centuries, that we alone, or our desires alone, are sufficient to make our self-empowerment true empowerment. Appealing as it may be, there is an inherent fallacy in the idea that we can be empowered without it being given, that we can be virtuous apart from grace, or that we can become our higher (divine) self without the Divine. The empowerment, the virtue, and the higher self must come from and be accepted from the Source.

As we explore the theophanies of empowerment, we seek to examine the source of empowerment given by and accepted from the Source. The dream sequences in this chapter include some very short, some without "words" and some with interpretations. All to illuminate the greater meaning.

Tackling the world

The Dream: I was going to a place where the activity had started before. I was in the hallway of a hotel. I saw a shadow of a figure out of the corner of my eye. I saw it and grabbed it with my legs. I subdued it and tore it apart. I identified it with a large part of society. I was seeing it for what it was. I didn't want to take money from other people for the work I would do for them. I could now see things more clearly and in their natural state. Others expected that I could see because I was using deeper insight. I could see matter appearing.

Words that came with the dream: Upon writing the dream I heard the following: "Each day is like a lifetime. An opportunity to demonstrate your precepts. To learn anew and to uncover the God within self. Unity is the key. Understand that diversity is but a shadow and that each thing glows with the same inner light of the Creator and is a part of the Creator. The observer watches and waits to join the pieces of the puzzle of Creation. Learn to see how each piece fits, not how each piece is different. Learn what is common. Lose judgement and prejudice."

Following this I received this additional insight which is carried within as I journey throughout the world… "Take time to learn how to use your gift of sight to benefit others. Forthwith you will see as your soul chooses to open its sight for you to see. But, lo, don't use it to hurt others or gain advantage for yourself. Spiritual sight is precious but gold does not buy it. Love will keep it open and awake."

Altering the power

<u>The Dream</u>: A woman had locked herself in an office and was hiding. I happened to also be in the room but she did not see me. I heard a telephone answering machine start and the voice on the phone was trying to help her. I was not visible to her but was present. I could see everything but had part of myself there and part in another place.

<u>Words that came with the dream</u>: "Carry yourself up to the dimensional state where you can see spoken words passing by, words are vortexes of swirling energies. Look for the colors that surround thoughts and words. You can place yourself in a waking trance state. A continuity of the thought field. This brings an extra-dimension into the conscious reality."

The covering of form, which you are taught
It is not rigid material, but guided by thought
Carry a clear image, within your mind
Then it shall manifest, this you will find

Alteration of form, this is part of the plan
A gift of God, to the co-creator Man
How do we manage, our spiritual gift
For the benefit of others, or do we just drift

The world's an illusion, you don't seem to break
It is images of solids, that you do create
Break these illusions, we know that you can
It is very easy, for the spiritual woman and man

The world is a thought, projected through all
It is a teaching aid, to help you re-call
Awaken your vision, to an inner sight that is clear
Then you and the Creator, become very near.

Power of the moon

The Dream: I was notified of a special game. I was invited to play. I was in the outfield and was chasing down the moon. It was coming down. People couldn't believe how quickly I was running to make the catch of the moon. I was standing right where it was going to fall, but it moved at the last second and fell to the ground as a round ball. I then kicked the ball to the 3rd baseman who tagged the runner out. The players on my team and the crowd, couldn't believe the play, they were applauding.

Words that came with the dream: "You get into rapport by assuming and resonating at the proper vibration field. There are great halls of learning in the spiritual realm. These are records of history. If you desire to see a time in history, visualize the period until you feel a change of state and a book opening. When you look at objects you will see dual images. It is the astral and the physical."

Claiming the empowering love

The Dream: I went to see a new house with my mother. We tried to get into the house through a door located in the garage, but couldn't get in. I could hear the sound of a young boy and young girl in the house. I tried to push the door open but then decided to knock. Then suddenly, the door was opened when I knocked. A voice inside said, the door was unlocked all of the time. I noticed that there was no door handle on the inside. My mother and I looked around the rooms. It was a beautiful house with blue and white walls. There wasn't any furniture and I knew that I was going to be furnishing the house. I told my mother that I certainly could be comfortable living there.

Words that came with the dream. "With the Christ self, there is the possibility of greater love, wisdom and peace for the weary ones whose trials and tribulations have become almost too great for them to experience alone. More than just religious, it is the ultimate reality and final goal of existence. You voiced before going to sleep, asking about the influence of spirit upon the material plane. The material plane is a part of Spirit and under complete sway. Those on the earth plane are temporarily subjected to the lower frequency of earthly life, the material world which allows them in physical form to act out the precepts that were discussed in spirit life. Do not fear the events or situations you face…your world is subjected to making the dramas for spirits to act out on the physical level. All is the play to move you on as you experience the lesson you are to learn from the experience.

There are no miracles, only the quickening of spirit on the material world bringing the situation which is desired. Miracles are the determination of spirit to alter a situation associated with that particular person in order for a lesson to be learned. Place yourself in the position of recognizing the lesson or truth being displayed, created or observed and you become one with the observer portion of self and the inner reality of the form or action. Follow the course of an activity but rise above the stream that nourishes the situation."

Dream Interpretation: This had to do with working with my Divine Feminine (mother) in finding and furnishing a new state (home) of awareness. The door was always open. When one knocks, they do receive an answer.

The Philosopher

The Dream: I was sitting talking about life with a group of older women at a park table. Two older ladies were reading want ads which were sitting on the table in front of me. The newspaper fell off the table and when I picked it up the ad that one of them was reading was no longer visible. It had folded back. One woman said it was still on the ground. I joked, maybe the position has already been filled. A woman to my left was reading some papers including one of my works. The paper was brown in color because it had been written long ago. I explained that I lecture on these subjects. The women were saying it was a little difficult to understand. I began to explain it. I glanced forward, one woman was listening sitting to my right under a lamp post. Then a dark skin man (from India) came over. Do you think the world will end, he said? I said, with the continuation of the spirit, what does it matter. He said that he felt women would run the world in the future. I said, 'why worry, you'll probably come back as a woman then.'

<u>Words that came with the dream</u>: I saw a philosopher with a white robe who said:

The creases in the robe, like the never-ending sea
Roll back and forth, in eternity,
Time is a stead, which races fast,
From anywhere in the future, to anywhere in the past,
Imagine where, you want to be,
Ride her stoutly, and you will see,
The concept held, about the life,
Can be dissected, with a knife,
Slice it up, and you will see,
It's all a piece of eternity,
Crossing the great void, will bring you home
You will find, you were never alone,
Another soul, has sat by your side,
When you had, much to decide
A provision of God, has placed them near,
So you should never, have any fear.

The thing that means, the most you see
Is do your best, in all you be
Live your life, and learn all you can
To bring out the meaning, of your Master Plan
Look deep within, and you will see
The returning glance, of eternity.

Faith is empowerment

The Dream: I was taking a long journey with a group of people. It was another country or perhaps another planet. It was an experience that was foreign to me. While there I had greater abilities that I was able to use during my journey. We were all walking and then sometimes I was on a bicycle. During the journey I had thoughts that I could move objects with just my mind. I could move chairs with my mind. I knew that it was merely an action of extending the force of my hands. As I awoke, I knew that I could still do it through thought and desire to do it.

Words that came with the dream: Words as I awoke: "Through constant mental thought all things on your earthly plane are possible. It is accomplished by those who know they can do it. It is sure knowledge and expectation, unshaken by any intruding belief to the contrary. It is not just a focus, it is a sure understanding that it shall be done. You must see it done in your mind, know it in your heart and see the action take place. The All is in all and all is in the All. All is in the thought stream of God. For some it is a form of self-hypnosis that has allowed them to have absolute faith in their accomplishment. See it, be it, do it. All materiality in this plane is moldable clay material."

All are welcome to board

The Dream: I was running in an airport to make my flight. I had been someplace else and I did not have my luggage with me. I was worrying about not having my luggage and walked into an enormous room with many people moving around. It was a room filled with luggage stacked in shelves. I finally saw my Kluge bag but then I realized I did not have my briefcase. The briefcase had my flight tickets. I thought, 'How can I board a plane without my tickets.' A stewardess said, 'Don't worry, you really don't need your ticket to get aboard this flight.' I really didn't believe what she said because you always need a ticket before you can board an airplane.

Elongating consciousness

The Dream: I was sitting in a jeep in front of a forest. All of a sudden I realized I was stroking the face of *Miles*, the man who ran the transporter machine, from the television show, *Star Trek, The Next Generation*. I was a woman and there was another woman present next to me. Then I realized I was not where I thought I was but really there, together with her, even though she was away at a great distance. It is possible to be in consciousness with the other person no matter how many miles away. Miles started to walk around the jeep so that he could be at my side. This was unbelievable, the ability to have the entire body projected at a distance. Could it last, and then suddenly I woke up.

Thoughts and Actions: This dream related to the aspect of how one can transport themselves to any distance or *miles* and be fully conscious. Later in my life I would bi-locate twice where I was in one location and people physically saw me in another location many miles away. (Padre Pio – elongating consciousness)[xviii].

Empowering your higher self

The Dream: I was driving to an old neighborhood that I used to visit. I drove up to an E-Z Storage building that was several floors high. The whole neighborhood was run-down and dilapidated. I was driving at first and then was on a skateboard. I notice that there were gang members living in some of the spaces. It was a tough looking area. I didn't go in but an official came out to talk with me and assure me that he was in control and he was not crooked. In the background I could hear the sound of breaking glass. The man very upright and watching over people's interest.

Words that came with the dream: "I am your Higher Self and I am the official who is still in control and watching over your situation Steve. Look within and know that I am with you. The sound of breaking glass is your outer world of change. Despite outward appearances your inner remains the same…fully diligent and in control of your life's direction. Your spiritual gifts are there and to be used to help all people."

Wise and regal

The Dream: I was with some people working on new ideas and projects for the future. In my home was a large snake, probably 50 feet long. It had a wonderfully shaped head and lay coiled in a very regal and stately position.

Words that came with the dream: "Your dream represents a big change in your activities and it will include greater wisdom and expression in your life."

The meek are empowered

The Dream: We were outside possibly at sea but also, we were in a gym. There was a tremendous light and waves of steam upon the sea. Tremendous clouds were leading to the formation of something. There were storm clouds that were building within the area. I heard the words, Little Man Tate.

Words that came with the dream: "Size and strength are not important. It is the ability to face and harness God's great Creative Energy. The substance of all Creation. Walking tall is the key."

Recognizing empowerment

The Dream: I was with a group of people as we listened to a very tall young man speak and try to teach people about his spiritual contacts. He was sharing his experiences with how the spirits were around people to reach and contact. He mentioned that he had spoken several times in the Valley but didn't do well with the people listening to him and understanding. I finally went up to him and said, why don't you walk with me. I told him that he was very brave and did well. He lit up and thanked me. He went to touch my shoulder and he felt an electric shock. He knew that I had strong abilities and was connected to the Source. I told him that I had studied over 30 years and I felt he was brave in what he was trying to do. He listened as I mentioned some of the healings I had been involved with. He felt much better about himself. [I am this man.]

The signet of power

The Dream: I was given a very big ring. I wore it after I picked it up from the table. I was with a woman and we began playfully hugging and kissing. Then I was near a golf course and while I was looking to line up a putt to the hole, the ring was so big that I couldn't see where I needed to look. It was a royal ring in gold and red.

Words that came with the dream: "Steve you are playing in life. It is okay but not enough. I Am that I AM sent you. You must realize the ring of truth. Look to be committed to what you need to do. Align with your goal. You are looking into the aspect of invisibility. This can be an accomplished ability. You must aim at your goal. It isn't happening because you are not aligning yourself with what you need to do."

Waking to subtle powers

The Dream: I was with a large group of people in a lecture hall. I was speaking to them regarding attunement to the forces and energy patterns that surround them.

Words that came with the dream: "You need to connect with the intelligences that exist throughout nature. It is not enough to live, you must live wisely. It is not enough to teach, you must be an example. Everything around you is a life living vibration which circulates throughout nature to the beat of the Creator's Heart. You attune to it by sitting humbly and asking to become one with it. Pursue your studies with vigor but have patience. You have been asleep and now you are awake. (Anthony DeMello) Wake up in your more subtle bodies where the real life exists. Sing with heaven and all the angels sing with you. You have the tools and you have the key. What remains is your desire and Will to formulate your thoughts into manifestation for the betterment of your fellow men and women and the planet."

Power in the dark nights

<u>The Dream</u>: I was one on one facing against a magician. Then a lady was standing to my side as I was in the face off. The magician continually changed appearances and costumes. He then stood with his arms outstretched at his sides like a cross. Then I noticed six bodies of people, all alive and moving under his grasp. They were tangling from his outstretched hands like puppets. The lady who was standing next to me began mumbling words, turned and handed me something and then she walked away from me, past the magician and disappeared. I was then standing alone again facing the magician by myself. A man came up to me and said he was there to help. I was looking at what the lady had given me. It was a gun that had blue Kleenex attached to it. I was trying to pick the Kleenex off of the gun. I was explaining to the man about what the magician was doing regarding changing appearances. When I looked down at the ground, all the light was disappearing and everything was becoming dark as the darkness crept across the land toward the magician. I then heard very loud rock and roll music playing from the direction of the magician. The man next to me said that I should quiet it down.

<u>Words that came with the dream</u>: "Appearances, shadows of realty, the unreal, the show that is the passing parade of life. It folds and unfolds, it is a play of lights, tricks of the mind and sleight of hand. The closer that you look, the more it changes in appearances and form. What is man or woman? Fear not dear one, we are always here. We love you and we protect you. So be brave, be true, be real. You must go through the philosophical death (i.e. spiritual death). It is not about being a man or a woman…it is about being reborn into a new image. Handle the gun carefully and turn off the noise. You will be in the place where the

light transcends the darkness into a new awakening. It is the Dark Night of the Soul."

Dream of beauty and possibility

<u>The Dream</u>: I was traveling through time and space but if I nudged or touched anything I would be sent back. There was a dangerous little bottle or liquid or gas. I could affect it mentally and arrange the molecules and atoms.

<u>Words that came with the dream</u>: "Through desire, intent, will and imagination a strong movement will take place to shift the picture. Become aligned to your goal in the dream state, then in the dream state, picture and imagine your goal. This will help in your physical reality. Dream of beauty and human possibilities. The game of life is a demonstration of creative energies. Beauty begets beauty. I-magic-nation, Imagination is the magic key. You accomplish by Just Doing It!"

The frequency of power

<u>The Dream</u>: I was observing a group of scam artists. They had taken over a business with the intent of scamming people. But instead the business became truly successful. In fact, one of the owners came in during the scam and instead of being mad at the people who were playing and running the company, he produced a check for $1,000,000. Then other shareholders came in showing they had also received large sums of money from the newly successful company. The scam group couldn't help themselves because they were in the proper vibration for success. While this was going on and they had become legitimate the lead man in the scam became sad. His fun and challenge in life had been to choose his mark and to scam his mark.

<u>Words that came with the dream</u>: "When you change your perspective and become aligned in a vibration field this changes your perspective and results in physical reality."

Faith is greater than courage

<u>The Dream</u>: I was in a glass aquarium with fish and people and we could breathe without any problems. Then I was at the entrance and exit door but I knew if I just opened it to walk out that I would hurt the people and fish because the water would pour out. I did not want the people to suffer. I had the realization that I needed to just pass through the door using my consciousness. Change my conscious state and I would pass through the door to the other world outside the aquarium. Just do it between states.

<u>Words that came with the dream</u>: "It is not about getting the courage to believe, it is about building the faith to know."

Empowerment is egoless. Empowerment is not something we simply claim, but it is something that we can claim simply when we recognize that it has been offered. It begins and ends from beyond us, while being fully captured within us. Empowerment is something in which we participate, not something that we possess. Our empowerment rises to the level in which we cooperate with its revelation.

Chapter Five - Love

Love is not real love if it is based on any expectation. In love the lover becomes one with the beloved. There is no spiritual practice greater than love. There is no law higher than lover, and there is no goal beyond love.

- Maharaj Charan Singh Ji

From the moment of our creation, humanity has been seeking love and trying to understand the fullness of love, the meaning of love – love of self, love of others and love of God. But what can be said of love that hasn't been already said throughout the eons? Perhaps it simply is to know that God is love, and like God no description of love will ever fully capture what love is. As with the trying to define the Divine, the Creator, the Source, maybe love can be better understood by considering what love is not.

Maharaja Ji helps us do that when he says that there is no expectation with true love. True love is simply true love. The highest spiritual practice where the lover becomes the beloved. Among the most well-known biblical passages on love is from Ephesians were Paul provides a litany not just of what love is, but equally (or maybe more) importantly what love is not - it is not jealous, not boastful, not proud, rude or selfish, not easily angered, it keeps no record of wrongs, love does not gloat over other people's sins, and love does not rejoice over wrongdoing.

Seemingly everywhere in popular culture (movies, music, TV, books, social media, etc.) the question continues to be asked, "what is love". In that deeply spiritual and philosophical movie *Wedding Crashers*, they ask the question - "What is true love?" In a remarkedly thought provoking answer, the lead character replies that "True love is the soul's recognition of your counterpoint in another." But as plausible as that answer may be, it only answers a small fraction of the questions about love. It speaks to the love of another – not any love, but romantic love.

When we consider love, we have to consider the totality of love. The loves that the Greeks spoke of. Philos – the "brotherly" love of all of humanity. Eros – the romantic (and sexual love) of a partner. Agape – the unselfish, unexpecting, complete, full and unassuming love. Agape is the mutual pure love that God has for humanity, and they for God. When we dream of theophanies of love, we can encounter all of these. Our joy in life may be largely dependent on how we respond to love.

Christ consciousness

The Dream: You walk hand in hand with God, every minute that you love. Love is the state of holding hands and Christ Consciousness is the aroma or essence generated as you walk together hand in hand with God. You activate love when you are in tune with, in harmony with, at understanding with, your fellow men, women, animals and nature.

Love transcends

The Dream: The truth of the ages, or law transcending laws...love is the key, the loving energy of the Creator of the Creation. All are One. Summon the healers of all times, places, realities, spheres, dimensions and planes. The essence of Love is never lost. Love made manifest in a single spot, place and time leads to the highest aspects of healing. One will feel a vibration in the solar plexus, a wave of energy and a thread of light directed by truth and love. So Steven, be love, live in love and heal with love, in love and through love. Attuned to this, now comes the gift of love from the Creator. A torch of love passes forth to you from all times. We heal the body, mind, heart, soul and spirit. Step into the light and be One with those you meet, always visualizing peace and love.

Love in Grace and action

The Dream. I was thinking upon the life of Jesus and was near him as he walked through the countryside...

<u>Words that came with the dream</u>: It isn't enough to learn something through books, you must put it into practice. The human race has moved forward from Gifts of the Spirit. One needs no rituals, rings nor magic incantations to reach a state of grace. Imagine that your actions will benefit humankind and all the forces from spirit will come to assist in the materialization of your intended desire. All people can be moved to greater heights. Use your hands of light, your gaze of truth and bring forward the beams of wisdom. Stay neutral but know that the Christ consciousness is the glue of love that holds all things together. Jesus awoke to this state of Divine Grace that is little understood. It is a State of Awareness. An estate of wealth that each person possesses.

Alchemical love

<u>The Dream</u>: The master alchemist is the power of Love. The crucible is the body. The magic power of transmutation is love in action. Beyond earth love, this love is the glue which holds your world. Make fast these broken ones by gathering once again, those random energies into a complete whole. To stabilize those you meet, smile with your fingertips and love with your eyes.

Love healing

<u>The Dream</u>: You heal by love from the ocean of spirit. Don't be afraid to kiss them with the breath of life from the Creator of the Creation.

You are connected to the healing stream of the Father of Creation. Works come from the strength and mighty power of the Father's Hand…there is no abracadabra. Love and Beauty are the Father's tool. God breathed into the nostrils of the first Human and God's sigh rocks the heavens. Your Father loves his children and provides examples so people can understand their true inheritance. The stream of life is the consciousness of God made manifest in nature.

Ask in love and you receive the love power emanating from the Creation or the creative energy of existence.

The wellspring

The Dream: Surround all things in love. The vibration of love is a part of all creative activity. The key to the lock is love. The key to healing is love. Love is a constant energy pattern that has many offshoots in many realities but its creative and healing essence never changes. Through love you are aligning with the Great Immortal Founts of Creation.

The patterns of love

The Dream: Was I dreaming? Delve into the mysteries of life. Climb high. The truth is demonstrated by the healing touch of the ages. I am an energy pattern of love associated with the Master Jesus. I have existed before the beginning of your time. This is not a dream that you are having. I am here to activate a germ of love that will spread throughout your body. Every atom of your being can be a source of power and energy. Touch me and become one with the light. Give yourself in love to each of your fellow souls here on earth. I live in each soul looking to foster the germ of love and fan it into the flame of God's love and Mercy. I become more alive and active with each thought of Universal Love and unselfish works. Can you be one with me? Yes! Be in love, dream of love and support love. I am with you until the end of your time.

All entities eventually unfold the vibration of love that resides within them. It may happen as though a switch is pulled and suddenly there is a realization of the Christ (Love) energy pattern as demonstrated through Jesus. This is a fruit of the Divine, a part of the Tree of Knowledge. Love has existed before the creation of mankind's belief systems. A static aspect of God's glory exists, held in repose, when it is not being lived. An aspect of love is the glue that binds all matter. Love is the attraction of particles, duality is parts of essences looking to reconcile themselves in love. When you live in love, this static essence turns into a living essence and you become one with the principle glue of all life. What do you do? Love.

Healed in love

<u>The Dream</u>: I was in a house. A woman was there and she was reaching for a shotgun. I ran down the hallway to get away. I called for my mother to come quickly before the woman started shooting. I went into my bedroom and closed the door. I thought that she might shoot through the door as I was closing it. The door started opening and the woman came in, but she didn't shoot.

<u>Words that came with the dream</u>: "The woman in the dream is your feminine part of self that must be opened up. The love that must be gathered together is a part of your goal. Your palms will heat and your solar plexus will burn with the fire of love and the healing stream of God's creative healing force. I Christ come from the great void. My love passes all understanding. No one has healed by any means that I was not there in love. My Mother/Father God in spirit blazed me to life and love was born in the world. All the great healers have been love. You must wish to be of service and place yourself within the vibration of helpful and loving assistance to all the children of God. With a wand the Master Musician conducts the music that makes whole the spirit, mind and body. Harmony and balance obey the lines of force. The answer to a riddle is found in the question."

Love in all things

<u>The Dream</u>: I was walking with two people, one was a doctor of Eastern philosophy and one was a man from the West. I looked around and saw thousands of homeless children that were sleeping in the fields. Then I heard a voice say it would be good to help even one child to a better life. Adopt the children of the world.

Words that came with the dream: "Return love to love. Return love to hate. Create love from the stillness. Charge the atmosphere with reverence, beauty and love. Learn to see the good in each person, object and situation. To help each person to a good, happy and loving situation brings a person closer to becoming an angel."

During the journey

The Dream: I rented a stagecoach to drive in the desert. At a rest stop, three of the people who were part of the staff were wondering if I was too lenient with a fourth member of the staff. The two women and man, who were there, asked me why I was so relaxed and let the other man of the staff take it so easy. I told them it really was not so important to worry about such things.

Words that came with the dream:

> Service to others, rather than self,
> Brings you a bounty, of spiritual wealth,
> Giving of yourself, to offer a hand,
> This you must do, as you cross over the land,
> Keep your demeanor, on an even keel,
> Though the wind blow contrary, to how you might feel,
> The journey is really, the trials that you face,
> The goal is not the arrival, at any particular place,
> Life is a journey, so keep a good pace,
> Don't push or shove, as if in a race,
> Keep true your heading, to gain what you can,
> Tis the experience for your soul, that is the Plan.

Gentle universal love

The Dream: A group of men were in the park sitting on benches. They were all different cultural races talking with each other. There were street people, destitute people and many others in various conditions.

I was interviewing them about their lives. They were sitting very close to each other having off in two different groups. Each trying to represent what they thought the other side was talking about. I was interviewing one of them while I was being one of them. I was an outside reporter. They had difficulties with a concept of their well-being in life and then an afterlife heaven. I was like these men, but not like them. I was one of them.

Words that came with the dream: "You must love them all as children of Mother-Father God. All people wish for greater happiness, peace of mind, love, desire food to eat and a roof over their head. Each one of them is learning, growing and experiencing for their own greater and expanding awareness. Love all people, share with all people and be one with all people. Love them as I love you. And a child shall lead them. Humbleness toward and non-judgmental of their past is important for you to understand. God loves them all. All are his children and your brother and sisters. You come to see the human condition. Each is unique and guide them home with the light of love.

Not through gimmicks, systems, gyrations, standing on your head or special breathing will develop you. It is through the understanding of the Extra Dimension. It is through the rolling away of the rock and removal of the burial cloths that have stifled the awareness and understanding that you will learn. Cultivate a greater love for humanity. LOVE THEM AS I LOVE YOU. HELP THEM AND SUPPORT THEM WITH UNIVERSAL LOVE. All won't desire or come to the understanding that you wish. Love them and bless them always and be there for each. What you do unto the least of these you do onto me. Live, love and be happy.

Jesus stirred their God-self within. Not through breathing, incantations or exercises. He loosened the burial cloths that they had place on themselves through their contact with materiality. Arise oh soul! He created a stirring through resonance. Jesus was a tuning fork and caused sympathetic vibrations of love. The key is love, God is love. So simple. We ask you to go amongst people as a beacon of love.

A vibration enhancement will come from spirit and a collection of energy patterns of love from other planets, planes and dimensions and flow through you. The people you meet will feel a stirring within. This is far more vast then your finite conception of love. Don't hold strongly to any conceptions that you might have for that limits the possibilities. We ask for your willingness to be a channel of expression. You are not the expression, but an embodiment of that expression. All people can and will be the embodiment of love. Live the vibration, feel the vibration and be one with the vibration."

When the power of love overcomes the love of power, the world will know peace.

- Jimi Hendrix

Chapter Six - Patience

*"Patience serves as a protection against wrongs as clothes do against cold.
For if you put on more clothes as the cold increases, it will have no power
to hurt you. So in like manner you must grow in patience when you meet
with great wrongs, and they will then be powerless to vex your mind."*

– Leonardo da Vinci

Entire spiritual movements and practices have emerged solely for the
purpose of developing patience. Among the earliest of these were the
ascetics, monks/nuns and hermits of the Egyptian desert. These Desert
Fathers and Desert Mothers left the major cities of northern Africa,
Rome, and the Holy Land in the 3rd century to find a place of quiet
contemplation. A place where patience could abound as they sought
connectedness with Divinity.

From the 4th century Eastern world and embedded within the yoga
sutras of Patanjali are Santosa and Tapas in which commitment and
persistence enmesh in the spiritual practices. These practices which are
part of the second yoga path (the Niyama) and provide guidance in the
habits, behavior and observances to instruct the personal growth of the
searcher.

In an interesting contradiction from the expected, the early movement
in the West tended to be more mystical and contemplative, while that
of the East was more physical; albeit one where the physical was mixed
with the spiritual and intellectual (mind, body & spirit). Both however
also tended to be practices "outside" of daily life – from that which
some would call "normal life".   Perhaps the best practices are those
which provide an integration of these "separatist" spiritual pursuits
with the realities of daily life.

In this chapter, Steve's dream sequences will showcase revelations from
both sides of this spectrum. Being called apart from the world, while

being fully immersed in the world. By becoming a "monk in the marketplace", patience can emerge, grow and mature naturally.

Glide or screech

The Dream: I saw a beautiful swan floating in a lake with such grace and ease. But then I heard the loud sound of a cockatoo with its shrill echoing in the scene. Despite the noise the swan continued with all its beauty and grace.

Words that came with the dream:

> Don't hurry through life, as if it's a race,
> Meet each challenge, with beauty and grace,
> There is no winner, at a finish line,
> As you come to the end, of your allotted time.

> The swan or the cockatoo, to glide or to squawk,
> Do you move in harmony, or is bitterness your talk?
> It was all in the journey, each step that you made,
> Did you plant flowers, or bring others pain?
> Glance back at your pathway, look where you crept,
> Did you flow in harmony, or were you heavy in step?

Also I heard:
> The music of life, the continuing song,
> Plays its melody, your whole life long,
> Some notes are high, and others are low,
> But the melody continues, as long as you go.

> So, pick up the tune, and sing with each stride,
> Your choice is the movement, and your feeling inside,
> Lively or slow, it's your choice to make,
> Don't rush or be hasty, it's your time to take.

Clearing the storm

The Dream: I was being confronted by various situations. I faced different scenes where elements were placed before me which had to be navigated properly. By asking in a nice way, the jumbled elements and stormy conditions all became clear. The controller of the situation came out of the storm and confusion and I saw their picture clearly. Then the various elements were set out neatly and I walked a path through the maze.

Being dispatched

The Dream: I was a policeman in the police department. A call came to the dispatcher and we were being sent out. Groups of officers were forming, some in police cars and others on motorcycles. The members of my team were not ready even though I was. I would wait until we could all go together. One member of our team worked as a mechanic in the motor pool. He was a balding man who was out of uniform. He admired the fact that I would wait for the rest of our team members. We would make the best team when we were ready.

When the time is right

The Dream: I was standing on the beach waiting to play in the next volleyball game. Some people were discussing what teams would play next and what players would be on the teams. I was hoping to be picked on one of the teams but it is not the time for me. Nobody chose me for the next game. Everybody had already made up their minds about where the players would go. I noticed that Coach Thompson (Georgetown University) was watching the action. He would see me soon.

<u>Words that came with the dream</u>: The beach dream was telling you that several different combinations are being looked at for your future work. You had voiced before bed time if you would have some activity you would be starting.

Released to the wind

<u>The Dream</u>: I was with a crowd of people in a park. I looked up and saw people in a hot air balloon. One man released his yellow shirt and it floated down directly into my hand. I had dinner with three of the people from the balloon and after dinner I brought them to a friend of mine who owned a mine. We all walked into a room that looked closed on all sides. One of the walls was actually a projection of a wall and it was the real entrance to the mineshafts. As my friend led the group, we entered a passageway where the wind was blowing so strongly against us that we could feel the force upon our bodies. My friend was pleased because the people I brought had the money to buy new equipment that was necessary to continue operations. Now all of us could work together.

<u>Words that came with the dream</u>: This is about letting go and allowing yourself to relax and commit to the guidance around you and trust that you will see through illusion. In the mineshaft was a great wind and represents a great force that is to be released. Channeling this great energy is important. Allow the rising of a greater awareness which has been out of your view to take place. Allow all things to commence and have trust.

Patience wins the race

<u>The Dream</u>: I was going to work. I had to go over beach sand and obstacles of concrete. I was following a woman and trying to catch up with her. There was another man at my side who was racing with me

to get ahead. I got ahead of the man in the sand and the eventually passed the girl. People couldn't believe I was able to get ahead and pass her. She said, 'I always win!' I said, 'I'm still going to let you win.' I then climbed the barriers to the top.

The small corrections

<u>The Dreams</u> (two together): [The first dream] There was a man who was singing country western songs. We heard him and assumed that there was a large audience he was performing in front of. As we crept closer, we saw that he was singing in a field with nobody around. There were many fences and fields, and the man was singing but there were no other people round throughout the countryside.

[The second dream] I was with some men who were playing some type of volleyball amongst some extremely tall buildings. The ball needed to be passed three times on our side and I was trying to help but lost sight of the ball as it bounced back behind me. I just never saw it and nobody was talking very much about what was going on.

<u>Words that came after both dreams</u>: Find the little things to correct. There is power in thought and belief. Your system is overloaded. Don't push or coerce…love your body and talk to it. You must talk to your body-mind. Go easy and believe. You are now very sensitive and the small things are important. Try to slow down and relax.

In his book *Power vs Force,* David Hawkins describes levels of consciousness attained (or attainable) within the human experience. Each level corresponds to higher levels of "spiritual vibration" and are reflective of the realization of higher consciousness. The low vibrational levels (shame, guilt, apathy, grief, fear, desire, anger and pride) are described as "force levels" governed by individual will. The higher "power levels" (courage, neutrality, willingness, acceptance, reason, love, joy, peace and enlightenment) are governed by surrendering to natural and higher power — being in harmony with power versus trying to drive (force) it.

For Hawkins, as with many others through the ages, enlightenment is the pinnacle of human experience. The penultimate however, is peace. A high vibration characterized by blissful emotion and life view of perfection. Patience shares these characteristics that Hawkins describes. Patience is permitting one's self to enter into a trans-cronos realization, where time is not the governing factor of apprehending an expected outcome. Patience is entering the "flow" of the natural unfolding of things. Patience has a different affect (vibrational energy) than perseverance or persistence. Perseverance and persistence tend to be egocentrically driven, maintaining commitment to a determined course of action. They overcome obstacles in a steady and unwavering (unalterable) move toward the desired outcome. Patience by contrast, entertains the possibility that there are multiple paths to a desired outcome where obstacles will be removed (versus overcome) and/or that the outcome itself is not fixed. That there may be multiple (and equally beneficial) outcomes, some of which may be yet unseen. With patience, greater possibilities exist.

> *"If there be one attribute of the Deity which astonishes me more than another, it is the attribute of patience. The Great Soul that sits on the throne of the universe is not, never was, and never will be, in a hurry. In the realm of nature, everything has been wrought out in the august consciousness of infinite leisure; and I bless God for that geology which gives me a key to the patience in which the creative process was effected."*
> – Timothy Titcomb

Chapter Seven - Joy

"The fact is always obvious much too late, but the most singular difference between happiness and joy is that happiness is a solid and joy a liquid."
— J.D. Salinger

To know joy is to know serenity. It is to lead a life of completion, where transfiguration of person reflects the selflessness of the human essence. Joy takes root from within, emerges from one's spiritual and sacrificial experiences, and is imbued with gratitude. In joy, one is closer to the Divine and to others, where delight is the reward where none has been sought. Joy comes from the selfless acts of charity to which, often through sacrifice, there no intention or likelihood of personal gain. Joy seeks justice and rejoices for the triumph of the less fortunate.

Joy stands apart from happiness. Joy is expressed inwardly as peace, serenity and contentment – although it can bring great ecstasy. Happiness is expressed outwardly as delight, jubilation and euphoria, and it too can be experienced as tranquility. Happiness is typically fleeting and based on external circumstances. Joy is usually lasting, with internal conditions as its foundation. Still, both can remain present in the ups and downs of the human condition, resilient in the delights and sorrows of life.

Steve's theophanies of joy seek to share this experience with you. To help you see in your dreams the reflections of joy, the subtle stirrings that joy animates in your spirit.

Release yourself to the Joy

<u>The Dream</u>: I was sitting in a big auditorium. A man came up to me and told me it was my turn to sing to the group. I could barely get the notes out of my mouth and the sound was terrible. The man leaned up next to me and whispered for me to be less self-conscious and be

in joy. All the people in the auditorium were beginners and really didn't mind how I sounded.

<u>Words that came from the dream</u>: Life can be like being in a small dog house, which is on roller skates that is moving quickly downhill. Or life can be joyful and fun if one is less self-conscious.

Seeing beyond the obvious

<u>The Dream</u>: I was out with the team and coach. People were lifting weights of 350 to 400 pounds. We were dropped off at the coach's house. I was just a regular person but I was lifting over 450 pounds. There is no limit to what could be done with intention and joy. Everyone was amazed.

<u>Words that came with dream</u>: Seeing is very often a function of what you expect to see, rather than what is always really there. Clearer vision comes from seeing the deeper reality. Allow things to emerge rather than anticipating or expecting something to be there. Don't strain to see.

Realizing Joy

<u>The Dream</u>: It was the biggest turnout that had ever been assembled. There were young people everywhere over the playing fields. There were sports teams that had come early to hear us. There was a band that was also playing as an introduction for my mother and me. I was waiting for my Mom to speak. My shirt was out of my pants, my jacket was crooked and my shoes were off. I was trying to get myself together as Mom was finishing and I knew she would call on me to talk. My mouth was so dry I could barely move my lips. I was pacing in the hallways. I tried to speak. I looked at all the faces of the kids who were watching me. They would begin their sporting events as soon as I finished.

Words that came with the dream: I finally said, "Work hard and you will realize your dreams. Don't work for others, but work for yourself. Be good, have fun and live life in a joyful attitude.

Mist in the valley

The Dream: The mist in the valley rose up to caress the ever-loving sky. The day began with thoughts of joy and herald the dawning of a new era. Bring forth thy soul by full art so that you may become a brilliant light on earth.

Words that came with the dream:

> Let swing the change of pattern
> Make haste to come up new
> Cleave not to things of old actions
> But harken upon the new.

Shimmering essences covered by the earthly garb. You are immortality. Above thy head whispering of angels call you homeward.

Anger, impatience, and greed are velcroed onto each on the earth plane. With a little effort know that you can remove these attachments for they are not a real part of each person's true essence.

> Climb the steps, which lead you higher,
> Out of the source, of earthly fire,
> The loving arms, of spirits await,
> To help you pass, through Heaven's gate

> It all depends on your state of mind,
> An important truth, you're sure to find
> Trifles of life, kept you spinning
> Causing you to forget, your spiritual beginning.

> Looking for home,

You've wandered and roamed
Head toward Truth's gate,
Your Heavenly Parents await.

Light shines on the path

The Dream & Words that came with the dream:

The stars are placed, in the sky
By the Creator, from up high
They do twinkle, with a light,
Which can be seen, in day or night
The path of light, can be found
You can find it, from the ground
Think how happy, you can be
Once you finally, learn to see.

Deep from within

The Dream: I was walking through an airport terminal and then through a mall. As I walked, I noticed that the people I would pass would break into a large smile that came from deep within their soul. They had to smile and would become peaceful and happy. All people, both men and women, were smiling. Some glanced in my direction and they knew that their feelings were coming from my touching them at a deeper level. Then I thought I should radiate a deliberate thought of greater happiness for them because I was having this happen in a passive manner.

Love, Laughter & Joy

The Dream: I was in a room full of people who had health problems. I immediately noticed that all of the people had very sad faces, there was no joy or happiness emanating from them. Then I saw letters forming over their heads…some had L's, others F's and some had E's. All the letters were very light and I wondered what that meant.

<u>Words that came during the dream</u>: The letters stand for Laughter, Excitement, Fun and Love. Check out people's emotional quotients and understand that the physical problems that come are results of a lack of joy in one's life.

Joy, real joy, can seem to be an unobtainable goal – beyond our reach or beyond our understanding. Something we desire but not likely to achieve. Many confuse joy with the things, experience, or people that can provide happiness. But happiness is not joy. Joy leads us internally, to the examination of self. To understand our history, our purpose, and our place in the universe. The Divine may be the source of our happiness (or may not), but the Divine is manifest in Joy.

Robert Louis Stevenson, the 19th century poet and novelist wrote that "to miss the joy is to miss all." He knew that in the human condition, we forget the joy that escapes us and instead we tend to settle on the sweet morsels of happiness that temporarily satisfy us. Settling for happiness may be to deny our destiny. At the Yale Divinity School's Center for Faith & Culture, contemporary theologians explore "Joy, Human Nature, and Human Destiny."[xix]   These three conditions progress in harmony as a single movement – destiny realized in the fullness of the completed act not in its individual parts.

> *"And, the true realism, always and everywhere, is that of the poets: to find out where joy resides, and give it a voice far beyond singing. For to miss the joy is to miss all. In the joy of the actors lies the sense of any action."*
>
> – Robert Louis Stevenson

Chapter Eight - Peace

"Lord, make me an instrument of your peace. Where there is hatred, let me bring love. Where there is offense, let me bring pardon. Where there is discord, let me bring union. Where there is error, let me bring truth. Where there is doubt, let me bring faith. Where there is despair, let me bring hope. Where there is darkness, let me bring your light. Where there is sadness, let me bring joy. O Master, let me not seek as much to be consoled as to console, to be understood as to understand, to be loved as to love, for it is in giving that one receives, it is in self-forgetting that one finds, it is in pardoning that one is pardoned, it is in dying that one is raised to eternal life."

– Prayer of St. Francis
(Fr. Ester Bouquerel?)

What could be more appealing and at the same time more fleeting than thirsting for peace? Peace of spirit, peace of creation, peace of mind, peace of emotion, and peace of humanity. Has there been any greater pursuit in human history? We might ask how can there be a universal desire for peace, when after 6 millennia of human civilization peace has yet to be achieved?

What is the essential nature of humanity – to seek peace or succumb to conflict? In nearly every cultural and faith tradition, creation myth narratives chronicle very similar stories of [divine] creation followed by battles, wars, upheaval, a fall, and then the ongoing struggle to restore peace.

But what is peace? Is it simply tranquility? Lack of conflict? What does God reveal to us when we speak of peace? In our world today, we cannot speak of peace without speaking of justice – but justice beyond the courts, beyond the superficiality of "social justice". Peace framed in justice speaks to the highest self. The highest form of peace is based in equality, righteousness, and morality. While peace is found within it is manifested externally.

Steve's dreams of theophany about peace draw us to the loftier heights of peace. It's a meaning beyond tranquility. Greater than calmness. Peace in which we rest in the embrace of the Divine.

Sure Wisdom

<u>The Dream</u>: I had been driving on the road and notice how all the other drivers were being erratic and not thoughtful of others. This got me very upset and I immediately looked to do some retaliation of cutting off people.

<u>Words that came with the dream</u>: Sail your ship through the ocean of spiritual awareness. Come forth from your old concepts and those of your brethren. Love your neighbors, be more patient when you are driving. It is an opportunity for you to level out your anger. Does it really matter what someone else is doing regarding laws? Go forth and rise up to wisdom. You affect your reality by your thoughts. Focusing the thought stream, you create your belief to that concept. Everything is your belief system. Now a lesson in manifestation. Don't accept or expect what others might conceive as a resulting outcome. Excitement and anticipation lead to the belief taking place…the expected outcome. You must picture the outcome at the time of initiation so that it will be done. Give thanks that it will be done before you see it. Your thoughts and sure wisdom it will be done supersedes other's expectations.

Beyond the projection

<u>The Dream</u>: I was with a group of people doing bungee jumping. It was not something I felt comfortable doing as I was going up and down in a very rapid cadence. As I was moving up and down, I heard the following…

<u>Words that came with the dream</u>: Take time to learn of the transparency of this reality. It is all a projection from the real to the shadow. You come to the earthly school to learn your lessons. Your earth life is only temporary, so only a fool mistakes the tool for the All.

Bring it all together as you traverse this time world. Lift up to see through the cloud of unknowing to recognize the Great Being. Isolate the moving pictures and the sounds that you see. You have two halves of the brain. You can listen, but don't fall into the motion picture of life. Guidance comes from your inner self.

A prayer of Thanks

I thank you God, which dwells in me,
The blessings of wisdom, you allow me to see,
I open my mind,
To which I find,
You blessed my being,
With the gift of true seeing,
I will walk the path, as straight as can be,
We take it together, both You and me.

The shining light

The Dream: In my dream I saw: A little child walked the path. The shining light beating down upon his pathway illuminating every step. The child grows stronger with each step in life. Learning its way and strengthening his conviction and resolve.

Words that came with the dream: Take your steps Steven, have faith and know you are a child of the light. A stream of steady consciousness emanates from the Godhead like a beacon. It is the creative essence. The healers and philosophers found the stream through realization…they felt the presence and acknowledged its life and expressions. The benediction of the Saints…God Loves. A part of each of you is also a part of God. There is a frequency that resides within you that is the radiant frequency of the Divine.

The man of love and peace passes forth in Beauty and Truth. The wise come to the fount of wisdom, love eternal.

The Great Spirit

<u>The Dream</u>: I saw four giant birds flying together and then I found myself on top of the birds. I heard the following from the heavens:

> Four great birds, carrying totems from each direction,
> Guide the seeker, towards inner perfection,
> White, Brown, Yellow and Black,
> United they must fly, as if one pack
> Unite the winds, and people each,
> Towards harmony and inner peace,
> The Great Spirit, in his robe,
> Blesses your work, from his abode. This is the Great Spirit which
> dwells atop the inner pole of the circle.

Simple acts of kindness

<u>The Dream</u>: I was jogging trying to join the other people. While I was running, a man riding a motorcycle came next to me and we were talking to each other. Then he pulled up to a woman who was standing next to her motorcycle. They then got into a sports car. Then I came to a big field where people were playing soccer and volleyball. My brother's niece said, 'ladies and gentlemen this is my uncle'. Soon a group of people gathered around to see me. I began talking about the effects of the planets upon people. I was explaining the effects but there was some static as I spoke and people could not hear because I was beginning to wake up. I told the people I would talk again. The moon effects the tides, the sun affects the growth and decay of elements and radio waves. The planets have effect on matter and people.

<u>Words that came with dream</u>:

> Simple acts of kindness, toward your fellow man,

Move the soul towards greater heights, and you will learn the Master
Plan,
Bring to each the gift of love, and the mystery becomes quite clear,
That all are not so really distant, but actually all are near,
The pull of matter brings us close, to actions that we might fear,
But the heavenly bodies that we see, bring love and guidance clear,
God lays out the beacon light, to guide us day and night,
Though hardships are so ever near, feeling the light will penetrate the
fear.

Live your life

The Dream: [As I was going to bed, I was asking about how one should
lead their life here on earth. What is the purpose?]

I was walking with a girl over someone's property. Then I was in a
room with my mom watching television. The girl that I was walking
with came into the house and over to us and said that someone was at
the gate and wanted to come into the property. I walked with the girl
over to the fence. There was a man who was crouching down low and
had a large straw hat covering his face. I had to bend down low to see
who he was. Then all of his friends broke through at another area with
their cars, sleds and skis on snow that was there on the ground. The
girl and I figured we had to tell someone about these people. We
passed a manager's bungalow figuring it was better to go right to the
owners and tell them. Then we entered into a house. I was then
observing a man who was very nervous. It was me but then it wasn't
me. He was nervous because he didn't belong on the property either.
He had cords draped over his head and we tried to align the chords
over his body. Then a policeman came in and tried to align the straps
over the man. Then the policeman said, "We should figure it out by
asking, what God would do if he was here? How would God handle
it?"

<u>Words that came with the dream</u>: The answer is in the question. The purpose of life is to live the life. Try to align all factors and learn to see all the viewpoints of those who live on earth.

With the right words

<u>The Dream</u>: I was in a room with several people. I said something to one of the people and a very big and mean man came to defend the person I was speaking to. At that same time my father came to defend me. I didn't want to cause a problem or start a fight and have my father involved. My father was very strong, big and stood eye to eye with the other man. I decided to say something that would ease the situation without bringing my father into the fight and because of the right choice of words everyone became friends.

The Creator Light

<u>The Dream</u>: I was arriving just in time for the marriage ceremony. I also was telling people about the importance of life. I saved the city because of my quick action that was done spiritually.

<u>Words that came with the dream</u>: Look to the golden light of peace and plenty. Traverse the world and always trust yourself. Raise your vibrations to greater activity.   Bring more people together for greater enlightenment. Always ring true. Ask for help and the great Hand of the Creator Light will pull you up and assist you through love.

Feel the breeze

<u>The Dream</u>: I was in a courtroom waiting for the decision of the Judge. I moved to the back of the room as the decision was told whether I would have the immediate spiritual contact. But, even after the decision was made, nobody moved or said anything because they didn't

know what the decision was. I said, 'nobody knows what the decision is?' Then somebody said, 'I know what it is.'

Words that came with the dream: Don't strain to see us. Relax to see us. Relax because we are always here. You can see us, relax. We are like a soft breeze that blows over your face. If you move too quickly you can't feel the breeze. You must expect to see us. We come in love to awaken knowledge of the Spiritual Dimensions. We come to assist humanity for greater growth. The veil between worlds is becoming thinner.

Become a great healer

The Dream: I was standing in a line of people who were waiting to have someone count the loose change in their pocket. When I got to the front, someone told me that the machine was broken. I went to another place, just to my right. I asked the lady if she counted change. She said, yes. The bank we were in looked more like a bar than a bank. She was hand counting, rather than using a machine, so I was concerned if she was going to short change me.

Words that came with the dream: Change your earth rage and impatience to become one of the great healers on the planet. You must always have the air of expectancy.

Release the emotions

The Dream: I was standing with some people in the front yard of a house. I looked into the garage and saw a beautiful race horse standing there. I knew we should exercise it. I opened the door to get into position but was worried that it might bolt out of the garage once the door was opened. A woman came out of the front door of the house and offered to help. At that moment the horse came walking out of the garage holding all of its gear in its mouth. It was so well trained that it just walked over to me with all of its equipment and was ready to be saddled.

Words that came with the dream: This represents bridled emotions and the importance of not being emotionally out of control where it might affect others.

First create peace

The Dream: I approached a building that had suffered great destruction. There were people in charge trying to figure out what to do for repairs. It was a government building. I returned with my girlfriend and we needed to go to the top floor to help. We approached an elevator as two men ran out of it to get away. We went in but realized it didn't go up high enough. We got out of one elevator and followed two people who looked like officials into another elevator and we all rode up together to the top floor. Then we were out in the countryside and saw the building from a distance. I held my hand up so as to see only what lay between my hands. I told everyone that this is how you learn to see only what you want to see within your vision. Rather than look at this building you limit your view to the beauty of nature. Then I turned to approach the building and helped with the repairs.

Words that came with the dream: Complete the task at the highest level. Go to the top and clear the confusion below. First create peace at the top of any situation and stretch out and survey the entire countryside to help carry out the pictured goal that you wish to achieve. Rise to the highest level and align yourself with beauty, nature and love.

Transformation to conscious living

The Dream: A ray of thought that goes on as you follow it through life. People had this thought or guidance around them that is part of their life. It directed them into new ways of thinking, feeling, learning, acting and moving. This transformed people as it taught them prosperity, love, hope, harmony and peace. Here was a new way of being, feeling, expressing, living and thinking. It was self-existing, self-activating and self-supporting. You became it and you live it. It transformed people into more conscious living and gave them confidence and changed every part of their being, thinking and expressing.

<u>Words that came with the dream</u>: It was more than a concept, it is reality and it provided for each in their life. It moves on to greater heights as a person follows the pathway within their own self and holds on to this idea and conception within their life.

<u>Poetic dreams of peace</u>:

The road of eternity

> High and straight, be sure to face
> Compete with none, tis not a race,
> Born to flesh, that is a cover,
> That is sparse, you'll soon discover.
> Your light is clothed, with a Gentle Hand,
> Built from substance, of the earth land,
> It melts away, upon your death,
> Flowing back, to clothe the next,
> Then once again, in spirit you be,
> Traveling on the road, of eternity.

Life is a classroom

> Carrying forward, on through the night
> The love of the Deity, enlivens the sight,
> Turmoil and stress, the plight of the lost,
> Turn inward and upward, for this there's no cost.

The heartbeat of matter, is spirit you see,
To reach this awareness, just use this key,
Look for the inner, the driving force,
It's the handiwork of God, your spirit of course.

For each there's a pathway,
So seek it each day,
It might become visible
At work or at play
Life is a schoolroom, lessons to learn,
Competing with others, should not be your concern,
Locate the pathway, and you will find,
Your journey homeward, leads to peace of mind.

Upon the waves of love

Float upon the waves of pure love.
Become one with the Choir of God.
See the swirling energy behind the material life.
What is seen covers a glowing ball of energy.
Mix the waves of light as a conductor moves his orchestra.
The baton brings the instruments into harmony and so the person
with spiritual awareness can bring forms into closer harmony.
You bring the energies of the Creator into harmony using the
elementals of the earth, air, fire and water.
Constantly illuminate your body and soul so you shine with radiance.

*"Never be in a hurry; do everything quietly and in a calm spirit. Do not
lose your inner peace for anything whatsoever, even if your whole world
seems upset."*

– Francis De Sales

Chapter Nine - Kindness & Goodness

"Kindness in words creates confidence. Kindness in thinking creates profoundness. Kindness in giving creates love."

"Treat those who are good with goodness, and also treat those who are not good with goodness. Thus goodness will be attained."

– Lao Tzu

When we speak of kindness and goodness, what is it we are truly speaking of? And why kindness *and* goodness, aren't both the same thing? In the mind of man/woman we try to capture the mind of God, and kindness and goodness gives us a pathway to glimpse into the "mind" of God.

Kindness speaks to us of the nature of who we are, of what is at our core. If we embrace a more ancient and spiritual language, kindness can be spoken of as being a divine virtue. It is the height of our moral standards that elevate the spirit and soften the heart of those we encounter each day. Drawn from grace, kindness is part of our very nature, reflecting back to us our attitude toward the world - and demonstrates to act out of "an instinct that is the noblest part of yourself."[xx]

By contrast, goodness is the external manifestation of our kindness, more about the things we do for others. "Goodness", and indeed *good* itself can be a bit tricky to define as it is (can be) dependent upon the perception of both the giver and receiver of the goodness. In fact, there is probably no other topic in ancient Greek philosophy that has been examined more than the idea of "good". Inevitably and unsurprisingly, throughout time, cultures have come to see good as inseparable from the Divine. Goodness can then be said to be holiness in action. In this, the Divine or one's own holiness are not the most important; *action* is that which brings goodness to life. Goodness always requires one to act — to act for the benefit of others.

As we delve with Steve into his dreams of kindness and goodness, we are given a unique opportunity to explore within ourselves that which is our "essential" self, and the vitality of our goodness. We should neither be trapped in endless "navel gazing", that is in endless interior self-exploration; nor in "moral therapeutic deism" where good acts serve as therapy to ease our self-confusion. Our kindness and goodness should walk hand in hand in a life of purpose.

Sands of the mind, sands of the Divine

The Dream: I found myself walking and talking with a large group of people. I was discussing how thought is the key to produce and experience actions within different states and times. The amorphous strata are like a fine sand. Each thought produces patterns that remain imprinted upon the plane. As you reinforce this earthly dimension it brings greater energy to form. This is the laboratory that leads to material creation.

Words that came with the dream:
Kindness and charity, are more than just words,
They distinguish the spiritual, from the masses and herds.
Each spirit is clouded, in its view,
Due to its covering, it knows not the true.

The herd is a group, of spirits you see,
Who have lost the sight, of whom they might be,
Ture spirit is Godly, of substance so fine,
A part of the Creator, the ultimate Divine

Amidst the barren earth

<u>The Dream</u>: Buffalo were walking slowly across the plain. The heavens opened up and rain began to pour down as the buffalo slowly walked along. Then the thunder spoke in colors of a rainbow. Yellow, then green, blue and finally white. Ants were on the plain and build a lodge toward the sky. They were industrious toward the goal of uniting the earth and heaven. Then the elk came to bring their gifts. The rains came down again and everything on the earth washed down in a whirlpool into a worm hole.

<u>Words that came with the dream</u>:
> The sun blazed hot, and parched the land,
> As Spirit waved, its mighty hand,
> The new flowers sprang, amidst the barren earth,
> And they all sang the tune, of a new rebirth.
> You will gather, the medicine you need,
> And provide its magic, to all who heed,
> You need not become an Indian now,
> But you do sit in Council, during each Pow Wow.

Giving of divine gems

<u>The Dream</u>: I found a cache of diamonds. Once we determined that we could take them, I put them in my pockets. They were small slivers to full size. I gave a large diamond to a man who was helping me. I started to put them into baggies to protect them.

<u>Words that came with the dream</u>:

> Some view life, as a continuous struggle
> Through quick sand and turmoil, they must muddle
> Others glide over, the swells of change
> Calm and strong, they seem to remain
>
> The shadows of form, we try to hold
> Have very little meaning, as we tend to grow old

The rings we reached for, as the carousel spun around
Have turned into dust, and merged with the ground.

Use your inner vision, to seek what must be found
What has substance, and is truly profound
What are the baubles, that form into clay
As you complete the Great Cycle, of another earth stay

Open your vision, to a sight that is clear
Spoken so often, by each spiritual seer
Harmony and love, with each that you meet
Carries you from the surface, to your spiritual seat.

Reverence, beauty and love

The Dream: I was with my friend and a doctor of philosophy. There were thousands of homeless children that were sleeping in the fields. My friend said that it would be good to help even one child to a better life. He said he would adopt one of the children. I said I would take care of the rest as the darkness was falling.

Words that came with the dream: To see the good in each being, person, object and situation helps one toward Mastership. To help each one to a good, happy and loving situation leads a person to become an angel. Return love to love. Return love to hate. Charge the atmosphere wherever you go with reverence beauty and love.

To give what you have

The Dream: I was walking along streets with another man. I was finding money when I was looking down. I found a $10 coin piece. When I found another one, I gave it to the other man. I also found dollar bills along the way. Another two men were walking ahead of us. I shared money with all the people I met. We walked to a store to meet our contact. He looked very nervous as he told us to wait in the store. I decided to leave, as I knew that there were many people looking to shoot to kill me in the streets because of my sharing with others.

<u>Words that came with the dream</u>: Jesus also rested. He lived a regular life where he also worked and rested. Steve…live your life and help when you are needed. Have love in your life and give much love when it is needed. Give what you have in your life when you are asked. Support all when it is needed. As you walk through life notice all the treasures that are around you. Observe the workings of the Lord.

Never forget

<u>The Dream</u>: I was with a family who were running a business. The husband, wife and daughter had finally reached a level of profitability. I was reading a book that was telling about the history of the family and their business. They came out of a meeting and a few people walked by and saw that I was reading the book. Everyone knew that this book would become very valuable. I mentioned to people that one should never forget their beginnings.

Become the help

<u>The Dream</u>: I was a player in a tennis tournament. It was due to my action, where I sacrificed myself in the 4th round, that Jimmy Connors was able to make it through the tournament and win the title. It was upsetting for me at first because of my competitive nature but I wanted to help. I was the only one who could help him. Soon others found out what I had done to help in the situation.

Find Kindness

<u>The Dream</u>: After a dream where I saw that I did not control my temper and I felt an earthquake...

<u>Words that came with the dream</u>:

Fettered brow, awaits at the gate,
Hoping the Father, will not be late,
Bringing us wisdom, and guidance so near,
To handle the stress, and ease our fear.

Rumble and tumble, off goes the quake,
It is a message, to get you awake,
You must understand, what matters to see
True life is not baubles, but spirit it be.

What has true value, in life's great plan?
Is it money, or your piece of earth land?
Is it the trinkets, or car that you drive?
Or is it the spiritual, which resides deep inside?

Extending your hand, to help those in need,
Remember this schoolroom, provides lessons to see,
Be not worried, or panic as you live,
Only the earthly shell, will eventually you give,
For grander you are, and always shall be,
Go within, to acquire the key.

<u>Poetic dream of kindness and goodness</u>:

Service to others, rather than self,
Brings you a bounty, of spiritual wealth,
Giving of yourself, to offer a hand,
This you must do, as you cross over the land.

Keep your demeanor, on an even keel,

Though the wind blows contrary, to how you might feel,
The journey is really, the trials that you face,
The goal is not the arrival, at any particular earth place.

Life is the journey, so keep a good pace,
Don't push or shove, as if in a race,
Keep true your heading, to gain all you can,
It is the experience for the soul, that is the plan.

Mixture for the Salad of Life: The leaves and greens are the people of
the world. The dressing is love. The tossing tools are gifts of the
spirit. Always be blending for harmony and flavor.

Nearly everyone would consider themselves to be kind, and
perhaps nearly as many as good. Kindness [to be kind] challenges
our understanding of who we are. Goodness, beyond being (or
acting) good, but goodness in action toward others challenges
how we live. Kindness, including gentleness of spirit and person,
may be more prevalent in our culture than selfless acts of
goodness. But goodness is returned with goodness. Theologians
say that God is kind to all; while philosophers would say that
goodness comes only to those who are worthy. We say that all
have the capacity for kindness, the duty to demonstration
goodness, and the opportunity to receive kindness and goodness
from others.

*"God's dream is that you and I and all of us will realize that we are
family, that we are made for togetherness, for goodness, and for
compassion."*

– Desmond Tutu

Chapter Ten - Gentleness

"What keeps faith cheerful is the extreme persistence of gentleness and humor. Gentleness is everywhere in daily life, a sign that faith rules through ordinary things: through cooking and small talk, through storytelling, making love, fishing, tending animals and sweet corn and flowers, through sports, music, and books, raising kids—all the places where the gravy soaks in and grace shines through. Even in a time of elephantine vanity and greed, one never has to look far to see the campfires of gentle people. Lacking any other purpose in life, it would be good enough to live for their sake."

– Garrison Keillor

What speaks to the human condition more than giving and receiving gentleness? When we hold a newborn, gentleness pours forth from even the most hardened person. There is something natural about gentleness, something that just feels right. But when we open our front door and walk into the world, it feels anything but gentle. When we are there, we feel anything but gentle. In fact, it feels more like a constant battle just to survive another day.

Like many higher aspects of our being, gentleness is often misunderstood. Too frequently and by too many gentleness is confused with weakness. Indeed, gentleness is meek, gentleness is mild, gentleness is tender, and gentleness is compassionate. But gentleness is also strong. Think again of the gentleness poured out to the newborn, and to that child as it grows. The newborn is held in the strong but gentle embrace of its mother and father. As the child grows, gentle and firm direction guide the child to better choices.

When we approach the world and those in the world gently, we create an energetic relationship with all that surrounds us. We form a symbiotic relationship where what we sow will be what we will reap – what could be called karmic gentleness. The Chinese author and physician Han Suyin stated it simply: "There is nothing stronger in the world than gentleness." Whether we are accepting gentleness from others, or providing it to them, it is important to remember that while gentleness is always tender, it is also firm.

Perhaps most importantly, gentleness should be understood not to be only externally oriented. We need to be gentle with ourselves. Arguably, never in human history have we ever been as harsh and unforgiving to ourselves as we are today. Our internal dialogue is not one of gentle compassion, encouragement and correction. It typically is more like an endless chatter of criticism, condemnation, and unforgiveness. This is not the internal dialogue that reflects our divine nature, nor that which brings us into deeper union with the rest of humanity, creation, and the Source. We cannot be gentle to others if we are not gentle with and within ourselves.

Theophanies of gentleness range from discoveries about the Divine, about ourselves, and about our place in the creation. These dreams may help us discover where our gentleness excels and where it needs improvement. They may tell us how to receive gentleness, and how to be gentle. Perhaps you will find in Steve's dreams allusions to your own dreams and your own experience in gentleness.

The essence

The Dream: When you can look at each person in their essence, when physical characteristics are not so important, when a diamond is a stone and money just a piece of paper; when the body is just clothing, then you have learned the lesson.

Always loved

The Dream: It is clear through history that there have come those of your race who have been face to face on a vibration level with the God, the Creator of all things. Catch a glimpse of His presence in every sunset, between every respiration and between sleep and wakefulness. Listen for His voice in the wind. Begin to feel His presence with you at every step, breath and through every movement. The Creator of the creativeness of the world is ever present and near to each and every person. Now you must not feel unworthy or small to be recognized. You are always loved.

Lift the veil

<u>The Dream</u>: I pulled into an alley near a gas station. I then pulled into the station. I was looking out my back window at a building. Then I turned to face forward and a bum was washing my front window. Then another man stuck his head into my car. I said, 'give me a break…it's been a bad day.' Then another man was taking a pin and needling me.

<u>Words that came with the dream</u>: Love your neighbor, honor your neighbor. The rewards are great, you are all travelers on the road. Know this, the hemispheres of your brain can function independently as well as together. You must concentrate to learn and feel each hemisphere as it is functioning. Relax to initiate but strive to feel the aspect of each and you will come into rapport. Everything is in the thought stream of God, everything! Feel what each person feels. Laugh with each person. None know the Father, but those who become sons and daughters. Forgive each and bless them for in this action that you take there is greater strength and awareness. Lift the veil Steve, you have much support on your journey.

Walk softly

<u>The Dream</u>: I walked into a restaurant and heard someone say, call Him. I called and Jesus popped up from behind the counter in the restaurant.

<u>Words that came with the dream</u>: Trials and tribulations are a part of this world. Look deep within to a place of guidance that you can encounter. You have second sight if you need it. Walk softly with your eyes of love, a voice of kindness remembering how the feet of the

Master crossed many lives. One does not need a system to go through life, it is how you handle life as it comes to you. Look to higher sources for guidance and enlightenment.

Fighting with self

<u>The Dream</u>: I was watching fighting taking place. Arnold Schwarzenegger was fighting many people including parts of himself that looked exactly like him. The fighting was taking place with knives being thrown at distances and also close fighting between his parts was taking place. All had some aspects of him and after it was all over, they were all still alive.

<u>Words that came with the dream</u>: Fighting against the self is not something that brings results. Home is where the heart is. Look for the real and finish what you start. Unfoldment of higher truth is possible when you align with the real. There is no acting or show but a constant pursuit of the truth.

In the yogic tradition, practitioners are taught to "soften their gaze" in order to see the "truth" more clearly. This practice helps to recognize the "vision" beyond sight. Seeking to see both unity with the universe and also beyond the external to one's internal essence. Gentleness is similar since softening one's heart and attitude creates the space in which the person and world we want can come into being.

> *"Be gentle and forgiving with yourself, abandon any and all shame, and refuse to engage in any self-repudiation."*
> – Wayne Dyer

Chapter Eleven - Gifts of the Spirit

"When a sunbeam falls on a transparent substance, the substance itself becomes brilliant, and radiates light from itself. So too Spirit-bearing souls, illumined by Him, finally become spiritual themselves, and their grace is sent forth to others. From this comes knowledge of the future, understanding of mysteries, apprehension of hidden things, distribution of wonderful gifts, heavenly citizenship, a place in the choir of angels, endless joy in the presence of God, becoming like God, and, the highest of all desires, becoming God."

– Basil the Great

In this chapter we subtly depart from the structure of the previous chapters. We begin with a longer dream, really a direct revelation, about recognizing and receiving the *gifts of the spirit*. We don't approach this from a theological or doctrinal perspective, but from a spiritual perspective. The difference in these approaches is that the theological/doctrinal stem from the intellect. While potentially inspired of the Spirit in the spirit, the source is typically the mind, from logic, interpretation, and deduction. The spiritual approach pursues this from the soul perspective; from a place that transcends the mind and transcends logic. Understanding the gifts of the spirit from this perspective recognizes the differences and distinction of mind, body, and spirit.

As we've walked through the first 10 chapters, we approached Steve's dream sequences within the framework of the commonly understood gifts of the spirit. In this chapter, Steve shares his theophany of the gifts of the spirit meant specifically for him. We depart from the past approach with the suggestion to you that you may have your own unique spiritual gifts imparted on you by your higher Source. To be spiritually aware and spiritually awake is to be vigilant to the theophanies that surround you, embrace you, and compel you to wade into deeper spiritual waters.

As you read Steve's dream sequences consider, and perhaps meditate on the gifts that may be speaking to you. Find within this sequence reflections of your own spiritual journey.

The Dream/The Revelation: It now appears that your interest has been quickened. The truth you are looking for are those activities which transcend the physical being, and the activities of materiality are a presentation from the Deity.

Now you may find this sort of presentation from the Deity being very effective for the activities of Christ and the Disciples, you can find that in the New Testament. Near every one of the miraculous activities that you find in the New Testament, we find in the Old Testament.

Now likely there would not have been the piecing together of the philosophies of the books that went to make up the orthodoxy that Christendom grew out of, were it not for those individuals who had Spiritual Gifts; nor would it have been possible for there to have been the activities of the Man who came to be an example for others, and those individuals who followed Him had it not been for "Gifts of the Spirit." There would not have been the effectiveness of His ministry without them. If we move into the Hindu, we would find the activities of Buddha in the revolution that he fostered in that faith, were supported and carried along by "Gifts of the Spirit."

The true concepts of spirituality are guidance from the Deity as presented to the individual self and if that guidance is followed, and followed rather religiously, individuals would develop something that would transcend their physical self. Now those individuals that have activities which are transcendent of the physical self should rather consider that they have a gift from the Creator, and they best have care how they use it.

Elemental energy

The Dream: I was practicing levitating objects using mental and spiritual energy. These objects and their actions could be used in a positive or less than positive action. Then I saw the number 10013623 on one of the tools connected to a motor.

Words that came with the dream: You must think of the elements or elemental energy and command them to work as you wish or desire to accomplish something. Remember that the air element must do air, the earth, earth and so forth. Each element does what it is programmed to do, however each element does contain an aspect of the other elements. Don't just stare and wish for something to happen, know that it will be so. [Then still dreaming I saw a fork dancing on a table. I could raise and lower it as I attuned myself.] The subatomic particles are the elements. You must direct them with positive and authoritative commands to act. You don't change fire but command the fire elementals within yourself to align with the fire outside yourself and the subatomic particles become active to your desire. Don't hope something happens, expect things to happen as you wish.

Become the Christ in Action

The Dream: I was walking along a dock. A man forced me to jump into the ocean water that was full of sharks. He would only let you live if you survived the shark-infested waters. I saw other men being chewed up and there was blood in the ocean. I dived in feet first and was all right. The man said, he wanted me to dive in headfirst. I then dove in again but then as my extended hands and arms hit the water, I slowed everything down. I was in slow motion and gently and quietly entered the water. I then came out completely unharmed because I was not exactly part of the action.

Words that came with the dream: Demonstrate principles of equality, love, harmony and balance. We watch over your Steve. You are a vehicle to transmit relative philosophy to help others live a healthier and happier life. To Christ yourself you must resonate and become the Christ in action, word and deed. To transcend the self you must find the spark of divinity residing within your soul-self. Listen and look to hear and see the workings of the God-self within. Become a mirror to watch all the action in a slowed down version. Meditate on these things. All people are divinity in manifestation. You must face and proceed forth to all actions that will allow you to channel love, truth and compassion toward your fellow men and women. Behold miracles and look to Gabriel, Raphael and Michael, energy patterns as you and others become Christ like in your actions. Live the life to allow greater expression of your Christ self.

Seeing the signs

The Dream: I was sitting opposite a stage that was set up in the middle of some buildings. There was a family on the stage and I was looking at the older lady with white hair who was sitting looking at me. The family members were answering questions from the audience of people that were around the complex. The older lady then looked right at me and called me Steven. I then realized that I had been face to face with her earlier. But I was till surprised that she knew my name. She spoke very softly and someone had to tell me she asked what Steven means. I mentioned that it, or I, meant a searcher for knowledge, a seeker of truth. I heard the people around me commenting on how nice that is. Then I said, 'I could give you the biblical meaning?' Then, up over our heads a gigantic sign was rotating...it was extremely high up and it was a grouping of letters. It then began to swing and the letters were falling from the sky and would crush people if it hit them directly. People began running and screaming as pieces began raining down on everyone. Then I saw planes coming in, helicopters coming in and even missiles coming down on people. I was dodging everything until something just grazed my right calf. I then began limping slightly but I was a bit more dramatic than the actual pain I was feeling. I saw a purple and pink welt.

<u>Words that came with the dream</u>: Complete the task assigned to you. Look for signs of guidance. We are always near. Speak the truth, live the truth, be the truth. Listen for the humming in your ear and follow your intuition.

The right angle of consciousness

<u>The Dream</u>: I was going into a room full of people to present a lecture. They were expecting something to happen. I thought I would discuss the Multiple Wave Oscillator so I went to get the device but then I saw there was another lecture hall where I was to speak. I went into the second hall and saw people streaming by. They were not physical people but spirits. I could see them perfectly clear. They would walk, talk and then I found that I could trip over them and interact with them. Now that was very interesting. One lady had a birthday cake in her hands. Then again, I thought, why not? Then the thought came to me that they probably would be attracted by the electrical current put out by the Multiple Wave Oscillator. They would then have to go to the other lecture hall and be present.

<u>Words that came with the dream</u>: You will eventually see us clearly. You must be in the right angle of consciousness. We live in our world as you live in your world. You can see us as streams of light until you see us clearly. You will see us so you will have a better understanding of the continuation of existence. There is a reason for life on earth and all must work hard. To see us then think of us and know that we are around. Believe but don't strain to see us. Talk and share with us as you would talk to anyone else and we will become clearer to you. To see us, expect to see us and always be in joy and fun.

Pathways

<u>The Dream</u>: My brother and I were on the grounds of a house. There were pathways with different symbols and I heard the phrase,

'pathways like Tibet.' I was having a heck of a time following the pathway, as it just kept crossing over itself.

Words that came with the dream: You have the capability of using several areas of your mind almost simultaneously. Both the right and left hemispheres working at the same time and being in a waking meditational trance state. Not just one or the other working on its own and switching very quickly, but in unison together thus being in constant communication with your Higher Self and the Spirit World. This gives you a direct spiritual link. The teachings in the temple activities during the Mystery Schools, thousands of years ago, was to reach this true dual simultaneous conscious state. You must learn to cross the Euphrates and synchronize your left and right side to the vibration of love.

Frozen in time

The Dream: I was with a woman in the job of life. I was driving a car with her as a passenger and we were talking. The streets looked like the Hollywood Hills and as we turned a corner a big truck pulled into the roadway in front of us and I knew we would then be going very slowly. She mentioned that when she was with her man, he just went at high speed and passed the truck.

At that moment we were talking on a stairway going down and all the traffic became a line of books on the stairway. As she and I passed the line of objects they had all become frozen in time. I had frozen all movement and there was a little flash of light reflecting off the objects as they were frozen. The lady realized I had frozen all life and were moving around it. She was in shock and asked how I could do this. At that moment the little flash came and all things started to move gain.

Words that came with the dream: A sequence of musical notes enveloped her. This sequence was the key to the opening of the security around them. There are words of power that have been spoken since the beginning of your time. It is elaborate symbology of visualization. An out-picturing of your thought with intent into the physical sphere of reality.

Vanishing

The Dream: I was sitting in a chair at the entrance of a store that was located in an airport terminal. While I was sitting there a group of reporters came up to me to get an interview. The woman asked a question and I mentioned something about a television show that I had seen. The reporters wanted to show me actual footage of some show to get my comments and reactions. I was talking about one show but the reports were talking about a show concerning the Challenger. Another reporter asked me what it was like to have come this far in my life from where I started. I decided to completely vanish, before their eyes, while they were looking at me. I vanished before their eyes to another spot. From this other spot I could watch and see how they were reacting to my disappearance before their eyes.

Absolute faith, absolute will

The Dream: I was taking a long journey with some people. It was another country or maybe even another planet. It was a foreign experience to what I was used to. I had greater abilities that I could use. At first we were walking together and then suddenly I was on a bicycle. During this time, I had the thoughts that I could choose to use my abilities to move objects. I could move chairs with my mind. It is accomplished merely by conceiving of extending your hands.

Then the whole group of people were riding bicycles. There was a lady riding close to me as we were now riding downhill. I noticed ahead of me was a construction area with black tar being placed upon the roadway. I was testing the break handles on the handlebars. I almost jack-knifed the bicycle but came to be moving slower.

The whole group was now standing in a hallway waiting for the next movement. We were in a room and some people were looking out of the windows to see the landscape of the new planet. I made a joke about the air where we were and what the atmosphere was like where we left. This is what I came for I told the lady who was now standing next to me. Let's check it out! I could hear the sound of a bird making a long clicking sound. [As I awoke, I once again thought about moving objects with my mind, and had a desire to do so.]

Words that came with the dream: By faith you can move any obstacle and change its position. Absolute knowledge that you can do something. Regazzoni knew he could accomplish whatever he placed within his consciousness to do [This was an amazing hypnotist from the 1800s in France.] Faith, absolute faith leads to absolute Will, unbroken resolution will lead you to foster changes upon this earth planet. Through constant mental thought all things on this plane are possible. Find the book, *Fascination*, read and understand that it is sure knowledge and expectation…unshaken by any intruding belief that leads to accomplishment. It is not just a focus, it is a sure understanding that it shall be done, see it done in your mind, know it in your heart and see the action completed.

The All is in all and all is in the All within the Thought Stream of God, the Creator. For some it is a form of self-hypnosis and that has allowed them to have absolute faith in their accomplishment. See it, be it, do it. All materiality in this lane is moldable clay material. This is the schoolroom where materials are to be created and fashioned - through knowledge it can be done. Think of the action of placebo. Humankind does not imagine clearly and therefore the results are not clear. Forget the boundaries of sense perception. Imagination surpasses the senses.

Look into the healings of Jesus and the words that were expressed between Him and the person to be healed. 'Do you want this to be?' Not what you see now but do you believe that this new picture can take place? If you believe in the new picture it shall come to pass based on the picture that you want. Read the exchange with the centurion. The centurion did not want what was present but what could be. Jesus remarked that he never had seen such great faith. The centurion is a big key.

So let it be written

<u>The Dream</u>: The task was to move a car from the bottom of a hill to the top using only psychic abilities. While other people would move it along the winding road to the top, I was told to just raise it from the bottom of the hill right to the top and not move it along the road. It is the final accomplishment and not how that is the most important.

<u>Words that came with the dream</u>: I will accomplish by conceiving that which I desire and then knowing it shall be done. Lo, however, it must never be used for selfish material gains. I am being given this gift to help the world. Your gift and support come from the Father of All Things. It is done to assist your earth plane. Apollo is around to help. Conceive of a round circular area that is bordered by white columns. In the middle is a pedestal. What you manifest there is from the fount of all Creation. Then a new creation appears in your plane through your love. So let it be written, so let it be thought, so let it be done NOW! What is created in thought remains in thought until brought into your sight on the earth plane. The matrix continues to exist. You must choose and decide what will help in your presentations. Moses made his own choices. They were not our choices but his choice on how to use gifts of the spirit. We helped in the manifestations. Aaron's staff was his support. Read the metaphysical meaning of Aaron. You are crossing from two worlds. Two worlds that will become One. You are shaping the desire in thought leading to manifestation. Steve, be truth, love beauty and become beautiful. It is not just by saying beauty but being beauty.

Vibration of love

<u>The Dream</u>: I was standing next to a low rock wall. A bull walked up to me and placed its head in my chest. It was being very loving although it was a very strong and tough bull. Standing behind the bull was a horse. I had been with the horse before. People who were standing around watching kept saying, 'how could this be that even the animals just come up to you?' I just smiled. The bull was now so tame that he let me rub his back and he was making loving sounds.

<u>Words that came with the dream</u>: Steven, animals, people and all objects are within your light. You shine your aura and nature dances to the vibration of love. So let it be written, so let it be done. Behold the miracles. All is well. From the Mighty Hands, bolts of energy descend upon your world. A whirling beam of light forms. You are overshadowed by three great Beings of pure light, love and harmony. Follow our guidance and don't question, alter or direct. We lead, you follow. Trust in our guidance. Pegasus is symbolic of the altered reality. During your Ayahuasca experience, a ray of light descended from the Great Light Beings around you. Feel it and allow God's truth to channel through you.

On current of air

<u>The Dream</u>: I was in a courtyard. I felt a tightening taking place around my chest and then I began to rise above the ground. I could fly on currents of air. I stretched out my arms and I was rising quite high. I knew that others were observing what was happening. I knew that I could levitate at will. So could others.

Keep your heart open

<u>The Dream</u>: I was walking with a close friend of mine through a shopping mall. Then I was in a hotel. I was looking for a place to sleep and then be on my way. I found myself walking through a place with

a lot of people who were walking or standing. I felt it was important to hold my space and get respect so I puffed out my body as I was walking through the crowd of people.

Words that came with the dream: Send your green ray to the green life of plants. May the plants be healed from the destructive vibrations of humankind that looks to destroy green for profit. Honor the green plants and all vegetation. Keep your heart open and not body puffed out to bring love and life to all you cross paths with. Say the following mantra, my body, heart and soul radiate the healing vibration of love. Send this out to all life upon this earth plane. Steven you have hands of love. Be open, be brave, be love. The same love that came through the Master Jesus when he brought forth the Christ, which is love supreme, is available to all people.

Only the now

The Dream: I was sitting with 3 people. The three people were asked about accomplishing a goal using their particular systems. But I knew that they couldn't accomplish the final work doing it the way they were saying. When I asked them various questions, they couldn't answer because they did not know the answers. So, I decided to go out on my own.

Words that came with the dream: In every age there are individuals who accomplish the great work using systems that fit within their time period and fit their personality. Materializations on the earth plane are not an automatic response that fits some pattern. You on the earth must have some help with accomplishing larger concepts. The individuals who do materializations are not always sure what will materialize. It is accomplished with help on our side. Some of the important factors are the need for the final materialization and the use of intent and love. If we feel that the materialization is beneficial then we will pump energy into it from our side in spirit. You must realize you are a focal point of energy. Do you believe you can do it? The energy to make it happen should be conceived of as an ocean of unlimited resource of power. The waves and currents are the delivery system of unlimited supply. To the level of your understanding so shall it be done. This was the admonition of Jesus to each that he healed. To the extent of their faith and understanding of the new picture He was presenting, so it would manifest. Doubt is what stops the entire process from manifesting. There is no time, space or place, only the NOW. The YOU does not age, only the garment that covers you ages. You are always young. Now imagine in your mind the picture that you are and want to be. It is your picture, your reality and your time.

The gifts of the spirit bring into being that to which we are destined. When we accept these gifts, our spirits are divinely energized. We enter a new vibration, a new understanding of our existence and purpose. The challenge becomes recognizing those gifts within your sphere, those meant for you. Understand, meditate, embrace and enliven these gifts.

"Do you wish to be great? Then begin by being. Do you desire to construct a vast and lofty fabric? Think first of the foundations of humility. The higher your structure is to be the deeper must be its foundation."
— Augustine of Hippo

Chapter Twelve – Contact with God

"There is an indefinable mysterious power that pervades everything, I feel it though I do not see it. It is this unseen power which makes itself felt and yet defies all proof, because it is so unlike all that I perceive through my senses… Just as my denial or ignorance of the existence of an earthly power will avail me nothing even so my denial of God and His law will not liberate me from its operation, whereas humble and mute acceptance of divine authority makes life's journey easier even as the acceptance of earthly rule makes life under it easier…For I can see that in the midst of death life persists, in the midst of untruth truth persists, in the midst of darkness light persists. Hence I gather that God is Life, Truth, Light. He is Love. He is the supreme Good."

– Mahatma Gandhi

"Contact with God" is an idea that can be experienced simultaneously appealing and intimidating, pleasing and daunting, clear and confusing. Yet even with this range of conflicting emotions humanity has sought this contact from its beginning. Even those who don't believe in a god still seek a higher sense of purpose, a deeper sense of understanding, and fuller sense of belonging.

Gandhi understood this beyond any particular faith, beyond any particular tradition. He knew that God existed, despite the differences in tradition. Perhaps in his view we might think of "religions" stemming from our attempt to understand the unknowable. Yet even if unknowable, God can be known through our encounter with Him. Of this Gandhi said, "Where there is realization outside the senses it is infallible. It is proved not by extraneous evidence but in the transformed conduct and character of those who have felt the real presence of God within. Such testimony is to be found in the experiences of an unbroken line of prophets and sages in all countries and climes. To reject this evidence is to deny oneself."

Dreams of theophany are nothing if not contact with God. We make this contact through the senses, even if the virtual senses. We may feel

God, hear God, see God, experience images or visions brought on by God, be given the sense of the presence of God, and many other ways of experience. Often, we may experience "contact with God" without even knowing it's God, of God, points to God, or inspired by God.

The new age spiritualists may call these the "clairs" and attribute them to individual intuition. The most commonly known of the clairs are: *clair-cognizance*, meaning intuitive knowledge where you possess knowledge of something without clear reason or cause – often described as an "inner knowing"; *clair-audience* where sounds or words are perceived – the ability to "hear" messages, perhaps from angels or guides or spirits; *clair-sentience*, this is the ability to "feel" – may be vibrations, temperature changes, experience a "gut feeling", etc.; and perhaps the most well know, *clair-voyance* – the ability to "see" spiritual things, which could be actually/physically or in one's mind. Often, dream experiences are considered clairvoyance.

Instead of attributing these intuitive experiences exclusively to our own abilities, we offer the idea that KNOWING, HEARING, FEELING and SEEING are more than tapping into to an undiscovered sixth sense. They are the manifestations of contact with God. As we open ourselves to the possibility that contact is possible, contact occurs more often and more clearly. Steve shares his dreams about contact with God.

Currents of understanding

The Dream: I was an assistant to an older man who wrote and presented lectures. It was time to stop his lecture. He would continue next time with lecture number 1034. Then two walked away together. A younger person was there and lost the grip on a camera that he had. He tried to pick it up from behind an obstruction but the lens cover came off. He looked, then pushed the button slightly until the green light was building in intensity. He would then face the camera toward himself and this would send him into a different dimension.

Words that came with the dream: There is an inflow and outflow of currents throughout the day and night. Let's begin with you understanding them. They are carrier wave frequencies that alter matter and your reality. They can be modified and held solid by thought which is aligned with Spirit. Align yourself with the Deity God thought. Your linking with the Creator or the One Field of ultimate strength means that all things become possible.

The Christ envelope surrounds each person. We live, move and exist within this vibration envelope. All things are involved with this vibration. Imagine standing still in this light, it intensifies as you become one with the Father of Light. The Father of all laws and times. The key is to intensify the light, love and harmony that surrounds you until you radiate this light. All may radiate this light because you are the light. Our Father resides in and is the light, your vibration is sacred. You must quicken your heart, mind and love until you fully exude this light. Intensify your awareness until you see, know and feel this presence and demonstrate it to your brothers and sisters.

Become this light by holding this though of light coming out, through and around your material presence. You are the light, you are all packets of light. The light is held in a frozen state or slower motion and things appear solid. Intensify your light that exists and 'the light shines in the dark, but the dark comprehends it not.' You aren't given the light, you are the light. During your meditation, see this light and be this light. By desiring to align yourself with the Deity, by going within the self and finding your link with the Creator and becoming a servant thereof, will bring energy flowing from the Spiritual realm down to reinforce your activities in the physical realm.

Salutation to God

The Dream: I was in an office with other people. We were all leaving and the boss was also going to leave for the night. I grabbed a little map that looked interesting. It was a map of a cultural park but it was mostly writing without any pictures. Now I had to try to fold it properly while closing it back up. I had some difficulty getting it folded back and didn't have it like it was. Everyone was out the door except the boss who saw me drop it on a podium near the front office. He joked and said, "I saw what you did with that!" Then we all had a good laugh.

<u>Words that came with the dream</u>: Begin your day with a salutation to the God of the World! The Spiritual Essence of all life. Take four deep breaths and feel the movement inside of you and carry and sustain it throughout the day. You are a part, as all are a part of the Divine Essence.

Message is always clear

<u>The Dream</u>: I was on the ground looking up in the sky. Ron Morris, my closest friend when I was growing up was standing next to me. I saw a jet airplane flying high overhead. His mother, who passed away many years ago, was a passenger in the plane. There was also a circle of stars around the plane. I was trying to get a message to the plane by throwing something high into the air. I was throwing the message all the way up to the ring of stars. I could see the airplane was adjusting position and heading toward the point where my message was reaching the stars. I could see that the plane knows and sees what I am doing. Then I was worried perhaps something would explode because the plane would lose direction and go off course. There was no explosion.

<u>Words that came with the dream</u>: We always hear you Steve. No matter how you communicate your message is clear to us. Bring your thought in rapport with us. WE fly in a ring of stars. We bring you peace, love, hope and life from other dimensions. You will show the world we exist in all of your lives. We are present and death is only a change of consciousness.

Lift up your vision

The Dream: I was with a team and we were on the top of a building. The Coach was watching and even though I was a pitcher, they wanted to see how I could bat left handed. Many people and players were watching. The pitcher threw the first couple of pitches but I didn't swing too well. At first, I thought the Coach was handling the catching but then I noticed a different person was behind the plate. It had been a former player from the far past. His first comment to me was that my mother had mentioned that I should take the chewing gum out of my mouth. I said to him, 'what do you think? What would your mother say?' Then I realized that this person never was born from a mother. A couple of moments later I took the gum out of my mouth and buried it in the sand near home plate. I was then looking through a window and it had gotten late into the night. Someone said it is 9 and we need to get going to see what happens. Then the catcher looked at the record and said, 'of course this has to be…the dotted lines in the record showed a long home run to reach the left-field porch. I knew that this tremendous hit would travel across the sky over the city buildings and hit the window far away. All would see and know that I could do it. I also knew the catcher was a special Angel. I knew this is Melchizedek. He was behind everything and the Angel would make it happen. The Angel saw it all must happen according to the record. The catcher told me to hit it to left field along the line in that area because it was open and it would be very dramatic. He told me to wait just a little longer before I swung, don't be so impatient and it would go in the right direction. I would swing on the 3 and 2 count and the Angel knew everything that would happen.

Words that came with the dream: Have faith son. Knowledge that all things come from the Deity, all things come from the Maker. You are guided properly. Accept and go with the action. You hold the bat; swing and we deliver. It will happen and 9 is important for completion. I am the Angel of Truth. Lift up your vision and check out the field of play. Relax and know it shall be done. So it is written, so it shall be done. The Order of Melchizedek is real and still a vibrant area of

Spiritual Masters. Bring your awareness to higher frequency by coming into the vibration/intent of contacting your True Being. Everything is your choice. Surrender your desire to control the movement of life. Have the awareness that this is the intent of the Father in the Great Heaven of Being, the Creator of the Creation.

Over the horizon

The Dream: I was Moses and I was observing what was happening. The Man of high authority came back and found the World Research Foundation green receipt book on a rock pedestal in the middle of the temple grounds. There were other writings on the stone pedestal and everything was in the open air. He was very upset and asked why it was left there as it could be ruined by the weather. Moses had been away on business and was the person who would normally have this work. A woman had been in charge while we were gone and the man and I went to find her. At that moment the man picked up something and threw it with great force over the horizon. I said, 'what a good throw.' Then I noticed that the man was now a woman. We went to the gym to find the ladies that were left in charge of the city. Only Moses should have touched the book. I was Moses. We found the ladies sitting on the floor of the gym and they were all laughing and smiling and were very cool about the situation. They didn't see anything wrong with their being in charge.

The umpire of life

The Dream: A man who was very spiritual was walking with people and telling them about their responsibility in different actions of their life. [He had been the Umpire in the previous dream] The Umpire of the game of life. He was sharing with different people while speaking but then he wanted me to know something and he mentally projected his thoughts to me while speaking with other people. The thoughts of his mind, took form on a tablet in front of me at the same moment.

They were Sanskrit symbols. He was so very wise and these were very ancient, as he was. A woman who was nearby steered the direction of the group in such a way that it was of benefit for me to work with the deeper meaning from this Man, who was I.

Listen to our voice

The Dream: I was in my SUV and my Father was trying to fix something. He kept dropping from the top down into the front seat where I was sitting. He was working on something on the top and underneath the dashboard. My Father was higher up and when I looked up, I saw daylight between the dashboard and the outside. I finally decided to get out of the way so my Father would be comfortable not have to lay on top of me and still try to fix the car.

Words that came with the dream: It is important for you to listen and decide who is driving. Listen our child make your choice of who is driving the car. Who is in the driver's seat? Listen to our voice and guidance. Our suggestions are from everlasting to everlasting. Practice discernment in all things you do. Many are chosen but few come forward. We surround you during your activity. You help all people. Where there is no Wisdom, there is no God, where there is no God, there is no Love, where there is no love, there is no Wisdom.

Speak into existence

The Dream: I am a counselor for special men. I was discussing a case with an African American woman doctor. I stated that we needed to add fun to the men's life. She didn't believe that it would work but she said, 'everything you seem to do Dr. Ross, always works.' I said, 'just call me Steve.'

Words that came with the dream: God spoke the worlds into existence. The thoughts, imaginations and pictures are commanded into existence through the phrase, 'Let There Be,' and it is done. You must state the purpose of your creation, the reason for such to now exist and there is a decision in spirit to help if needed. Is your creation aligned with beauty, truth, love and harmony? Align with the Creator of the Creation, the Father of God. Bring a beautiful heart, an open mind and a humble spirit. Through love and a desire to be of service, humble without earth ego, confident that you are a part of the Divine Plan conceived of by something greater than yourself.

Contact with God provides us hope, provides us knowledge, provides us understanding that we are the main players in a "theo-drama". An unfolding of our story within the universe. By, through and in contact with God the universe expands as does our role within it, and we expand within ourselves.

> *"Instead of an intellectual search, there was suddenly a very deep gut feeling that something was different. It occurred when looking at Earth and seeing this blue-and-white planet floating there, and knowing it was orbiting the Sun, seeing that Sun, seeing it set in the background of the very deep black and velvety cosmos, seeing - rather, knowing for sure - that there was a purposefulness of flow, of energy, of time, of space in the cosmos - that it was beyond man's rational ability to understand, that suddenly there was a nonrational way of understanding that had been beyond my previous experience."*
>
> *– Edgar Mitchell*

Chapter Thirteen - Prophecy

"Prophecy is not an art, nor (when it is taken for prediction) a constant vocation, but an extraordinary and temporary employment from God, most often of good men..."

– Thomas Hobbes

When we speak of prophecy what exactly is it that we are talking about? Is prophecy a way to talk about the future, to predict what is going to come to pass? What do we make of intuition or "second sight", where do they fall in the spectrum of prophecy like experiences? Are "seers" like Nostradamus examples of prophets, extolling their prophecies to mankind? Or is prophecy more – theophanies of what *might* be?

In our minds eye, we likely see prophecy as a grand vision, given only to a "chosen" few; those who possess extraordinary gifts. Despite our expectations, we are all given the ability to share in this gift and receive prophecy. In fact, it is likely that we receive prophetic messages often. Yet we don't acknowledge them because our expectations don't allow us to see prophecy in the ordinary, nor recognizing them coming in subtle ways.   It's much like the way in which Hebrew scripture describes hearing the voice of God, not in the strong and violent winds, not in an earthquake, not in the fire, but in a light and silent sound.[xxi] In the same way, we need to look for our prophecy in the ordinary, and in the quiet voice of the Divine. The extraordinary, the grand revelations will be apparent on their own.

Like many things in the spiritual life, prophecy has been made uninspired; its mystery dissected into manageable pieces of decipherable elements.   The majesty of the source of prophecy diminished with commonality as to make it little more than superstition As a result, although integral to every faith tradition, there are more who doubt the reality of prophecy than those who believe them still possible. We are witnesses to the reality and grace of prophecy. Our witness can be our advocacy for prophecy in the Divine.

The Oracles of ancient Greece may have been the precursor to what we now understand as prophecy. The seeds of prophecy can be found among the Oracles, although the fullness of prophecy was not realized. The Romans drew one step closer as expressed through the words of Cicero in 44 BC. He wrote of "an ancient belief, handed down to us even from mythical times…that is, the foresight and knowledge of future events…giving to this most extraordinary gift a name, which we have derived from divi, a word meaning "gods.""[xxii]

Prophecy becomes the fullness of the ancient practices when the Divine becomes both the source and the purpose of prophecy. The purpose of prophecy is to understand the role of the Divine within our lives, our world and our destiny. Our future, emerging from our participation with and within the Divine, becomes known. The French cleric Henri Dominique Lacordaire described prophecy as "that universal and perpetual torch by which faith is enlightened."

As we explore Steve's theophanies of prophecy, we wish to capture prophecy in its fullest sense, including through the ancient understanding that prophecy is "to foresee, to be inspired by a god"[xxiii].

Walking in time

The Dream: I was in the back yard of the house on Satsuma where I grew up. I was able to walk back and forth through time. It would happen when I passed by a computer screen that was on a laptop. There was a man who could see me on both sides of the time line. He was a scientist who was leading the experiments from the house. He talked to me as I was walking from him and crossed passed the screen. He said I was in the year 4035. He could talk to me in a continuous manner in whatever time period I was in.

Words that came with the dream: Mistrust will be a keyword of the future. Steve you will see true but only use it for the highest and best and take not for yourself. Protect all people from the misuse of prophecy. Believe in all the possible uses of spiritual insight. Be not afraid to look into the still waters and see the future at the right time.

The record plays

The Dream: I was watching a man, in a business suit, during his activities. Then I saw the man repeat his activities following all the exact actions that I originally saw. I knew that I was able to know in advance, exactly how all the actions would take place.

Worlds that came:
    The song of life, like a record plays,
    As each rotates, throughout their days,
    A groove is followed, as the record spins,
    Originally recorded, as each begins

    Imagine that you, can replay,
    The thoughts or actions, of any day,
    Travel forward or backward, without any risk,
    You locate a period, then play the disk,

    Think of a time, or place to see,
    Create the moment, and let it be,
    The song remains, as a great imprint,
    In the record player, of God's Firmament,

    Voices, actions, smells and thoughts,
    Can all be found, if that's what is sought,
    The Masters of time, will see you through,
    Come quite humbly, to see what is true.

The future is in the past

The Dream: I was walking with some school friends in the past, or I was projected back into the past. As I joined them in the past time, I asked them what the date was. They were telling me the day of the week and the month but I wanted them to remember what the year was at that moment. As we tried to figure it out, I told them that they must remember that I asked them, so that in the future I would remind them that I had asked them in the past about it. I had jumped back in time and then forward and I knew that they would remember in the future what I had asked them in the past.

Be present in the experience

The dream: I woke up to tell my parents that I saw in my dreams pictures of life that would happen and also the pictures would appear in the newspaper. I could not show my parents the pictures because I had seen them in my dreams live but did not have a physical picture to show them.

Words that came with the dream: Even the most dramatic actions wouldn't exist if one was not present to experience it. The picture of life is only real if you experience life and own the picture of life. The Hawaiian healer does not choose to see any other picture then what he chooses to see. He does not see a broken bone if someone is brought to him, he sees only a perfect leg.

In the first dream sequence, you see Steve being admonished to "protect all people from the misuse of prophecy." It is important to distinguish between what *is* prophecy and what *we think* is prophecy. When one receives what they consider prophecy, if it is for their own aggrandizement or gain at the expense of another it might be from their ego more so than from their highest Source. Any prophecy requires discernment of the source, the purpose and the receiver. The fullness of prophecy occurs where self-seeking knowledge is surpassed by wisdom, and benefit replaced by purpose.

> *"We must believe what is good and true about the prophets, that they were sages, that they did understand what proceeded from their mouths, and that they bore prudence on their lips."*
>
> – Origen

Chapter Fourteen – Divine Physician

"There are two ways of healing sickness, material means and spiritual means. The first is by the treatment of physicians; the second consisteth in prayers offered by the spiritual ones to God and in turning to Him. Both means should be used and practised. Illnesses which occur by reason of physical causes should be treated by doctors with medical remedies; those which are due to spiritual causes disappear through spiritual means."

– Abdu'l-Bahá

The passion and purpose of Steve's life has been the discovery and rediscovery of healing modalities. In his 2008 book, *And Nothing Happened...*, Steve unravels the "mysteries" of modern healthcare and the interests that seek to interfere with their availability and use. There are forces in the material world and the spiritual world that work to suppress that which allows us to live to our highest potential – physically and spiritually. Humanity that is healthy in body and spirit is one that allows realization of its fullest potential. It is also one that threatens the profits of others – albeit physical or spiritual.

In this chapter, Steve's theophanies draw together the physical healing (and healers) and the spiritual world in which they are revealed. Conceived as the "divine healer", Divine intervention and participation share in the healing of the body. Wholeness of mind, body and spirit are attended to by the divine physician and the **D**ivine **P**hysician.

Just use love

The Dream: I was talking with a woman as we were walking in opposite directions. We were using a telephone. She was a very well-known lecturer in the health field. She shared with me her information regarding healing. I finally said to her, 'You make it too complicated! You just use love.'

<u>Words that came with the dream</u>: J.R. Newton gave of himself and he believed in himself. He created within his awareness the pattern of the Great Healer, Jesus, and then stepped into the pattern within his life. You step into the pattern that you wish to create. Remember, to love all people as I love you. Love is the key. There are planes and planes of life. Leave yourself open to spiritual guidance. You will see into the Spirit Realm when you know that it is there. Make straight and one-pointed your vision. Believe and trust yourself and ask in the name of the Father and all is given onto you. J.R. Newton reinforced his intent with will-power and love.

Lifting the veil

<u>The Dream</u>: [When I went to bed, I wondered about the great healer J.R. Newton and if he would come to me to help me heal.]

A man was in an outdoor area that was part of a church. He was wondering how to conduct everything that he needed to be a part of the church activities. But everything just started on its own and was taken care of. The man was very amazed at how things were functioning. [That man was me.] Then a woman was playing on the piano, it was the proper time for the piano to be playing even though the woman didn't play well. Everything was taken care of.

<u>Words coming with the dream</u>: Never before have I, J.R. Newton, come back through to anyone. Lifting the veil is what I want to do and be one with all people. I come to you as a humble servant of God, our Father, and of our brother Jesus the Christ. My brother Steven, what do you desire? [I would like to be helpful to my fellow people and assist them in healing their maladies.] Then lift your veil of unbelief. Know that I speak with you now and your wish will be assisted by those patterns of healing that have visited the earth from times past. We acknowledge your feelings and know that Love is what drives all to completion. Healing is not about learning a system, it is about attunement and learning to attune and synchronize vibration rates.

The shell is cracked

<u>The Dream</u>: I was in an apartment with several people. We were just sitting talking. Two teenage girls were standing close together while playing near the window. They lost their balance and fell out the window. The man next to me thought there was a balcony there. He then realized that they had fallen many stories. We all looked down, the girls were lying on the ground. It was very far down to the ground floor. I knew I had to get down to the ground floor to heal them. I could save them and bring them to life with my hands.

<u>Words that came with the dream</u>:

> To each their gift, and share of life,
> This mortal plane, of stress and strife,
> Lessons come, in a variety of ways,
> Some last years, and some last days,
> Behold the victor, whom has gained,
> Some great new measure, in mortal frame,
> The shell is cracked, out streams the light,
> The spirit now makes, its return flight.

RELEASE!

<u>The Dream</u>: My friend Sandee and I were walking with a friend of mine so we could be in front of a classroom of children. My friend was wearing some type of costume. One of the kids, as he was walking toward the front of the classroom, suddenly turned to reach for a knife on a table to kill himself. I started after him by walking a parallel course to reach the knife before he did. I noticed a still picture, in a frame, of the Archangel Michael. Then I heard the word RELEASE. I had been touching the boy to heal his mind and I was being told to release my hands from the boy. Whenever I do touch healing, I need only wait to hear the word RELEASE. Everyone was saying it was a miracle. The

kids did not have the ability at that time to go directly for their own healing, I had the energy coming through me to teach them.

Words that came with the dream: Sandee was the good spirit trying to lead the class. Steve, your unwavering desire to help others to freedom, love, truth and healing has placed Raphael, the healing spirit of God, to overshadow your activities along with Michael and God's strength. Michael slays the dragon of ignorance. Bring them home to truth and not error.

Help from the spiritual world

The Dream: I was sitting with a large group of people in an auditorium. I was at the back of the room watching and listening to the people. I glanced to my left and I saw two men outside bringing something to the door. The wall was made of glass so I could see they were rolling a large blue trunk. I got very excited because I knew it was filled with special papers that I was going to be able to examine and research. I then glanced up to the front of the room and the man in charge was sitting on a chair and he made eye contact with me to let me know that I would be able to check the contents of the trunk. I got up and started to walk to the front of the room and l looked down and saw my shoes were off and I was walking in my socks.

Words that came with the dream: Carry on your activities of healing all things, people, animals and nature on your planet. Visualize and conceptualize, we who help you from the spiritual world, standing behind and next to you with our forces gathering in resonance with those energies you are projecting during your healing work. Behold miracles in action on your earth plane. Work with light, sound and love. You are a priest of light. A Priest after the Order of Melchizedek. It is not by rings, dear one, but the love that is projected as light. The green ray comes from your left palm and it is the ray of growth, the right palm is the purple ray and it is the ray of power and transformation. Come with a beautiful heart, and open mind and a humble spirit. Listen to all people and reinforce them with love, energy and truth. The blue trunk of truth, knowledge and wisdom is your Ark of the Covenant. Release some of your old energy patterns and take on the new as you come to hallowed ground.

Bridle the energy

<u>The Dream</u>: I was driving to a house that was in the country. I was going to meet some people who lived there. There were beautiful trees that surrounded the roadway. The garage was opened and I was walking toward it. I thought I saw a car driving toward me on the road ahead. It was a horse that was running down the street toward me. Then I noticed there were many horses running free down the road toward me. They had escaped their harnesses and I thought someone would be upset that they were loose and running free. Then I thought, I wonder if they would come to me in a wild manner and rear up?

<u>Words that came with the dream</u>: The horses represent deep emotions that run unbridled, free and out of control. People are coming to you with a lot of energy that is running wild and unbridled. You must help to bring them under control. The energy you use to help others is love, energy and light. The same in substance but in different degrees. Keep yourself in the consciousness of helping others and being of service to humanity. All the Revelators of your earth carried within themselves the strong emotional desire to help their fellow man and woman. Place yourself in a receptive state. Your dream also represents the activities of the enlighten souls before you to were assisted by the energies of Creation that came down to them like charging horses in your dream. It was up to them to harness and channel the energies of Creation that would be used in their healing work. Do not be involved with politics. This is a childish game of the physical world. Do not desire those things that are possessed by another. Seek those things from above and not below. Do not belong to groups but support with energy those activities that are of the highest and best for all upon the earth. You give love. Be brave and be true.

Life can be hard

The Dream: I looked into the back seat of a car and noticed two children with Down's syndrome. It was very obvious to me that they had a health challenge. I looked into their eyes with love and then mesmerized them into complete peace and quiet. At that moment some other mothers were bringing their children to school and they knew of these two children. I was wondering if these children would be taken care of if the parents had the money to do it.

Words that came with the dream: These are aspects of life that are a part of the learning experiences. Some people must work very hard and have some experiences that appear to be worse than others. You will always know what you can and should do in every situation. Be open to guidance.

Embodiment of love and light

The Dream: There was a tremendous celebration at a big park. I was being celebrated by thousands of people who were there. It was a celebration of life and accomplishments of beauty and love. The celebration consisted of hundreds of thousands of balloons of many different colors. The first set of balloons that were released carried small signs of what had been done with people of various colored balloons. I was sitting on a beach chair watching the action.

Words that came with the dream: You are supported in every endeavor with the embodiment of love and light. When you become the embodiment of love, light, truth and beauty you become one with the Spiritual Entity that surrounds you at this time. You must become one with, live one with, bring love into your heart and become a Christ. You are not being honored for the past, but for the future. There is a wind of change coming and you must become like onto the Christ. Now you must have a leap of faith with love. Green in your left palm and violet in your right with a golden white light in your heart. You can create, correct, conceive, pattern and build. To develop your Will is to develop power over your life. Let fly your courage and fly like the eagles. You are a son of God. You must go higher within yourself beyond conscious thought. You live in a world of Maya, it is a thought form world of mirrors. Keep still and calm. All is created out of mind-stuff, which never runs out. It is the fabric of creation, the loom of life.

Give power back

The Dream: I was lecturing in front of a group of people when suddenly it began to turn into a healing event. I spoke to the people because I was inspired. I was told by the woman who was with me to stand up and talk and she would ask for donations and take their money. She would pass the hat for donations for my healing work. No, I said, I don't take money. This surprised the lady. I closed my eyes and spoke to the group. I said the power to heal does not come from the healer but it is within the person who is seeking healing. As I looked at the people in the audience, I could see a green luminescence in the places in their body that needed healing. I could feel the healing energy building up within me as the green light within them became more illuminated. I told them it is you, look within yourselves. Then I told them I would return tomorrow. As the people were breaking up to leave a man came up to me and said out loud to the people, 'do you know who this man is?' I thought at first he was talking to put me down and reveal something that would not be complimentary. Actually, he was trying to build me up as a great healer so I could get money from the people. I said, 'I am only me!' You are healing yourselves. I just help your power. As I spoke a group of athletes in wheelchairs passed under my outstretched hands. There were in a line moving quickly while wearing protective hats. Then I told the people again, 'I don't take money.' The man was shocked as he thought it was a way for me to get money.

<u>Words that came with the dream</u>: Blessing our son. Be there for all people, Heal in body, mind and spirit. Give back to others the power in their life. Calm and soothe all people in beauty, love and truth. Live, love and be one with God, the Creating aspect and truth of life. The healing balm is love. No money is needed to buy love. Push through your heart and hands the current that is directed by the Creator of the Creation. So let it be written, so let it be done!

Begin in beauty and explain to people the course to take. Share with them your story. Live and climb the mountain of your own disbelief and conquer your fears Steven by becoming one with Divine Power, the Source of Creation.

You will see the areas marked in green. You will see their need and where the love is to be directed. You must push the button to start the elevator. You must believe for things to start to move.

The healing prayer

<u>The Dream</u>: The following was given to me while I was in the teepee of a group of American Indian Chiefs. This is the prayer to help heal others.

<u>Healing Prayer that came in the dream</u>: Oh Great Spirit, manifest your loving energy to your children. Make whole this broken one. You are the glue that binds all life together. You are the force which drives all toward completion. You are the warmth that heats love, the voice of thunder and the light of lightning. For you all is done.

Dream and create

<u>The Dream</u>: I was sitting in front of the old philosopher Paracelsus from the 1500s. He said, "Your imagination has not been properly understood or applied. Here is the secret to master transcendency of

the physical materiality. Creation begins in the higher realms of vibration. Creation in your material world begins with thought. Can you build anything without conceiving? Can you even begin without dreaming? Listen well! To build, to construct to frame anything you must first conceive and imagine what you desire and then add faith with will power. Thought forms…thought, forms, thought does form. Have the faith that it shall be!

The shadow

The Dream: I was in a hotel lobby in what appeared to be Las Vegas. When I went out of my hotel room I met a tall basketball player. He was talking about hypnosis. I mentioned that I had some books dating from the 1600s that he would find interesting. His wife joined us and we were talking about how the early hypnotists in the 1800s helped the people remove their senses from their body. They were able to realize that there was more than just the physical body. I told her that this was a great bit of knowledge.

Words that came with the dream: The physical is a shadow. All materiality including fire, cold and all other forms are shadows. Dwelling within the spirit and pulling slightly away from the consciousness of the body allows for the cessation of feelings and reactions in the shadow world. The shadow world of materiality has no reality unless you place yourself there.

The fount

The Dream: I was receiving answers to my questions about my ability to heal from dreams taking place within this dream.

Words that came with the dream: The fount of God, the Creator of the Creation is a substance that is flowing energy which permeates all matter. It is in continuous movement, it is in the air we breathe, the water we drink, it surrounds us at all times. It can be accelerated in its activity by thought, desire and faith. It can be activated by touch, speech and sight. Not material wealth, but source and spiritual wealth. None knows the Father except all of his children.

Melt the illusion, clear the third eye,
Symbolically the physical, goes on to die
A robe of glory, within you mortals be
Hidden from view, soon you will see
Spiritual essence, flowing with light
In a world, with no day or night
Clear the vision, so you will see
Reaching a vibration, of loving energy.
Aspiring soul, into the night,
Leave the body, you do take flight
You will find new awareness, and bring it to view,
Cleansing and helping, all to renew.

Religious mythos says that the ills of humanity began at Eden, when we sought to be like God. For "punishment" of that desire we were cast out of paradise to experience pain, illness, suffering, death and sin. Since then earthly physicians have been working the cures for our illness. But those physicians have separated the physical ills from the spiritual ills, unable to provide the healing we required. The Divine physician came among us to heal those illnesses. As inheritors of the Divine physician we too can be divine physicians when we open to the theophanies of healing.

"We are not human beings in search of a spiritual experience. We are spiritual beings immersed in a human experience... Once you believe in yourself and see your soul as divine and precious, you'll automatically be converted to a being who can create miracles...Everything in the universe

has a purpose. Indeed, the invisible intelligence that flows through everything in a purposeful fashion is also flowing through you."

– Wayne Dyer

End of Part I

Part II – Dare to Dream – Living a Divine Life

Introduction to Part II

The fulfillment of life comes not in simply pondering or thinking about life itself, nor even in dreaming of it. Fulfillment comes in the living of life. And living life is likely to be as simple and ordinary as it is to be exciting and meaningful. It is easy to sense the transcendent, feeling the Divine in the extraordinary moments in life. But it is in the ordinary where we lead our lives and where we need to discover the Divine and the divine moments.

This is what Steve shares with us in Part II. The moments of ordinary in which theophany becomes reality. In the ordinary, extraordinary and transcendent aspects of life, Steve encounters the Divine. In his work, his research, his relationships and his transcendent moments. Of particular importance is his experience of healthcare discoveries and rediscoveries, and ultimately his ability to provide healings to many of those who came to see him.

In Part II, we will explore these times as a means to make evident those ordinary things in your life which make you extraordinary. To discover the "unimportant" experiences in which you begin to transcend the routine. To hear and see transcendence and ultimately live a rediscovery of your own participation in divinity.

Chapter Fifteen – My Early Years

My earliest recollections are of standing on the front seat of my parent's car while my Dad was driving. My father worked at Lockheed Aircraft and with each two or three-week vacation, our family would journey from my birth city of Los Angeles to some distant spot in the country. On some of our longer trips, dad would drive throughout most of the night and I would be standing on the seat with my arm around his shoulder. Usually during this time, my mother and brother would be asleep in the back seat.

My parents took trips every year, with my brother and I, and this provided an opportunity to visit almost every state in the continental U.S. I use to love looking at the world coming toward me through the windshield. These early experiences gave me the love of traveling and learning about the world beyond my home.

Even at a very early age my parents allowed my brother and I a certain amount of freedom that I did not find my friends were experiencing with their parents. My brother Barry and I were told that as long as we showed our parents that we could be trusted, and were respectful of other people and their 'things', that they would trust us with more freedom and would treat us like adults.

Although I didn't appreciate it at the time, my parent's style of sharing with us and the openness they provided for my brother and I to experience life, was instrumental in establishing my eclectic interests and desire to always learn something new.

My parents had a wonderful group of friends that would get together almost every Saturday evening. Their closest couple, Nate and Diane, would become the couple they would most often be with.

I would hear some of their discussions while I was in other rooms and I remember how much I desired to just sit and listen to their intriguing Saturday conversations about life, politics, religions and so many subjects. When Nate and Diane were coming to our house my mom would prepare the most incredible finger foods for snacks. I know how good they were because I was always figuring how to snitch some from out of the refrigerator and then pack them more tightly on the plate so it wouldn't appear any were missing. Mom always knew they were missing. Barry and I hoped that they wouldn't finish them all because they tasted so good on Sunday!

One day I asked my parents if I might be able to sit in their room and listen to some of their conversations. I used to listen close to the door, but I wanted to really be in the room. When I was old enough, they told me I could sit with the adults under the following rules. I would not interrupt while an adult was speaking…and I would only speak when someone addressed me.

Although I was constantly playing sports with my friends, either on our street, or at the local park, I prized this opportunity to be with adults.

When I was around eleven years old, I asked my parents what religion we were. They asked me what religion I would like to be. I told them I didn't know. They bought me a little book on the world's great religions and explained that I should read about some of the different faiths. My parents made the point that when I could explain to them what religion I would like to be and why, they would support my choice, and it was all right for me to practice that religion. They did recommend that I would never go wrong following the principles behind the Ten Commandments.

When I was fifteen, I asked my parents what political party we were. They asked me whom I would vote for. I told them I didn't know. They told me I should read the platform of the various candidates and determine which political party's precepts most appealed to me. If I were old enough to vote then this would be my political party.

My brother and I never had any real curfews. My parents told us that as long as we followed their rules, respected others and followed through with promises we made, they would respect us and allow us to go with the flow of what was taking place regardless of the time. We could stay up late if there was something that was important or interesting for us to watch on television. When we were tired and it seemed late, it probably was late and time for bed. In the early evening if we were with our neighborhood friends, called and informed our parents where we were, and how late we would be, then they were fine with that. As long as we did not get into trouble, did not embarrass them and they did not hear any complaints from our school, they would always be tolerant and fair with us.

We did not disappoint our parents and they were always fair and never disappointed my brother or myself.

Chapter Sixteen – On the Muscle

The $100 Long Shot

When we think of inspiration most of us think of encountering some deep mystical event. Something beyond most of us. Something we seek but never experience. For me, I discovered early on that inspiration is ever present in the ordinary. In those things that don't immediately remind you of the Divine or of the Source, but when examined more closely the inspiration is present all along.

One such example came to me in the early 1970s. I had admired the beauty of thoroughbred racing and the power and majesty of the animals, but never really understood how racing work or what made a champion in a champion. It would be in this early experience that I found inspiration in the ordinary, the Divine in the everyday.

In 1971 one of my childhood friends told my brother and I about his going to the horse races at Hollywood Park in Los Angeles. It sounded like it had a lot of action and was a lot of fun. So, my brother and I went with our friend to Hollywood Park to experience horse racing. I never will forget the excitement of walking through the parking lot seeing all of the people walking toward the entrance and then seeing the vendors selling various papers predicting the winners of the days racing. Our friend told us that we definitely had to buy the Racing Form so we would be able to see what the horses had done in the past.

Then we entered the facility and walked through the lobby and finally came in full view of the magnificent racetrack. There were tens of thousands of people with activity and action wherever you looked. By the end of the day I was definitely hooked on the races!

For me, it wasn't so much about money as it was about handicapping who the winner might be. The Racing Form was loaded with statistics, numbers, charts, formulas and it was a real challenge. If you were successful, you even made some good money.

It was summertime and I was working at a job where I could take the time to do what I wanted to do. So, now I was going to be a handicapper. I studied the form, bought books about how to handicap successfully and spent my time learning some of the finer points of the sport of kings.

After a few months, I believe that my brother and I became reasonably good at handicapping and making money at the track.

In Southern California the circuit for the horses was Santa Anita, Hollywood Park and then Del Mar. It was fun to go to the different tracks because each track was unique and offered different variables that needed to be considered.

The next year I was at Santa Anita racetrack on a beautiful Saturday afternoon. I was by myself and watching one of the early races taking place. One of the early races had just been concluded and I was fortunate to have the winner, at a very nice price. I was rooting my horse along down the stretch in a very quiet manner but probably using a lot of body language. When my horse crossed the line in front, I am sure I gave out a little shout. Then I caught myself and very quietly began to glance at the Racing Form for the next race.

I heard a voice ask me, 'did you have that winner'? I glanced up and saw a man standing next to me. He had a derby hat, a long trench coat and looked to be in his 70s. He was very neat, clean and dressed in all green. He was a complete stranger. I was a bit hesitant but nodded that I had the winner. He asked me if I had picked my horse for the next race. It was a tough race for me to pick a winner and I didn't have a choice at that moment. The man said, 'the winner of this next race will pay over $100 for a $2 bet. I snickered a bit and said, really! He said, 'absolutely'! Then he said, do you want to split the cost of the bet? I then began figuring he was very down on his luck and was just looking to get money. Before I could say anything, he explained to me that the winner of the next race was going to come out of the gate and take an early three-length lead. He would stretch it out to five lengths down the backstretch. The other horses would gain on him around the far curve coming within two lengths and then the horse would drive down the stretch and win going away by six lengths.

I really didn't know what to make of what he was saying. Then he said, here was his dollar and I could buy the ticket and hold the ticket during the race. I started musing in my mind, let's see…I'm going to bet one dollar, my horse is going to run away with the race and I am going to get $50 back. It took me a nano-second to say okay.

I believe the horse was named Santana Sands (this was almost 50 years ago). I looked at the tote board and he was going off at 50 to 1. I looked in the racing form and thought that there was no way this horse could do it. He was a sprinter (a horse that runs shorter races) and he was stretching out running a long distance. In fact, he had never run this distance before. The man told me that there was no problem, just to watch the race.

I bought the ticket and continued to watch the tote board. At post time, the horse went off at 50 to 1. The race went exactly, and I mean exactly, as the stranger had predicted. We received $102 for our bet and needless to say I followed him around as if I was a fly on flypaper.

He told me his name was Brad and he had been a long-time horse trainer in his past. He explained to me why our horse had won. He was stretching out to a longer distance and there were no other speed horses in the race. He was able to go out and get a lead, take a breather during the race and then use his speed down the stretch. He then told me that the horse's body was really conducive to running a route (distance) and that he would have no problem with his wind or breathing over a longer distance. Brad showed me horses in later races that would have their tongue tied before the race. That some horses have their tongue block their windpipe and midway through the race they slow down because they can't breathe. Bettors would see the horse slowing down in the race and then not bet on the horse the next time it ran. Now the odds would be higher and the stable or owners would make more money if the horse won. They would tie the tongue to the lower jaw of the horse and instead of it stopping at the same distance it would carry on.

Brad taught me about the class of horses as well as training methods. When we came to the feature race at Santa Anita, he would continue to prove his knowledge. There were two horses at very low odds and then there was Kennedy Road at 5 to 1. This was a great price for this horse. He was the third favorite. Brad explained to me that the horse had been in some difficulty lately and had now overcome its problems. Brad explained to me how you can tell what shape a horse is in by looking at the muscle configuration on the hindquarters. These muscle structures would be a visible manner, for most horses, of determining how close they were to running at their best form. He called it, 'being on the muscle.' At the end of the day, Brad told me that he had enjoyed our sharing. I thought to myself, he enjoyed, I really enjoyed what he had shared!

I went back the next day to the track and found Brad once more. He continued sharing so many other aspects of the sport. I took notes and asked as many questions as I could think of. We had a fantastic day and his sharing really was a great adjunct to my handicapping from the form. After that day I never saw Brad again. I would always look for him but I don't believe he was there.

Later that year I decided to travel to New York and see if the information he gave me would work everywhere. I was fortunate to see an incredible horse called Secretariat. Secretariat was just a two-year-old and he was disqualified that day for running between horses. He was like a freight train. A big red beautiful horse. I remember calling my brother that night and telling him that I saw the most incredible horse that I believed would be unbeatable. Secretariat would win the Triple Crown the next year and run perhaps the most incredible race of all time in the Belmont Stakes.

I didn't continue with the handicapping because it was a lonely and quiet life. I had thought about going to different tracks and having fun but I knew it was not for me. After that I would go occasionally to our local tracks and always had a fun day at the races.

Fruits of this experience:

The adage of *never judge a book by its cover* is a lesson we should all heed. I found throughout my life that the "likely" sources of wisdom aren't necessarily the truest voices; and the least likely can be the most profound. Our society sometimes casts judgment simply from a person's appearance. The greatest prophets, sages and teachers have been of humble means. Even someone who looks down and out can possess great wisdom. There are always "monks in the marketplace" who can have a profound effect on our lives.

Chapter Seventeen – The Quest to Run

In 776 BC the first Olympic Games were held. The ancient Greeks understood the beauty of creation and the reflection of God in man. There is a sense of spirituality in the physical discipline, just as there is a sense of mystery in spiritual discipline. Mind, body and spirit come together in a wholeness in which a more complete picture or representation of our transcendent soul can be imagined. You do not have to be a world class athlete to experience this, or an athlete at all. This can be experienced in the arts, music, writing, love, and any other endeavor of "inspiration." Inspiration means to be "in spirit."

I've found my inspiration, being in spirit through many things. Leading among those has been athletics. The development of discipline for the body, strengthening the competition in the mind, and losing myself in the moment of completion. I've always loved to run. During my elementary school years, I can remember running from one side of the schoolyard to the other while counting in my mind. Rainy days were great as I could splash through huge puddles spraying water in all directions. It was during my elementary school days that I had my first competitive sport experiences. Roscoe Elementary had a decathlon, which was comprised of a series of different sporting events. I won my first award of any kind, a blue ribbon in 1956, at the age of seven years old. From that time, I utilized my speed in every sport in which I would compete.

I was blessed with an extraordinary amount of running speed for my age. My speed was always equivalent to that of boys two or three years older than I was. I never had any difficulty catching someone from behind, running past or just getting away from someone. It was a wonderful period for me in which I won almost 50 ribbons throughout my elementary school period.

After I graduated from elementary school, I attended Sun Valley Junior High School. I will never forget my first experience with the physical education coaches. The boys in my first physical education class were lined up on a cement running course. Ahead of us were six lanes outlined with yellow stripes. We were each to run a timed 50 yard dash. When it was my turn, I was so excited that I felt like I was going to run faster than the wind. I just kept pushing myself faster and faster until I crossed the line where the teacher was standing with a stopwatch. The man came up to me, with a funny look on his face as he glanced at his stopwatch, and told me that he had definitely made some type of error and I would have to run the course again. He told me to run back to the start and do it again.

I lined up in position to run and when he blew the whistle, I ran the same course as before. Again, the man walked up to me with a perplexed look and shaking his head. He said, 'A seventh grader does not run a time like this.' You must run the course again and I want you to run back to the starting line.

Needless to say, after the third straight run with no rest, the teacher seemed much more satisfied with the result of his timing.

My junior high experience was a happy time where I met many new friends who would remain in contact with me up until the time of this book. I had the opportunity to compete in several different sports against boys from many different elementary schools around our city. During my three years in junior high school I broke all of the sprinting records that had been set.

I entered John H. Francis Poly High School and had my first experience with organized workouts and a running coach who worked on my running form. It was an interesting experience because the track coach was very 'laid back' and didn't push any of his athletes very hard. Coach Vardanian was an extremely nice man but didn't have much fire or passion. It seemed that all the athletes on the team always tried to get by with as little training work as possible.

I was a sprinter running 100 and 220-yard dashes at the time, and the older boys were always showing me how to just cruise through our workouts without sweating or feeling tired. I wasn't questioning anything and just thought this was the way things were supposed to be. In fact, even though I was running 100 and 220 yards during the meets on Fridays, I was only running 20-yard bursts out of the blocks for my workouts during the week. While it all seemed like fun and games during the week, the 100 and 220-yard distances seemed like a mile during the competition.

During my three years in high school, my coach never pushed me and I never pushed myself. Later in my life, I have looked back at this time, realized that I really could have accomplished so much more in lowering my sprinting times, and perhaps even received scholarships from outside my local area.

Even so, for two years I received wonderful acknowledgement in my local newspapers. Both the Los Angeles Times and the San Fernando Valley Green Sheet had accounts and stories of my competitive experiences at Poly. I continued to improve despite my lack of hard work, had three great years at Poly and I was able to tie the school record for the 100-yard dash.

While I took school very seriously and had very good grades, my basic demeanor was very light-hearted and at times a bit silly. I loved to make jokes, do play on words and always loved to laugh and make people laugh. Yet, at the same time, I was painfully shy. Most of my friends have always found that hard to believe but I did not have a lot of self-confidence in anything other than my athletic ability. I received a lot of attention and found many new friends while I was competing. Most of the time people would approach me first to comment upon my athletic ability.

After graduating high school, I entered San Fernando Valley State College. Several years after I graduated the name of my college was changed to California State University at Northridge (CSUN). Despite my success in sports I had decided to concentrate on my studies and not compete in track and field. That idea lasted about two weeks because I missed the competitive aspects and the emotional release that I had received from sports. I located the office of Dr Felix Jummonville, the track and field coach for CSUN, and asked him if I could become a member of his freshman track team.

Coach Jummonville told me that he had been following my progress while I was competing at Poly High School and he was very happy to have me become a part of the track team. The year was 1967 and freshmen were not allowed to compete against more mature college students. First year college students could only compete against another freshman. That rule would be changed the next year throughout college sports.

I realized how serious college competition was when coach Jummonville had my first workout consist of running twenty 220s, one after another with only a 220 walk in-between. That first day about equaled all of my workouts during my three years of high school! I was doing my work out on the other side of the track from where coach Jummonville was standing and I thought I could get away with only running 19 220s. As I began walking off the grass area I was training on to go to the locker room, I heard a booming voice yell, 'that is only 19 220s Ross'! There were over 75 athletes training all over the track area and the coach was counting my exercises. I couldn't believe it.

Coach Jummonville was instrumental in helping me to become more competitive and take pride in my ability. During my first year, I not only broke the freshman records at CSUN, but my times were also faster than regular CSUN records in my events.

For several years I competed in indoor competition around the Southern California area. I ran short sprints at the Times Indoor Games and in other arenas. These short sprints of 50 and 60 meters provided me with some very good lessons about handling life. Virtually every one of these short races ends up in a photo finish. We competitors would wait until the finish judges would huddle around with a magnifying glass looking at a photograph of the finish line.

Someone would win by a chin, nose or puffed out chest. An athlete could place 4th or 5th losing by less than six inches or maybe a foot. This might be the result after training many weeks or months for the competition. After the results you would pick yourself up emotionally and begin thinking of your race on the next weekend. It was a great character builder to just look forward to the future.

It was during this time that I developed my own competitive philosophy. Rather than just competing against the other athletes, I began competing against myself. If I ran a faster time than I had previously, I considered myself a winner despite whether someone else had beaten me during our race. This would prove very valuable for me and always kept me on a level emotional state. I was never a 'trash talking athlete' but just always looked to improve my own self and I did not lose confidence in myself despite running against some better athletes.

During one competition, I sustained the worse defeat I had ever experienced. For the entire length of the 100-yard dash I saw the backside of one of my competitors and lost by a large margin. I was surprised when coach Jummonville came up to me and congratulated me for breaking the CSUN school record. I was in shock when he told me the time I ran and I immediately started to wonder what the other runner's time was. I was told that Kirk Clayton had just run one-tenth (1/10) off the world record.

STEVE ROSS

I would compete for four years at CSUN becoming a small college All-American for sprinting. Upon graduation I was also inducted into the CSUN Track and Field Hall of Fame.

Fruits of this experience:

When we strive to achieve great things, we need to be prepared for the work and perseverance that it takes to attain success. The joy we experience in the training, preparation, and event should be the same as that of the "victory" we desire.

There should be joy in the losses we experience in our life's journey just as there are in the successes, although admittedly this perspective is a challenge to envision and more so to embrace. In the times of "defeat" we perhaps learn more than if we should never face any adversity. They show the mettle that we are made of; they are the purification of our spirit, a purification of who we are. Even when you work your hardest, and lose the race by "a nose", you don't give up. You keep going, pick yourself up and might win the next time.

Chapter Eighteen – Only Bear and Bull in this Market

Each day we artificially separate our lives in the workplace from our internal lives. We become someone or something different; or perhaps we are afraid that our true selves will be rejected in the marketplace. But wholeness of person is more fully realized when the separation of our "avatar" (our external face) to our true selves is narrowed. We can accomplish this by embracing our work lives as symbiotic to and harmonious with our internal lives. Sometimes it is in the absolute failure of our professional careers, when our best laid plans fall apart that we discover by "accident" a better path or a more aligned opportunity. We often forget that in the spiritual life there are not accidents, just opportunities we hadn't yet discovered. Sometimes you just "know" when those opportunities come across your path. Your challenge is to be prepared to wade into the unknown waters without fear and dive in.

When I was sixteen years old, I came across a wonderful book that gave keys to successful stock market strategies. I found the book exceedingly interesting because of the type of numerical calculations and mathematical equations it utilized. I practiced running hypothetical investments for about six months. At the end of that time I felt I was ready to try it for real. I found a brokerage house, Glore Forgan William R. Statts, Inc. Because I was under age, my parents had to open an account. Wayne Wagner was our account executive and I explained to him that I was interested in trying my system. He was very nice, open of course to a new account, and understood that I was the person who would be making the decisions even though my parents would be validating the transactions.

I had a fantastic couple of years utilizing technical trading strategies. Actually, Wayne had me looking at several different stocks that he found of interest. I continued my trading throughout college and just assumed I would become a stock broker. I changed my major from science to business and couldn't wait to get into becoming a broker in the stock market.

Upon graduation I told Wayne that I was desirous of becoming a stockbroker and he set up my interview and testing with his company. When the results were back, I was told that I was going to be a part of their company and within two weeks they were sending me to New York for training.

Within that two-week period my world collapsed. Several brokerage houses went out of business with thousands of experienced brokers now available. I received the news that there were no new openings available for me. My dream of becoming a stockbroker was over. At the time it was devastating! In retrospect it changed the course of my life and I remained in Los Angeles.

The importance of this episode in my life is that what often appears to be devastating and a crushing experience can often pivot a person towards a different direction in their life.

Instead of going into the stock market I decided to go into business and work in establishing a cosmetic manufacturing facility. While I was involved with this activity, I ended up meeting an individual who would change the course of my life and have me paying more attention to my dreams.

Fruits of this experience:
While you may suddenly be torn away from your life's plan, there is always other ways to go. In fact, your "plan B" may be the destiny you were never aware of.

Chapter Nineteen – The Gardner and the Sprinkler

Our hands, and especially our finger tips are amazing things. They can feel and move something as small as a grain of sand, and at the same time be calloused and hardened by extreme manual labor. Life tends to be this way as well. We can sense the smallest things yet endure some of the most difficult times. For most of us, as we walk through life, we pay attention to the boulders along the way, avoiding the hardest path. What we don't realize is that often it is the small things that cause us to stumble. While we see the boulder, we also seem to trip over our own shadow. The pebble we slip on can slow us down as much as the largest bolder. I experienced this as a young man. Slipping on the pebble while avoiding the bolder. Fortunately, I listened to my internal guidance on my way to recovery, not to all the so-called "experts" who would have me believe the comeback was impossible.

As each year passed at CSUN (Cal State University – Northridge) I continued to lower my sprinting times and continued to receive a tremendous amount of publicity in various newspapers and sports columns. In my junior year of college, as we went into the Easter break, each athlete was to conduct their own workouts when they could find the time each day. Up to the Easter break we would normally have been doing mostly distant work and then begin our speed work after the break. Speed work was the time of the season where a sprinter would dramatically lower his sprinting times. In my junior year I was three tenths of a second faster than I had ever run before the speed work.

I had just competed in the Claremont Relays running the fastest times I had ever run for that time in the season. So, with much excitement I was eager to follow coach Jummonville's suggested workout at our practice site. We would work out on a grass field just alongside the track. I did some slow jogging and then lined myself up to run about ¾ speed 110-yard workout. As I came to the 75-yard mark, and in full stride, I noticed that there was a sprinkler head right where my left foot was going to land. While in full stride I tried to avoid the sprinkler head by extending my stride. I felt something pop and felt excruciating pain even before I touched the ground. My knee was burning, I felt like I had been hit in the stomach and wanted to throw-up. I let out a terrible scream but nobody was around and nobody heard me.

I tried to stand but it was impossible. I began crawling on my hands and knees, dragging my left leg toward the trainer's room in the physical education department. It was quite a long way from the track. I finally made it to the trainer's room and they helped me up on a table. The head trainer was very upset and obviously worried. He immediately went to the telephone to locate coach Jummonville. The coach came to the trainer's room and spoke with the trainer and told me they would have to send me to an orthopedic specialist. I was sent to the head physician for the Los Angeles Rams and L.A. Lakers. In fact, Dr. Kerlan (Dr. K) was one of the most renowned specialists in the U.S.

Dr. K's examination led him to tell me that without surgery he would not expect me to be running again. For a second opinion I was sent to the trainer at UCLA. The trainer's name was Ducky Drake. These were the years that Lew Alcindor competed at UCLA. Later, Drake Stadium at UCLA would be named after this great trainer. His diagnosis was that I would need surgery.

I was by now very dejected at my prospects. I would see myself through the puddles at Roscoe Elementary and my wonderful memories of playing football and nobody ever being able to stop me from catching passes. How would I ever be the same? I returned to my trainer's room and picked up a scientific magazine to read while I was there. Within the magazine there was the mention of a therapeutic technique that was being used in Europe. I thought perhaps it would work for my problem.

When I spoke with Dr. K, he told me that it was holistic garbage. It was alternative medicine that could not work. I asked him what he knew about it. He said nothing. Then I said to him, if you don't know about it how could you say that it wouldn't work. He said, "son, this is America! If we don't have it, then it isn't worth anything!" Even though I was 19, I thought that it wasn't right what he was saying. I decided to try it myself. I was fanatical. I was visualizing myself running and winning and breasting the tape in the lead while using the approach of alternating cold, thawing, cold, thawing non-stop for sometimes 16 hours per day. Throughout the day, throughout most of the night. I did this for three weeks.

I then went out to the track and began trying to run. I ran very slowly and then picked up the pace. I wanted to run and I wanted to compete again. One thing became very obvious to me. I couldn't run comfortably around the curve of the track. That meant that I couldn't run the 220 anymore. I had to concentrate on my hundred-yard dash and anchoring our 440-yard relay team. Later that year I would compete at the small college nationals and sprint my way into an All-American award.

Although the gardener had left a sprinkler head on the course, he had also planted a seed in my mind. Why did the so-called experts tell me that there was only one way of rectifying my problem? Why did the supposed experts tell me that everything else from around the world was trash and garbage? What other things might exist in this world that we are not told about here in the United States?

Later in life I have come to realizes that my visualization of running and winning may have had more of an effect than that of the physical therapy protocol.

Fruits from this experience:

Supposed "experts" only know what they know. Even they possess only a small portion of the possible knowledge. Trust must be placed in these men and women only for what they do know. Trust too must be placed in one's self to know what the experts don't or are incapable of knowing. There are many paths to the summit, some more traveled than others, but all available to those who seek.

Chapter Twenty– Wilt the Stilt

For each of us we have the opportunity to surround ourselves with a sacred circle of trusted friends, family and advisers. But as we begin to build this circle, the limitations of our own imagination tend to compromise the integrity of our network. Allowing the possibility of anything to take hold in our reality, frees us from the artificial boundaries of who we can encounter and who will play a leading role in our lived drama.

Within our life experience, when we see each moment as an opportunity, we are open to possibility. The adage that when one door closes another opens, when internalized, sets the intention that permits daily miracles to happen. I am undyingly grateful for the weakest moments of my life which resulted in the greatest opportunities. When what seemed to be failure became an undeniable success. And perhaps most importantly, to the people who walked through the newly opened door.

After having sports be such an integral part of my experience in school, I felt a very big loss upon graduating from my university. I had long found such a great release through my sports activities. During my last two years at CSUN I had discovered volleyball. I had to be very cautious about playing indoor volleyball because the track coaches did not like the idea that we might get hurt jumping indoors in the gymnasium. But I enjoyed the sport so much I decided to take the chance and play on Wednesday evening in the upstairs gymnasium. It was so much fun that a group of my friends decided to form an indoor team and we participated in volleyball tournaments in the United States Volleyball Association (USVBA).

We were a rag tag group of friends who had all been involved in other sports and wanted to see what we could do. We actually amazed ourselves when in one tournament, when the Athletes' Foot, sporting Goods Company, sponsored us; we beat UCLA and knocked them out of a tournament. I will never forget their faces when they kept looking at us and trying to figure out who we were. Al Skates was the coach and they had won the NCAA's the previous year. Coach Skates brought us down to earth when the team he was playing for, a master's team, knocked us out. But we had become legends in our own minds.

We were playing almost five nights a week after I graduated and my knees were beginning to get swollen all the time. So, along with my volleyball friend Dan Kellogg, we decided to try playing volleyball outdoors on the beaches of Southern California. We played a couple of times on the beach and very quickly found that jumping off the sand, with the wind blowing and sun in your eyes was quite a bit more difficult than the wonderful conditions indoors.

We decided to play in a beach tournament. We lost our first game 15-1. The only reason we scored one point is because our opponents felt sorry for us. We had been yelling at each other about our poor play - it was a demoralizing situation. I had been an All-American, I had set school records, I had played baseball, football, and tennis and achieved wonderful awards in park leagues, intramural sports and this was embarrassing. We were being schooled by our opponents and put in our place – a classic smackdown.

A couple of weeks later Dan and I wandered down to Manhattan Beach and found a nice group of people that played privately with their own nets and developed their game skills. So, here I met a new player, Ron Troester, and he and I began playing very often. We worked out the rest of the summer and throughout the winter.

Ron and I decided to enter a tournament the next year. It was the Santa Monica Easter A tournament. We were unranked and actually seeded last and scheduled to play against the first seed. We both played like we were possessed. We knocked off the first seed and were paid a visit by the tournament director. He asked me who I really was and whether I was playing under an assumed name. There was no way he would not have heard of me. We kept on winning over the next two days. I was a bit sports crazed and excited. I wasn't eating or hydrating from the excitement and was just lying in the sun getting a tan

We lost our first game late on Saturday night and went into the loser's bracket of the double elimination tournament. We ended up playing the first seed of the tournament again in the loser's bracket. They informed us of how lucky we were the first time and we would be going home after they beat us. We beat them again. We now were going to play in the finals of the loser's bracket with the chance to play for the championship of the tournament.

We were ahead 10 to 6 in a game to 15. I went up for a spike at the net and then felt both calves and thighs cramp up. The mega-cramp. I was literally dead in the sand. We had to forfeit because I could no longer stand up. People walked over to me and acknowledged how they enjoyed watching me play since none of them had ever seen me before.

I glanced up and saw someone hand me a banana. "You need to watch yourself during a tournament and get salt and potassium into your system. You need to be staying out of the sun during the tournament." It was Wilt Chamberlain. I was awestruck. He was so complimentary, and we would become friends at the Santa Monica Pier. Later. I would come to Wilt to make an unusual presentation that would change the course of my life forever.

That day of the tournament my playing status went from novice to an A rating. After that we played several times at Santa Monica during the week. Within three years I would go from the novice status to a AAA volleyball rating, which was the highest rating at that time in 1976.

Fruits from this experience:

You never know who you might meet and what might transpire at some event or gathering. Lying in the sand, with calves and thighs cramped, I met a giant of a man.

Chapter Twenty-one – The Quimby Manuscripts

Both the spiritual neophyte and the seasoned pilgrim will learn of the "subtle energies" that surround and engulf our lives. The ancient Christians of the East understood this when they described the Energies of the Holy Spirit. More than the theological teachings of the who of God, it described the way in which God permeated all of creation, including humanity. When this idea takes hold in our consciousness, the randomness of our interactions become "ordered". We come to understand that even the most random encounters are replete with possibility, pregnant with promise, and only a moment away from bloom.

It took only a few of these random encounters for me to appreciate what could happen. To embrace the moment and allow the natural flow of this subtle energy to create its own networks. If my divine energies intended something to be, it would be. This now probably describes the entirety of my relationships, those in my life, and the networks we have created.

During my recurring dream of being in a library and being told to study the writings of various personages from the past, in 1982 I heard the name of P.P. Quimby. Within days I met a woman, "DB", through a mutual acquaintance who would be the unexpected connection to the works of Quimby.

As a result of my meeting with DB I was introduced to the works and writings of Phineas Parkhurst Quimby. P.P. was an amazing healer that

lived in the 1800s. By profession he was a watchmaker but by the end of his life he would become one of the most profound healers of all time. He is generally regarded as the father of the New Thought movement. New Thought being defined as the mind-body relationship or the effects of thought on the body. DB gave me an interesting book on Quimby, which I wasted no time in devouring. After a few weeks DB set up a conference call between Erroll S. Collie and us.

Collie resided in Naples, Florida. Collie had been studying Quimby's work for almost 40 years when we spoke in 1982. He was one of the world's authorities on the work of Quimby.

In the author's preface of a book written by Collie he stated the following about Quimby: "The foundation principles of what we now term Mental Science are shown by history to have been largely understood by the philosophers of all ages. The first person in this age who penetrated the depths of truth so far as to discover and bring forth a true science of life, and openly apply it to the healing of the sick, was Phineas Parkhurst Quimby of Belfast, Me. Dr. Quimby was not only a philosopher but also a scientist, who formulated his theory of healing after long years of intensive experiments. He called his new method of curing disease by several names which included, 'The Science of Health and Happiness', 'The Science of Life' and the Science of Correcting an Error.' In a circular to the sick, Quimby said, my practice is unlike all medical practice. I give no medicine and make no outward applications. I tell the patient his troubles and what he thinks is his disease, and my explanation is the cure. If I succeed in correcting his errors, I change the fluids of the system and establish the truth or health. The truth is the cure.'"

Dr. Quimby died before he was able to organize his writings for publication and only part of the voluminous literature, which he had written in preparation for a book, was published. The Quimby articles were not published until 1921, fifty-four years after Quimby's death. They were published under the title of "The Quimby Manuscripts" and were edited by Dr. H.W. Dresser.

In 1930 Quimby's heirs presented the entire collection of Dr. Quimby's original manuscripts to the Library of Congress, Washington, D.C. Collie mimeographed the unpublished parts of these writings, which constitute the greater part of the collection, including approximately two hundred and twenty-five thousand words, in 1943 from the original manuscripts in the Library of Congress. It was due to Collie's efforts that the materials have been available in a form that can be read and studied.

After a few conversations over the telephone Collie invited me to visit him in Naples. I flew from Los Angeles to Miami and then took a connecting flight to Naples. The good news was that I finally had the opportunity to meet Collie. The bad news was that my luggage was not on the carousel. In fact, the airline told me that my bags had continued on to Bogotá, Columbia.

My next surprise was that Collie did not have a car. He was riding a bicycle and he had one for me. I so clearly remember pedaling through the streets of Naples. I spent a few wonderful days with Collie.

Upon his death, Collie's will stated that I was to receive certain materials from his estate. This included the rights to his book, Quimby's Science of Happiness.

Over the years I found philosophy of Quimby to be extremely valuable. I have put into practice many of the ideals that Quimby formulated. There is no question that Quimby was a beacon light and Collie was an able custodian of that light.

Fruits from this experience:

Our lives can be full of random connections (like DB) that can be an answer to or the path by which you can discover important truths. Truths of discovery mustn't diminish over time, but can flourish in each new generation.

Chapter Twenty-two – Dare to Heal

I could never quite understand those who are the most ardent fundamentalists, who could without hesitation site verse and chapter every miracle, encounter with God and healing, rail against those who possess the ability to heal (mind, body or spirit) today. They call them frauds, charlatans, cons, quacks or even worse. I believe in a Creator who was, is and will be present within the lives of all human creation. Certainly, there are those who aren't genuine, but they in time (often a very short time) will be known.

Healers may be miracle workers, but they often are simply the vessel by which energy moves and healing happens. I hold to the belief that all of us can be healers. While not all in the same way, or for the same reason, we none-the-less can be a channel for compassion, love, and healing energy. In my meditations I saw the message: "have a consideration like the disciples. They were so concerned with what was going on that their interest alone manifested with them the transcended condition. They couldn't focus on the how, it was beyond their understanding. They were left with the feeling of humbleness toward the activity." This is the mind we must wear to become healers.

Throughout my early years I was blessed with unusually good health. I didn't have any major health problems nor did any member of my immediate family. Although I was aware of the major type of health problems that people would have, it never really touched close to home. I was a member of an HMO because it was part of a plan that was available when I did some part time work during college.

I believe up until the time of my accident while sprinting that I assumed that everything was taken care of by the doctor.

I had been told by a good friend of mine, Edward Monroe, that from information he had received while in meditation that he knew I had some abilities that I was yet to recognize. He did not go into detail but told me that in addition to my dreams, I should pay attention to new thoughts regarding healing others that might enter my mind. When I asked him what he meant he only said that when it came to my relationship with people, that whenever I felt that I might be of assistance to help someone I should follow through with the thought.

In 1977, I was lying in bed when the telephone rang in the middle of the night. A friend of a friend of mine was calling and she was mumbling something about her brother. I told her to try to stay calm and she then related that her brother had taken angel dust and was having a bad trip. She mentioned that she was calling from a telephone booth. She was afraid to go to the doctor or tell anyone because her brother would get into trouble. He was out of control and she was scared. At that moment, I heard a voice within myself begin to talk to me. I could not determine if it was a male or female voice but it was calm, loving and I felt a presence associated with it that was indescribable. The voice told me that I could surround her brother with a loving protective cocoon and he would immediately become perfectly calm and coherent. At that moment I heard Marianne gasp. She told me that her brother just sat down very quietly and was smiling.

I was so overwhelmed myself that when she hung up, I was still spinning in my mind with what had happened. As I lay back in my bed, I heard the voice tell me that all was all right and I had done a good job. I really couldn't tell if the voice was outside of me, inside of me or both. It was almost as though there was someone else there with me.

Later that year I was out on a date with a woman who was a friend of one of my friends. We went out for dinner that evening and then we returned to her apartment. She was becoming very agitated and I asked her what was wrong. She mentioned to me that she had really enjoyed the evening but was sure that I was going to be like all the other men she had met and would be more interested in her physical then who she was as a person.

At that moment, I was feeling so badly for her that I thought about surrounding her with my arms and comforting her in a calming and non-sexual manner. We were sitting apart from each other. At that very moment she looked at me and said, you touched me. I was in shock! She said that I had placed my arms around her and she could feel them. She became very quiet and smiled. I became very nervous and immediately made an excuse to leave. I really couldn't explain what had happened.

In my dreams I would see myself helping people. From my reading of various books, I felt that I should always view myself as a conduit and realize that I was assisting some loving greater energy greater than I. While I was the conduit for the healing, I was not the source and should not take credit for these things that were happening.

From that time forward, I decided to follow my inner thoughts and try to assist people. In the years since I have been involved with many people and their return to health. Working with people they have had instantaneous remissions of inoperable brain cancer (diagnosed at UCLA medical school), breast cancer tumors (University of Kansas Medical Center) and other medical centers.

I did not work with the medical centers but with the patients. People have come out of comas, people were being given their last rites before dying, people have had many different types of health conditions that were immediately rectified. Not that they just thought they were rectified, but when they were examined again, the condition did not exist.

In all of the healing work I have done over the last 40 years, I have never charged any money or asked for anything in return. I know that the gentle, loving voice of the Angel of Healing has always been with me to help assist others in need. While there have been many healings in my lifetime, I have not included the many names or experiences. I do this because I want you, the reader, to become aware that you can manifest this ability - Trust yourself; Be still; and listen.

Fruits from this experience.

Everything is possible - nothing is impossible. You don't have to be perfect nor fully understand how a healing has occurred. Simply be open and desire to help those in need. Have a beautiful heart, an open mind and a humble spirit.

Chapter Twenty-three – J.R. Newton

What does love look like? I heard of love; I think I knew love; but had I ever really seen the face of love? When we project love, love is returned to us. When we seek love, love is returned to us. Finding the face of love is to recognize the various forms and expressions of affection. Love, and its face is more than mere affections, it is greater than emotion, and more evolved than even the highest self-surrender. Love is love in its sharing, in its selflessness, in its completeness.

These are all nice descriptions, but are they really attainable? Simply, yes. I have seen them throughout my life in various ways, and in various people. You know them by seeing them. But if you aren't looking you aren't able to see. Your projection of what love should be can get in the way of what love could be.

Over the years I have had a recurring dream where I was in a library and standing in a line of people. In one occurrence of this dream, at the front of the line was a man standing behind a very high podium. As I reached the head of the line the man behind the podium said, 'We would like you to study the life and work of J.R. Newton.'

I was not familiar with Newton but it was only a number of days after this dream that I was reading a book from the late 1800s which gave a country by country survey of people who had unique healing abilities. Within the book I learned of the man Dr. J.R. Newton. I conducted research in other areas and found virtually no information regarding this man who was born in the 1800s in Newport, Rhode Island. I finally located one other brief reference that mentioned J.R. and a book regarding his life. With all the many sources that I have to locate reading materials from around the world I was not able to find this book anywhere. It was titled, *The Modern Bethesda*.

I finally located a group out of New York that had the book. They made a copy and sent it to me. Many years later I was able to secure an original copy for myself.

What intrigued me about Dr. Newton was how he spoke of and demonstrated the power of love. This man worked with nearly 200,000 people during his life and the testimonials regarding his effectiveness in healing were extremely impressive. Within the book of his life were not only the types of health problems he rectified but also the people's name and address where they lived. The book was filled with notarized statements from city, state and national government officials who witnessed Newton's healings.

Following is the article which I wrote for the World Research Foundation News:

Dr. J. R. Newton and His Gift of Healing

Extracts were taken from his autobiography, *The Modern Bethesda, Or the Gift of Healing Restored* (1879)

"Dr. James Rogers Newton was born in Newport, Rhode Island, on September 8th, 1810, and was a lineal descendant of John Rogers, who was burned at the stake.

In his youth, Dr. Newton enjoyed all the advantages that competence and good judgment could confer. He early evinced a strong proclivity for the medical profession, or more properly speaking, an inclination to do battle with old Allopathy, to modify and improve, if not to entirely change, the prevailing system of medical practice, so as to make it more in accordance with nature's laws; but various circumstances combined to prevent the gratification of his desires.

At an early age he became aware of possessing the gift of healing, which he demonstrated amply throughout his adult life. He became conscious of new powers, new capabilities, wonderful and strange, and opening a glorious avenue of usefulness; and his young, enthusiastic spirit burned for the work. But meeting with no encouragement, he suffered his gift to lie cooperatively undeveloped until later years.

For twenty years, he was a prosperous merchant, during which time his peculiar gift was often manifested but never exercised to any great extent until the year 1858. He traveled through parts of Europe investigating hydropathic (water therapy) hospitals and improved his knowledge of healing.

Dr. Newton was a man of most pleasing presence and great manners and reports about him stated that he was very modest of his great abilities, and when he spoke he always acted as a gentleman of refinement and intellect.

He held none of his activities in secret, but welcomed scientific investigation and he always endeavored to promulgate to the world his principles of cure as well as to show how the life principle, or vital force, can be imparted by a positive will from a strong and healthy body to a sickly and weak one, producing an instantaneous cure of the most chronic diseases.

Newton disclaimed any miraculous powers, but declared that the results he produced were founded on philosophic and scientific principles which can, in a measure, be taught. He felt that his extraordinary powers over disease were due to the philanthropic idea of always doing good, projecting love, and his positive character.

In 1853, Dr. Newton was a passenger on the steamer, Golden Gate, from Panama to San Francisco. The second day yellow fever broke out among the 1,300 passengers which also included several physicians. The fever raged for eight days, with seventy-four persons dying and their bodies being consigned to the ocean. The ship's surgeon lost every patient but one that he attended. Dr. Newton lost none.

In 1858, Dr. Newton commenced practice as a public healer in Cincinnati, Ohio. Despite the usual amount of incredulity and skepticism attendant on the introduction of a new system of curing disease, virtually all who saw his work were compelled to believe. After performing some very wonderful cures, his fame and practice were so great that his rooms were daily crowded with invalids. His average number of daily healings the first several months was about one hundred per day.

The following people's cases were notarized and attested to by the most notable individuals in the city:

- John Hutchinson, Frankfort, Indiana; cured of paralysis in the leg in 15 minutes
- Miss Catherine Johnson, Cincinnati; blind for 15 years, restored in 15 minutes; and could see to read and work
- Mrs. Elizabeth Miller, Lawrenceburg; rheumatism for 20 years, restored to health in minutes
- William Rolls, cataracts on eyes; perfectly restored to sight in 15 minutes
- Mrs. Francesco, Cleveland; internal ulcers, discharging a pint daily; cured in 10 minutes (her husband was the sexton at White's Plymouth Church)

- Maria Louisa Crane, 320 George Street, Cincinnati; spine disease for over two years, legs withered and drawn up; 5 months previous to being cured, could not be turned in bed, but lay in one position; fully restored in 15 minutes
- Mrs. Bromwell, 293 George St, Cincinnati; had lost all use of her limbs by spinal disease, had not walked for 8 months; restored in 20 minutes and walked to her hotel
- George Bechtolds, Newport, Kentucky; daughter aged eight years, spine disease and had never walked, moved about room after 15 minutes of treatment
- Frances Harty, fourteen years old, 169 West Fourth Street; hip disease, walked on all-fours without a crutch, cured in 30 minutes and never used crutch afterward
- Mrs. Elizabeth Wallace, Broadway St; totally blind in one eye, and could not distinguish any person four feet distant with the other - both eyes fully restored in 20 minutes
- Jane Scott, Third St, Cincinnati; lame ankle, scarcely able to walk for 12 years, made to walk without halt or limp in 15 minutes

The case of Alexander Fairchild deserves special note and he wrote the following letter to the local newspaper:

'Two years ago, I was taken with fever, was confined to my bed, and lost all use of my legs, which were drawn up and anchylosed. So great was my debility that for five months my head was not raised from the pillow to receive nourishment. I am twenty-five years old, five feet seven and one-half inches high, yet my weight was then about fifty pounds. Midway between my knee and hip I could span my legs with my thumb and middle finger. It is over a year since I was given over as incurable.

'Last May you published an account of a cure performed by Dr. J.R. Newton, who was then at the Gibson House. My friends were thereby induced to have him come to see me. By the first treatment my whole system was vitalized and invigorated; then one leg was relieved and straightened; the next day the other; and the next day I walked. This was twelve weeks ago and I have increased in strength ever since. I now weigh 135 pounds. I walk out daily and am often in the office of Dr. Newton, and see much of his astounding cures of all kinds of disease.'

Dr. H. T. Child, an eminent physician of the Allopathic profession reported, 'I saw him operate on more than one hundred persons with various forms of disease. His rooms were crowded with patients who were lame, halt and blind. Of these cases I will mention a case of paralysis. An old man, a painter by trade, came hobbling in on two crutches. He said he had not been able to rise from his seat or walk without aid for eight months. In about twenty minutes he rose up and waked away, going up and down stairs without a cane or crutch.'

Austin A Hill, was Dr. Newton's personal secretary for many years. Mr. Hill wrote, 'I first met Dr. Newton in the summer of 1863, and since we both seemed to suit each other I became his secretary. Dr. Newton had large crowds that visited him on New York Street in New Haven Connecticut.

'Of the many people who visited him, the following stood out during my first year I met him:

Miss Caroline F. Davis, of Guilford, CT; was brought on a bed sixteen miles, afflicted with spinal disease and she had not walked for 6 years, or spoken above a whisper for 4 years; she was cured instantly. She walked away rejoicing and talked as freely as anyone. Miss Davis later visited the Doctor in New York. She said she came to thank him for what he did for her three years earlier.'

'Mrs. Wm. Toohy, of Hartford; was brought into our rooms in her husband's arms; she had spinal problems; she instantly was able to walk.

'Another case of equal prominence was that of Hon. D.L. Harris, formerly mayor of Springfield, but at the time was a member of the Massachusetts Legislature. Mr. Harris had been injured in a carriage accident and couldn't walk. In less than 5 minutes he could walk without any assistance.'

Mr. Hill also said, 'During my time with the Dr. Newton, the number of names of the people who registered with us was approximately 10,000, but fully nine-tenths were free patients, or those not liable to pay for treatment - the Doctor's rule being that if a patient was worth less than $1,000, he or she was cured, 'without money and without price.'

A remarkable case was reported by Mr. Hill as well as the Toledo Record newspaper. 'Margaret Fuller fell from a horse at fourteen years old and injured her spine that that her lower limbs were totally paralyzed. In this condition she succeeded in getting an education and became a teacher. Her brothers built a sort of 'go-cart' in which they used to draw her back and forth from school. Later, she finally married Mr. Fuller, and went to live at Tontogany, Ohio. She had eight children, two of which were in the northern army and became lieutenants. Not one of those eight children ever saw her stand on her feet or walk a step in their lives.

'In this condition she was brought to Dr. Newton, sitting on the hands of two men. In less than 10 minutes she came walking out of the treatment room. She came out saying, 'how strange this seems!'. 'The doctor told her to go down and have a steak broiled, and eat a good hearty meal, and fear nothing.'

After this case the rush of invalids was truly amazing. Six extra cars had to be added to the morning train to accommodate those wishing to visit the 'great healer.'

It was reported that when Dr. Newton visited Portland, Maine, he met with a young boy, who was about fifteen or sixteen years of age, who was a patient of Dr. Stone. Dr. Stone had known this boy from childhood. Both of the boy's feet turned in till the toes pointed nearly toward each other. Dr. Stone approached Dr. Newton at a lecture and asked, 'Can you do anything for this lad?' "Yes, come here, my lad.' Within minutes of touching him; the boys feet turned out and he walked perfectly with a wonderful gait.

Mr. Hill had the following to add regarding Dr. Newton; 'to me Dr. Newton was more than generous. He was noble in character and always just in his dealings. I could not help loving him for what he was. Though junior in years, he was like an elder brother or father. From his lips I never heard a profane or obscene word or expression, and nothing seemed to offend him. He was a man of powerful physique and strong passions, and when he heard the word humbug used and applied to him, the fire of those dark hazel eyes and a simple admonition were sufficient to make the stoutest and most hardened, quail and humbly apologize, or quickly leave his presence. He always retired by ten o'clock, unless engaged in visiting the sick or perhaps amused with a game of dominoes. No matter how hard he worked, in the morning he would appear as bright as the lark. When not feeling exactly well, he asked me to lend him my magnetism when I would sit by him, with my hand on his head, or his hands in mine, and in a few minutes he would be fresh as ever.'

When asked about his healing he would say, 'What did the Great Teacher say? He that lives as I live, the works that I do shall he do also, and still greater works.'

Dr. Newton's motto was, God is love, and love is the link that binds in one, all human souls to God. Newton had no doubts whether he would cure or not. 'The difference between him and us was that he was conscious of his power, while we were conscious of our want of power.'

At a meeting in England, Dr. Newton stated, 'As to the power of healing, it is merely an illustration of the power of love. When any sick person comes before me, I lay my hands on that person and feel that I love him; tell him I love him and if the patient is not antagonistic, he is almost sure to be healed because this opens their heart to me and the disease must depart.'

Throughout his healing career, Dr. Newton was very well liked by all class of people. He had no difficulty relating to anyone that he met.

Dr. Newton was engaged in three lawsuits during his life. Individuals who were jealous of his work did their best to impede his activities. During one case over one thousand people produced notarized statements of his healing ability and success with them."

J.R. Newton's manner of healing was totally based on a concept of love. I read and reread his autobiography many times and was thrilled and empowered each time. I have had several dreams over the years where I believe that J.R. Newton appeared to me and offered love, support and guidance. I have followed this concept of universal love and know that it has been a vital part of the healings that I have been a part of during my life.

Fruits from this experience:

Within life, nothing can contain the power or magnitude of love. Healing pours forth from love. Success comes from love. Life and relationship are rooted in love.

Chapter Twenty-four– The Vision of World Research Foundation

When we have dreams, we are usually speaking of our hopes and ambitions. Rarely are we actually talking about our dreams as we sleep. But sometimes those things intersect in ways we never anticipated. In fact, if we don't dismiss our own dreams and dreams, other in our lives will be more than glad to do it for us. We have to trust in ourselves, to have confidence in our abilities, to have certainty in response to our calling. We can love, respect, and appreciate the feedback from others but ultimately, we are responsible for what we do, what we think and how we respond.

I found it difficult when those with whom I was the closest were those who seemed to have the most difficult time thinking that the extraordinary was possible for me. While their concern for me was most likely embedded in their love for me, I came to understand that it was perhaps their insecurity or fear that they were projecting on to me, not a vision of what my life would be. When I took hold of my destiny, my future became unencumbered – free to flow in ways I never imagined.

In 1978 I was having a large number of dreams each night. Or I might say that I was recalling an even greater number of dreams. I was having particular dreams relating to the establishment of a worldwide health organization. Since 1970 when I decided to discover what other type of healing modalities existed that we were not being informed of in the United States, I had been looking here, there and everywhere where I thought I might uncover information. At that time there did not seem to exist an all-inclusive data center housing both allopathic and complementary approaches for all diseases and illnesses. There was a society or group for this topic and a center for that health problem but no place that acted as a general clearing house for health problems and therapeutic approaches for those problems.

One evening I was awakened with a dream of a worldwide health information network. I saw a picture of a world map with lights blinking at various cities around the world. The blinking lights were supposed to be offices of the worldwide network. Rather than us traveling all over the world to gather information, this organization would operate its offices around the world acting like little magnets to attract information. Centers would be located in the Far East gathering information on acupunctured, herbs, Qigong and other Eastern modalities. There would be a center located in Germany gathering information on homeopathy as well as a location in the Western United States gathering the wonderful information of the Native Americans and their interaction with nature.

At the same time I awoke, I had the thought that color therapy, using the visible light spectrum, was an important component to healing. Up until that time I had not heard of the use of color in healing.

The following day I visited my parents and told them of my dreams. My very practical Dad responded, "How will you ever start a worldwide organization like this? Where will you get the money for computers, desk, books, office expenses, salaries and all types of other costs?" He reminded me that he and Mom were not wealthy people. Next my Dad asked how would I ever discover what color works for the various health conditions, if in fact, color did work?

I believed strongly that it would all work out and I boldly told my parents it would happen. I also believed my Dad had brought up very important points. Within one year of our discussion, I would discover an entire system of color therapy that had been developed in the early 1900s.

In 1984, when my Dad was hospitalized and after surgery at Kaiser Permanente when my Mom and Dad were told that he might become a quadriplegic, I would end up using color therapy and my Dad would make a full recovery even though the hospital records had him listed as a paraplegic.

At the end of 1984, LaVerne and I would co-found the World Research Foundation. The World Research Foundation is an international non-profit health and environmental organization with offices and advisors located around the world where the blinking lights appeared on the map in my dream.

Fruits from This Experience:

Trust your dreams. Don't let other people dissuade you when you feel strongly about an idea or a goal. Picture what you want to accomplish and stay true to your dreams.

Chapter Twenty-five – The Color of Health

In the most recent incarnation of Alice in Wonderland, Alice and her father talk about their ability to think of six impossible things before breakfast. They believed by thinking about the impossible, it could become possible. It simply took trust, imagination, and commitment. I have found this to be a truism. We can make the impossible possible. When we pay attention to the muses of creativity that speak to all of us, we can discover the possible. Not only the possible, but the probable.

Many spiritual teachers, of this age and of old, speak of manifestation. Often it seems to be wishful thinking or foolish hopefulness; but when made part of our life practice, manifestation becomes real. The ingredients in this alchemical and metaphysical cocktail are varied, but common among them is the purpose and intent. When our intention is simply for our own gain, manifestation is fleeting or inadequate. When the intent is for the greater good of others, the creative energy abundantly fuels the manifestation and completeness. In this, I have learned that you don't have to worry about being the best because you are handling that energy that created the universe. Your creativity and creativeness, and the creativeness that is behind the idea, and the creativeness that is manifested in the organization that is associated with the universe is a pure creativity.

After I had the dream relating to the use of color and health, I began trying to find all that I could regard the use of color and healing. The colors would be part of the visible light spectrum. To my surprise I found that there was a tremendous amount of materials relating to the use of the visible light spectrum and health.

In several books that I read there was consistent reference to Dinshah Ghadiali and his Spectrochrome System of Health. Dinshah had begun investigating the use of color in the 1800s after reading the book, The Principles of Light and Color by Edwin Babbitt. Dinshah improved upon Babbitt's work by developing a 12-color system.

The effects of color and light on the human system are subjects of continuous scientific investigation. The research and experiments of the late Dinshah Ghadiali proved that the body could be tuned or adjusted from disease to health by systematically exposing it to colored light. An example of this effect is found in the medical practice of treating premature babies with Bilirubin Syndrome (jaundice) by exposing them to blue light, although the methodology is somewhat different from Ghadiali's.

Dinshah Ghadiali was born of Persian descent in Bombay, India, in the year 1873. At the age of eleven, he became assistant to the Professor of Mathematics and Science at Wilson College in Bombay. In his early career, Dinshah was Superintendent of Telephone and Telegraph for Dolphur State in India.

The year 1897 marked a permanent turning point in his medical career. The niece of a friend was dying of mucous colitis. The attending physician was using the then accepted drugs, to no avail. Having read Edwin S. Babbitt's work, The Principles of Light and Color, and Blue and Red Light, by Dr. Seth Pancoast, Dinshah was aware of the theory of chromotherapy (healing with colored light).

Dinshah treated the young woman according to Dr. Babbitt's technique. The light from a kerosene lantern, filtered through an indigo colored glass, shone on her. Milk was placed in a bottle of the same color, exposed to the sunlight, and then given to her to drink. Dinshah writes, "The urgent straining to evacuate, which occurred perhaps a hundred times a day, abated to ten after one treatment; after three days she was able to get out of bed." This case was the beginning of Dinshah's intense investigation into the effects of colored light on the human organism.

In April of 1920, Dinshah introduced his system of healing with colored lights to the world in New York City. (He had taken up permanent residence in the United States in 1911.) He named his development Spectro-Chrome. In the next four years Dinshah trained over 800 professionals and laypersons. He also designed and sold color projectors and accessories.

The first indication of opposition to Spectro-Chrome emerged in the pages of the January 1924, Journal of the American Medical Association. The article ridiculed Spectro-Chrome and its originator as being preposterous, closing with the statements, "Some physicians, after reading this article, may wonder why we have devoted the amount of space to a subject that, on its face seems so preposterous as to condemn itself. When it is realized that helpless but credulous patients are being treated for such serious conditions as syphilitic conjunctivitis, ovaritis, diabetes mellitus, pulmonary tuberculosis and chronic gonorrhea with colored lights, the space devoted to this latest cult will not be deemed excessive."

An indictment in Buffalo, New York in 1931 charged that Dinshah feloniously defrauded a purchaser by falsely representing SpectroChrome as a healing system. He defended Spectro-Chrome with the testimony of three physicians: Dr. Kate Baldwin, Dr. Martha Peebles and Dr. Welcome Hanor.

All three of the medical experts gave sworn testimony before the New York Supreme Court. Dr. Kate Baldwin, M.D., F.A.C.S., was Senior Surgeon at the Women's Hospital of Philadelphia, and had been using the Spectro-Chrome system for ten years. When the prosecution asked her if Spectro-Chrome would cure cancer, Dr. Baldwin stated that in many cases it would. She testified that she had used it to cure gonorrhea, syphilis, breast tumors, cataracts, gastric ulcers, and severe third-degree burns, "I may commence at the top of the head and cover practically every part of the body: ordinary inflammatory conditions of the eye, cataracts, glaucoma, hemorrhage into the retina and sclera, infection of the sinuses, bronchitis, pneumonia, pleurisy, tuberculosis, heart conditions (functional and organic), acute indigestion and ulcers of the stomach, asthma and hay fever, hiccoughs that had for ten days resisted all classical methods, cured in less than one day, all sorts of infections (local and systemic), abscesses, jaundice, kidney conditions, appendicitis..."

In fact, in an article printed in the Atlantic Medical Journal of April 1927, Dr. Baldwin stated that after thirty-seven years of active hospital and private practice in medicine and surgery, she produced quicker and more accurate results using Spectro-Chrome than with any other methods, and there was less strain on the patient.

Urging the medical profession to investigate the effect of color light on burns, she cited the following case history, "In very extensive burns in a child of eight years of age, there was almost complete suppression of urine for more than 48 hours, with a temperature of 105 to 106 degrees. Fluids were forced to no effect, and a more hopeless case is seldom seen. Scarlet was applied just over the kidneys at a distance of eighteen inches for twenty minutes, all other areas being covered. Two hours later, the child voided eight ounces of urine."

Dr. Martha Peebles also gave sworn testimony at the trial. Dr. Peebles was a doctor of medicine for twenty-four years, including twenty years working for the Department of Health for the City of New York. She was a physician for New York Life Insurance, and was a physician to the American Expeditionary Forces during World War I. During the war, she would attend up to 61 operations daily. She stated that she had been forced to retire due to ill health but using the Spectro-Chrome system had restored her health. She had used seventeen color machines over ten years, and had treated cancer, hypertrophic arthritis, poliomyelitis, mastoiditis, and many other medical conditions.

Dr. Welcome Hanor, M.D., a medical doctor for over thirty years, provided sworn testimony that he had treated cancer, diabetes, gonorrhea, syphilis, ulcers, hemorrhage, neuritis, spinal meningitis, heart disorders, uremic poisoning, and other medical conditions. The jury did not find Dinshah's healing system "preposterous." Ninety minutes of deliberation resulted in a verdict of 'Not Guilty.'

In 1947, Dinshah was tried in court for "mislabeling." Dinshah was found guilty and was forced to surrender all of the books, magazine articles and papers he had written on Spectro-Chrome to be burned! The estimated worth of the material that the government destroyed was $250,000. Dinshah was placed on five years probation, ordered to disassociate himself from Spectro-Chrome, and to close his institute. In 1958, the FDA obtained a permanent injunction against Dinshah's institute. He worked under the limits of the injunction until his death in 1966.

A very interesting statement was made by Dr. A. J. Ochsner, M.D., F.A.C.S., who was an author on several texts on surgery during those years, "In a personal experience with septic infection, the pain was so severe that it seemed unbearable. When the use of electric light was suggested, it seemed unlikely that this could act differently from the other forms of therapy that had been employed. Upon applying the light, however, the excruciating pain disappeared almost at once, and since this experience, we have employed the light treatment in hundreds of cases of pain caused by septic infection, and quite regularly with results that were eminently satisfactory, not only in relief of pain, but also because the remedy assists materially in reducing the infection."

Dinshah's son, Darius has written two books dealing with his father's work, "Let There Be Light," which was written by Dinshaw, and a reprint of his father's 1935 work, "The Spectro-Chrome Metry Encyclopedia."

Since I first learned about the Spectro-Chrome system I have had several hundred personal experiences over the last twenty-five years. The most dramatic had to do with my father Stanley.

In 1984 my mother and father went to Sedona, Arizona with the intent of possible moving there later in the year. They found a potential property that they were considering. Upon their return to Los Angeles my father was having back spasms and difficulties. He checked into his HMO for some examinations. Although the doctors felt something was going on, they couldn't quite figure out the problem. They asked him to remain overnight. By the next morning my father was having severe problems, which included paralysis taking over his body. Kaiser Permanente had done several tests including a spinal examination. Now they were calling my mother in the morning and telling her that dad was losing function over his entire body. They requested she allow brain surgery to take place to try to halt an infection. She gave her permission for the brain surgery to alleviate an infection. The surgery lasted six hours.

The head of neurosurgery, Dr. M, met with my mother to tell her that he believed their surgery went well but he was concerned and warned her that Dad might not regain any movement in his body. If this were the case, they would eventually place him in quadriplegic training. Several weeks went by and my father regained only a slight movement in a toe, but the doctors who came in told my patents that Dad would not regain the use of his legs due to the spinal infection. I met with the head of neurosurgery and explained that I did not like their approach and I was going to bring in color therapy into the hospital. We would not interrupt the hospital routines and my Mother would use it on my father. The doctor asked if it would disrupt the hospital, the electrical systems and the like. I explained we would bring a light source and a color filter into the hospital. We would use AC current and not disrupt any mechanical or electrical devices in my Dad's room or in the hospital.

We used the spectrochrome system twice a day and my father did regain the full and complete use of his legs. My father's hospital records are in the appendix. You will note the choice of the doctor's words. 'The patient has made a remarkable recovery from complete quadriplegia'. I have personally been involved with, and witnessed results in, the application of Spectro-Chrome in over one hundred severe medical conditions. In the majority of these cases, the medical profession had nothing to offer those who chose to utilize this therapy. I have seen the reversal of gangrene, arthritic conditions, and severe eye problems and on and on and on. Now, because of our legal system in this country I would add the following.... I am not diagnosing your condition nor recommending you try anything having to do with your particular problem. I would suggest that you consult with your physician or health care specialist. I would also suggest that you learn of all your options and determine your choice of action.

There are several hundred articles published in reputable scientific and medical journals relating to the effects of light on biological functions, such as Volume 453 of the Annals of the New York Academy of Sciences, "The Medical and Biological Effects of Light." Here is an entire conference dedicated to the biological effects from the use of light and color.

I believe that color therapy is one of the most successful, yet noninvasive therapies in the world! It is also one of the easiest to use; it can be done by laypersons.

The medical profession has utilized color therapy for many years, such as in the example given in the beginning of this article. They may not want to call it as such, but it is.

A couple of years ago, I was asked by my brother if WRF had information concerning a therapy for his injured dog. The young dog had broken out of the yard, and been hit and dragged under a car for approximately 90 feet. The dog was being brought to a veterinarian daily for fresh bandages. After my recommendation of using color therapy, my brother began color tonations about one week after the accident. After four days of color tonations, the veterinarian remarked that he had not witnessed an animal healing so quickly from that type of injury. When my sister-in-law began to explain what they had been doing, the veterinarian said that he did not want to know. His next statement was, "Keep doing it, whatever it is."

Fruits from this experience:
Encoded within our being are the archetypes of our creation. The natural healing modes inherent to all creation. Natural healing, in fact all healing enters through the senses, the bodily processes and our

innate ability to heal. There are far more approaches to healing then one learns from our medical professionals. Color therapy, and the color of health, are natural healing processes that undoubtedly work.

Chapter Twenty-six – Surprising Gifts

There is a story of two boys climbing coconut palm trees in the Caribbean to collect coconuts for their families when a tropical storm blows in suddenly. The boys keep working as the storm approaches until the wind overtakes them. Each of the boys' fathers come out to see that they were safe, and seeing them still in the trees calls out to them. The first father calls out to his son to hold on and he will be safe. He tightens his grip and is able to hold on as the winds blow through. The second father calls up to his son, "don't fall!" Almost immediately his son falls out of the tree.

When the storm is over the second father asks the first, how did your boy stay safely in the tree when my son fell. My son is as strong as your son; he is as experienced in climbing as your son; and is the same age. The father of the first boy explains to the second father that by telling his son "don't fall" put into his mind the possibility that he could fall. Before he could hold on, he had to process that reality and never could recover. My son, said the first father only had to think about holding on, and he did.

This is the story of our lives. We can either entertain the idea of succeeding or the possibility of failing. When we talk ourselves into success, we succeed. When we talk ourselves into failing, we fail. Henry Ford said that when you choose to do nothing you have already failed. The words, images, and possible outcomes you use and see is what you will experience. I have chosen to fill my internal dialogue with the language of success. What will your life be, the liturgy of success or the liturgy of failure?

Nicholas Eliopolous had a profound effect on the World Research Foundation in its early beginning. A mutual friend introduced Nicholas to LaVerne and I and we became good friends. One day Nicholas called and asked if he could bring a visitor over to the foundation. Nicholas came several days later and brought a very nice man who didn't speak very much. Nicholas asked if I would give him a tour of our little offices and LaVerne and I would share our philosophy. We spent about two hours talking and watching for some reaction from Nicholas's friend. At the end of the tour the man finally spoke and asked if we would like to go out for dinner. While we were out, he asked me if there was anything I wanted. I thought a moment and then said, if we had our own desktop publishing system I could print our newsletters on our own computers and not be dependent on anyone else. He asked how much it would cost. In 1985 a computer and software ran about $10,000. The man said, my accountant will call you tomorrow. I glanced over at LaVerne and raised my eyes in disbelief but didn't say anything. The next day I received a call asking for our address and the following day we received a check for $10,000 from Colin Higgins. He was a producer from Hollywood. We began printing the World Research News in 1986.

Nicholas was also instrumental in bringing Hollywood celebrities to assist us in our fundraising. Nicholas brought us Joe Bologna, Renee Taylor, Sharon Gless, Susan Strassburg, Diane Ladd, Lainee Gazan and several others. Nicholas not only brought people to us with beautiful gifts but he is a beautiful gift.

In 1985 we subleased a suite of offices in a five-story office building on the corner of Ventura and Sepulveda Boulevards in the San Fernando Valley, just outside of Los Angeles. A group of attorneys were moving across the street to a larger space and LaVerne and I were sitting at a conference table telling the partners that we would like to take this space. We had virtually no money in the World Research Foundation account and our foundation was so new that the ink was still wet on our business cards. In fact, I don't believe we had business cards at that time and we didn't yet have permanent offices. We received a great gift when they told us that we could sublease their office space. At that moment there was LaVerne and I and about twenty friends who liked the idea of the World Research Foundation.

We now had a beautiful office, but a library needs to have books, book cases and shelving. No matter where we checked the first week after moving in, every company said they didn't have enough cases on hand and they had to be ordered. It would be about six weeks before we might get shelves for our space. At the end of the first week in our offices a man walked in and asked to speak with the owners of our business. He was a nice man who told us that he was an attorney from Beverly Hills, California and he had just moved into the offices next door to us. He was having a problem because the special custom-made bookcases from his prior offices did not fit into his new office space. My eyes got very wide as he asked if we might have some need for them.

We received a great gift when his 13 bookcases were exactly the amount we needed to fill our central space in the office. Not only was he letting us have them but he didn't want any money for them. The only problem was that they were custom made and needed to have their headers and footers connected to them. The attorney gave us the name of the carpenter that built them for him so I could call and have the man put them together for WRF.

Upon calling the number I reached a man with an extremely heavy European accent. He didn't have much patience on the telephone and when I told him about the bookcases he immediately started telling me how busy he was and he just doesn't have the time to take on new projects. He is an artist!

I told him I understood and was hoping he could help us since we were a non-profit and looking to help people. It was Friday and I was hoping that he could get to us within a week. At the end of our conversation he reminded me again how busy he was but he would drop by the next day to take a look at the book cases and how they could be set up in our offices.

When he showed up on Saturday he was just as impatient and hesitant to commit to help us. Actually, he was funny with his antics and choice of words, but this was serious - we needed bookcases! He asked me what exactly we did and as I was explaining WRF to him, he said that he needed to call to confirm the first of three appointments for the day. When the first appointment cancelled, he said that he would place some of the bookcases and see what else he could do.

By the end of the day all three of his appointments had cancelled on him and he had erected all of the 13 bookcases into their proper places. He and I talked all day. I of course was talking so he wouldn't notice what the time was but I really didn't need to do it. At the end of the day he told me how much he enjoyed our conversation and $100 should cover his work. What a gift!

Elizabeth Karcher of Sedona. She was truly one of our greatest angels. Elizabeth took a great interest in the work of WRF when it began its Sedona office in 1985. My mother Adele ran the office and she and Elizabeth became close friends. Elizabeth's incredibly generous donations throughout her lifetime and in her will, has allowed the WRF to continue throughout the years. She was our wonderful Angel. Because of Elizabeth's donations the WRF was able to buy it's building in Sedona.

Fruits of this experience:
All things are possible and know that there is great assistance and support in this world and in Spirit for those activities that are in integrity and will benefit others. There are so many people who come at the right time, in time.

Chapter Twenty-seven – Antiquarian Books

I've never really understood why so many of us are afraid just to try. We see our weaknesses before our strengths. We see the someone else as the one who can do special things. We shy away from the potential embarrassment that we will be subject to if we fail. But what if we were detached from the outcome. If winning or losing didn't matter. What if we saw the joy in the experience itself?

My friend and co-author Jeff Wincel shared with me a story of exactly this. He is an avid, but not very good golfer. That didn't matter to him when he signed up for a club championship. He knew that there would be different "flights" where similar skilled players would be grouped together and play against each other. To his own surprise he made it through the first two rounds and found himself in the final. His challenger was clearly a better skilled golfer and likely to win. The caveat was that the final round had to be played on a specific day and time, no make ups were allowed.

Jeff's challenger wasn't able to play that day so asked the pro if they could schedule for another time – which Jeff was o.k. with; but the pro said no. The championship matches had to be as scheduled. Jeff showed up but his challenger did not. Jeff won simply by showing up.

At first Jeff felt that this was less than an actual championship win, but then as he thought about it, he realized that he had played the preliminary rounds and won; was prepared to play the championship round whether he could win or not; and showed up to play. He did all that was required of him, and won. The following year he played again, and the experience of playing under pressure served him well as he repeated as champion, this time playing all the rounds.

This, to me, is a great example of being an active participant not simply a spectator in life. You never know what may come of participation, of simply showing up. It can be great things. Greater than you may have ever imagined. I have learned that I need to show up every day.

When I put my life on "cruise control" it becomes less than it could be, and I become less than who I am.

In the late 1970s I was told that I should read and explore the writings of Manly P. Hall. Mr. Hall was the founder and President of the Philosophical Research Society, located in Los Feliz, California. He was a very highly regarded philosopher and I had noted his name and words being quoted in many times in philosophical publications.

I decided to visit his center on a Friday afternoon. That day there was a meeting taking place. It was called a Lyceum meeting. I entered a room with approximately 60 people. There was a blackboard at the front of the room with approximately seven points listed on the board. At the front of the room were some people who were speaking about Mr. Hall. Apparently, every Sunday morning he would speak on some philosophical topics. He had been presenting lectures since the early 1930s. On Fridays, people gathered together to discuss key points from his presentations on the previous Sunday.

At the front of the room on this day were two people from the Midwest who had been following Manly Hall's presentations since the 1940s. There was also a woman in the front who introduced herself as Pearl Thomas, head librarian at the Philosophical Research Society. I took a seat as far back as I could. In fact, you couldn't get any further then the back row where I positioned myself that day.

Some minutes later someone in the audience asked the moderators a question about one of the points on the blackboard. There was a moment of silence and then Pearl Thomas said, how about you there! I glanced up to see her pointing in my direction. I thought, she couldn't be pointing to me. But, as people in the rows in front of me shifted their positions either right or left, there I saw her finger pointing to me.

I started to speak but really do not remember what I said. The next thing I knew people were all looking at me and smiling. When the session was over and I was about to leave Pearl came up to me and asked me how long I had been reading the materials of Mr. Hall. I told her I had never read anything he had written. She then asked how many lectures I had attended. I told her I had never heard Mr. Hall speak. She then told me she was the head librarian of the Philosophical Research Society library and that she would like me to visit her tomorrow. I told her I would.

The following day I entered the most magnificent library I had ever seen. It was a two-story facility with floor to ceiling books, all behind glass. There were paintings, scrolls, busts and so many wonderful exhibits. It had beautiful wood bookcases and desks. It was a stately and impressive a facility housing approximately 80,000 books and scrolls.

A visitor tells the librarian the book that they wanted to view and the librarian opens up the locked book case and places the book on a reading table. There were materials dating to BC within the building; incredible parchments and scrolls, paintings and sculpted figures. One of the greatest collections on earth and Pearl Thomas told me that there was also an inner vault of extremely rare materials that were not available to the public. I spoke with Pearl Thomas most of that day while also checking out some of their holdings.

When I returned the following week, Pearl told me that when I wanted to look at one of the books, I could take the key myself and open a bookcase. What an honor this was for me. I was truly overwhelmed.

Mr. Hall had one of the most outstanding reputations in the field of philosophy and spirituality. He had more books in print then any living author at the time. As I began to familiarize myself with his writings, I found him to be very eclectic and he wrote in a manner that was easily understandable. He wrote on numerous ancient topics without interjecting long dissertations of his own opinion. When he did give his opinion, he made it quite clear that it was only his opinion. I also found that he was more concerned with helping people live a happier and more productive life rather than promising someone that he had the secret for the development of some ability where they could take advantage of another person.

When I came to the Philosophical Research Society, Manly Hall was in his 70s and still giving two-hour lectures for $1, a price he had been lecturing for in the 1920s. He would lecture without notes on any subject. When the material was transcribed it would be 12-15 pages single-spaced. He gave thousands of lectures and wrote nearly 150 books.

It was difficult to meet personally with him due to the fact that so many people were demanding to meet with him.

After three visits to the PRS I had a dream about Mr. Hall and his society. I knew it was important and so I gave it to Pearl Thomas on the Saturday following the dream. She said that she felt it should be given to Mr. Hall. As an aside, Pearl was in her 70s and had listened to Hall speak since she was in her teens. One week later I received a call from Mr. Hall asking me to come visit him in his office.

When I met Mr. Hall the first thing he said to me was, 'who are you? I answered that I was a student. He asked me what I wanted. I told him that I wanted to go into his vault and copy some materials. He asked me about my dream. I told him that it had just come to me. Mr. Hall explained, that he had a vision of the PRS about six years before he had built it in the 1930s. He did not build it in the manner in which he wanted to do to a lack of funds. My dream was how he had originally designed his facility to look like in the 1920s, well before I was born in 1949.

Mr. Hall remarked that my dream was a calling card and he gave me permission to go into his private vault and copy whatever I wished One stipulation he had was that I could not reprint any of the antiquarian books and sell them while he was alive. At that time, I was the only person that had gone into the vault, removed books and photocopied books of the Alchemists from the 1500s, 1600s and 1700s.

I knew exactly what to copy and did it for approximately six months. The only drawback being that because the books were so rare, so flimsy that I could not close the top of the copy machine and this did affect my eyesight for quite a long period after that experience.

From that time forward, I had access to incredible writings of the old philosophers. I also made these writings available to anyone who crossed my path. They would later be available to people who visited the World Research Foundation.

Fruits from this experience:
When given the seed of an idea to explore Manly Hall's work, I had no idea who he was, what I would discover, or even why I should care. But, when I stood for the first time in the doorway of Manly Hall's personal vault, I knew I was in the right place and the right time; a voice told me the materials that I should photocopy from within the vault, that they would be meaningful in my life and my work. I had showed up even when I had no previous knowledge of what the vault contained. The right direction and words were given to me at that Friday meeting of the Philosophical Research Society (PRS). Stepping into the experience apart from the outcome made all the difference.

Chapter Twenty-eight – A Pesky Fruit Fly

How often in human history has civilization succumb to "authority"? Where our common sense, our judgement, our self-preservation have been surrendered to those who we believe to have power over us. Power is rarely earned, and often taken. But what can we do about it? After all we are just the "little guy". Those we follow are smarter, more educated, more accomplished than I am, so how am I supposed to do anything?

Within us we possess the ability to overcome tyrants. We know deep down that our preservation lies only within ourselves. We have to step up and demand more…demand better. Confidence in these things only come with doing. We can't sit on the sideline and simply hope things get better. We have to become the change we want to see.

I learned this not by accident but by knowing I was right, that truth resided within my commitment to the cause I had to champion. It wasn't that I had the choice not to act, I had to act, and I was compelled to act. If I failed to act, I failed myself, and failed my community. Each of us have to ask whether or not we are prepared to act. Can we become a crusader for the truth?

It was winter 1989 and I had returned to my home from a trip to my office in Stuttgart, Germany. As I walked on my patio, I noticed some white powder on the black cover over my barbeque. I gently took the cover off and shook off what I thought was dust. The next morning when I woke up, I didn't feel very well. I was dizzy and sick but it didn't feel like jet lag. I asked one of my neighbors if she was aware of anything that had changed around our home.

I was informed that the night before helicopters had flown over our home spraying Malathion throughout our city of Granada Hills. In fact, she said the houses were shaking as the helicopters flew by.

Before I let on my trip, I remembered that there had been television commercials warning citizens, that in an attempt to eradicate the Mediterranean fruit fly, the California Department of Agriculture was undertaking a program of spraying an organophosphate poison (Malathion).

The radio and television commercials stated that it was perfectly safe but that pets shouldn't be allowed to run outside during the spraying and that paint on cars could be affected.

I talked with some of my neighbors who told me that they all stayed inside during the spraying with all of their windows tightly closed and their pets inside.

The head medical physician for the State of California was constantly on the airwaves stating that Malathion did not cause cancer and it was perfectly safe. He mentioned that thousands and thousands of studies had been conducted by the State showing that the Malathion was not cancer causing or dangerous to people.

But something seemed very wrong. I was not feeling well and since when is a poison not harmful to humans? I decided to gather all the information I could on Malathion and then present it to my local representative Congressman Bernardi. The internet was very helpful and I was able to gather all the studies that were done on Malathion going back into the 1960s. I then bundled the abstracts up and mailed them to my congressman. Two days went by when I received a call that some government officials from Los Angeles wanted to meet with me.

I met with councilman Joel Wachs who was absolutely in shock with the information that I had shared. During this same period many groups were protesting what the State of California was doing with its spraying. The more the people were protesting the greater the amount of propaganda the State was putting out regarding the safety of Malathion.

Councilman Wachs shared that state of California was concerned with the Mediterranean fruit fly and why the State was using this method of eradication. The bulk of agricultural crops are located in Northern California. If the farmers in northern California directly sprayed the Malathion pesticide on the crops then the various foreign countries that purchase the crops would not buy them because of the pesticide poison on the crops. So, someone came up with the idea to spray all the surrounding areas in California other than where the crops were located. In other words, attempt to kill the fly before it arrived in Northern California.

Every day in the Los Angeles area, we would hear on the news, that one or two fruit flies, not hundreds, but one or two, were found in a particular area of city and then spraying would take place in that area. A group of five or six helicopters would fly over the area where the fly was found and dump the Malathion over residential areas.

Originally the City of Los Angeles had welcomed the spraying of the city by a Los Angeles City Council vote of 8 to 7. The vote favored the political party that was power and in the Governor's office at that time.

As I explained to councilman Wachs, based on the studies I had accumulated from the internet, the danger was not necessarily of getting cancer but the studies showed RNA, DNA and all types of immune difficulties with Malathion. The only reason there had not been much information regarding Malathion leading to cancer was due to the fact that there had been only one peer reviewed study that had been conducted to determine cancer risks.

Strangely enough the State of California was saying they had thousands of studies and yet they had only one peer reviewed study. It was a 1980 report showing an increased risk of cancer from this Med fly eradication program. There was also information showing that the results of the study were altered from the author's original findings, infuriating him so much that he submitted his resignation. His superiors explained that the numbers which were changed were not scientifically significant. Their changes lowered the incidence of cancer in the study from 6 persons per million to one person per million. Also, there were peer commentaries that the entire study was flawed and not very well conducted.

The more I was hearing and reading the more I believed that something needed to be done. Obviously, the Los Angeles City Council officials had been 'handed a line' by officials from the Governor's office and they had not conducted a study or examined available information regarding safety to the public.

The information I gathered was forwarded by officials from the city of Los Angeles to the state capitol in Sacramento. A few days later the Governor's office in Sacramento stated that the data collected showing deleterious effects of Malathion was not really credible or what it seemed. Their reasoning was as follows; any study which shows it causes cancer is not really a good study because the State of California already knows that it can't possibly cause cancer. Also, research studies from foreign universities and genetic laboratories around the world stating that there was RNA and DNA damage were not acceptable because they couldn't be equal to the high standards of research which are a part of the California Department of Health.

This response was truly unbelievable to me. In my opinion, as well as the opinion of other scientists round the world, it was definitely the opposite. The foreign research studies were from some of the leading scientific and medical institutes in the world. In many cases the European studies were much more rigorous and unbiased.

Also, the State of California went on to say that just because there were some detrimental effects from in vitro studies doesn't mean that it could ever occur in the human body. This was incredible science and an extremely weak position to take. The Health Department of the State of California was not conducting more studies because they felt

Malathion was safe. This despite the fact they had never conducted a bona fide in depth study.

I decided to gather more information so I flew back to my office in Stuttgart and from there I would conduct personal meetings with officials from several different countries. I was able to make contact with the Head of Toxicology, Minister of Public Health of Belgium; the Head of the Department of Pesticide, Health Department of West Germany and the Federal Entomologist, Federal Research Station of Switzerland.

In audio-taped conversations each of the ministers told me, '…it is absolutely inconceivable that this [spraying pesticide over people] would happen in a city and would never be permitted in our country at any time!' Several of the individuals I interviewed believed that I was joking regarding a pesticide being sprayed on people, and that was at any dose.

After I returned to Los Angeles and provided the information to the City Council members, they decided to force officials from the Department of Health in Sacramento to defend their position, in open public hearings, on the safety of Malathion spraying. I was designated as one of the expert witnesses for the City of Los Angeles to provide testimony and Sacramento sent the head physician for the State of California.

Providing testimony in the hearings in the Los Angeles City Council Chambers were Dr. Adrian Gross, a pathologist and Senior Science Advisor for the Pesticide Division of the EPA; Dr. Donald Dahlsten, an entomologist from the University of California at Berkeley. He was the author of 135 scientific works. Also testifying was Dr. Sadun, a neuro-ophthalmologist and Associate Professor at USC School of Medicine and myself.

While information can always be debated and people have their own opinions regarding the interpretation of data, I believe that the information provided by the heads of the various governments that I visited was very impactful and armed with their comments and data I felt I was coming from a very strong position regarding the safety of Malathion.

During my portion of testimony, I had the opportunity to debate directly with the head physician for the State of California from Sacramento. I realized very quickly that he was not very knowledgeable.

This was surprising considering he was the individual speaking for the State of California's plan and the safety of Malathion and spoke on virtually all of the television commercials telling everyone how safe Malathion was. He actually inadvertently admitted he didn't have enough expertise to read studies and evaluate them. I asked him how many studies the State of California had conducted and he said several thousand. I mentioned to him that as of 6 PM last night there were only about 1300 conducted in the entire world since the 1960s so how could the State have conducted several thousand studies? He then stated that the State's unpublished studies were good studies. My response to him was that in these types of situations were health and safety were important, only peer-reviewed studies would hold any validity. That is the scientific way!

He then asked me what I had collected and I mentioned that I had the titles of all the articles on Malathion that had been published since Malathion was first introduced. [I had placed several boxes under the table before the two of us began our discussion. So, I reached down and brought up the box of titles only.] Many of these titles stating exactly what the health risks of exposure to Malathion would produce. He stated to me that those were just titles and perhaps would be misleading, he would need to see abstracts. I reached under the table where we were sitting and produced two boxes of abstracts. The doctor then stated, that he would really need to see the full articles. As I made a hand motion, which was a bluff seeming to bring up boxes of full articles, he stated that he was not qualified to read studies. Then I said, "But you are qualified to tell people that it is safe when you can't read a study?"

Congresswoman Molina who was listening to the debate asked me if I was being a bit hard on the State's representative. I told her that I was not the person who was making up the information regarding the studies. Just because of his position or title, we could not blindly accept or allow his words to turn a poison into ice cream. Soon after the presentations, the LA City Council voted 15-0 to stop the spraying.

When I returned to my seat, two men came up to me. We are disappointed in you and you did not play the game properly. I asked what game they were talking about. The Governor's office does not like to be embarrassed in a public forum like this. You should have sent your information and testimony to our offices before you made this presentation. I told them that the information was sent to their office. Several words were exchanged where I felt I was being threatened regarding my future involvement in the medfly issue. They stated they knew where I lived and my non-profit organization was allowed its exemption because of the graciousness of the State of California. My final words, "You have to do what you have to do and I will do what I have to do."

Two days later I received calls from several other cities in Orange County, California that wanted me to speak in front of their city councils regarding spraying in their cities. I spoke at La Habra, California and debated the Head of Agriculture for Orange County. At the end of our testimonies the council voted unanimously to stop the spraying. As I was leaving, the Agricultural Commissioner for Orange Country walked by me and moved his lips saying, 'thank you.' I knew that he was just using words that the State of California had given to him for his presentation. He didn't believe what he was saying but was towing the line.

The end results were that the State of California refused to stop spraying and threatened the City of Los Angeles with cutting off their highway and roadway funding if they blocked the spraying. The City of Los Angeles fought back as lawyers battled lawyers on each side. The State then took the position that the Medfly was an agriculture emergency and superseded health concerns. Eventually the cities won when they forced the EPA to get involved by sending information to them so they couldn't reply they were unaware of the situation. After they became involved the spraying program was shut down.

At that same time the walls had come down in Eastern Europe as the countries and people fought for their freedom. I can't help but remember my thoughts that here I was in California where my rights of life and pursuit of happiness were influenced by a pesky fly.

Fruits from this experience:
Nothing is impossible with truth. Nothing is impossible with perseverance. Nothing is impossible with commitment. Even when we feel we can never succeed, we are still able to fight the good fight. We can slay the giant. We can make a difference.

Chapter Twenty-nine – Qi Gong Masters

How often are we overwhelmed with the "holiness" of the spiritually accomplished? Seeing them more than merely human, almost super-human. When we are around them, we don't treat them as friends, we stumble over ourselves in reverence and insecurity. We don't see them as they see themselves, or as they want others to see them. We elevate them to a pedestal that they may not want to be on. We subject them to a higher standard of being than we are capable of holding ourselves.

Have you considered that perhaps the holiest of those around us, the most pious, and the most consecrated simply want to be seen as our brother or sister? To be with us, be like us, be loved like us. This is what I have discovered during my lifetime. Those who are more spiritually ascended are more humble, down to earth and "normal". They see in themselves who we are and who we can be. To embrace them like any of our other friends is all they seek. After all, when all else is stripped away this is all Jesus wanted.

During 1986 I had the opportunity to meet a fascinating woman from The People's Republic of China. Nellie Wong was a representative of the Central Government and her job was to help negotiate relationships between the People's Republic of China and people, companies, governments and groups outside of China who looked to develop inside of China. Nellie was introduced to me through my very close friends Phil and Allie.

Phil and Allie brought Nellie in to see me to ascertain if any of my business contacts would be interested in doing some joint ventures within China. It could have meant helping to develop raw materials, precious metals and stones or some other activities.

With Allie doing the translating I was asked if I had something I would like to discuss. Without any hesitation I asked if it would be possible for me to get in contact with the various academies of traditional

Chinese Medicine that dealt with acupuncture, Chinese Herbs and Qigong or energy practices.

Phil and Allie looked at me and wondered if I understood the potential that existed at this moment and was I sure that this is what I wished. I said that is what I wished and both Phil and Allie understood and supported my wish. Nellie told Allie that this was no problem.

Two months later I received a letter from the People's Republic of China inviting LaVerne and I to come to Beijing. Wow, this was one of the most exciting things that had happened to me. We were invited for 17 days in May to visit China. This was not a tour group but only LaVerne and I.

We made our arrangements including booking our flight and the next thing I knew we were on the final approach to Beijing. Then it struck us…who were we meeting, where were we staying and would we manage when neither of us spoke Chinese? I didn't really have a lot of forethought here. Really didn't even look up what the currency was. I think we were a bit 'star-struck' or should I say excitement-struck!

When we landed, we didn't see anyone that was looking our way or trying to get our attention. Now we really started to wonder about what we were doing here. We continued walking through hallways and passing checkpoints but not really knowing what lie ahead. After our third checkpoint we saw a group of people and one holding a sign that thrilled me to no end. The sign said ROSS. It wasn't a great leap to understand that there weren't too many Chinese with that name.

We were met at the airport by Yang Guozhong, General Manager of the Peking Union Medical Development Corporation. Yang Guozhong told us that we would be spending our first five days in Beijing and we would visit the Institute of Medical Information of the Chinese Academy of Medical Sciences. Prof. D. X. He would also meet with us as he was the Director of the Academy of Medical

Sciences. This was not the traditional academy of Chinese medicines but this was their orthodox mainstream medical institute.

We stayed in a dorm room located right next door to the Institute of Medical Information. We learned later that the suite that we were in was one of the best that they had available for visitors. It was all so very overwhelming! At night we heard tens of thousands of little bells ringing. These were the bells on the thousands of bicycles that were on the streets of Beijing.

On our first full day we met Miss Liu who was to be our translator and assistant. Miss Liu was a bit shy at first but proved to be a warm, loving, thoughtful and proficient person. She explained much about life in China including philosophy, social matters, the arts, politics and many other aspects. We grew each day with Miss Liu as we shared much about our life in the United States.

Miss Liu took us sightseeing and shopping during the periods we were not in meetings. Our meetings were with the highest medical authorities in China.

Some of the medical and health specialists we met included:

Dr. Liu Daqui who was a doctor of Pharmacy, Director of the Institute of Classical Chinese Dietetics of Shaanxi Province and Director of the Bureau of the Pharmacy in Xian Hospital and one of the leading experts of classical dietetics in China and Japan

Dr. Jin Yun Wang, M.D. who was Director of the Zhejiang Research Institute of Traditional Chinese Academy and the leading member of the Chinese Association of the Integration of Traditional and Chinese Medicine.

Prof. Dr. Ru Kuan Wang was the Vice-Director of the Institute of Medical Information for the Chinese Academy of Medical Science; ministerial level-expert of the Ministry of Health; President of the

Information and Library Expert Advisory Committee of the Ministry of Public Health.

Dr. Lu XiQian, M.D. who was the director of Public Health of the Provincial Government of Shaanxi Province.

Dr. Wang Xiufeng, Deputy Chief, Bureau of Science and Education of the Ministry of Public Health and responsible for the administration of all medical science and technology; formerly staff member, Office for Prevention and Treatment of Chronic Tracheobronchitis, Ministry of Public Health; former professor, Dept of Parasitology, Chinese Capital Medical College.

Prof. Jianchu Zhao, president of Shaanxi Provincial Academy of Traditional Chinese Medicine, Xian; professor of Research Department of Physiology; director and professor, Department of Basic Medical Sciences.

Dr. Gu-Fang Zhou, president, Chinese Academy of Medical Science, Peking Union Medical College; executive member of the Chinese Association for Science and Technology; professor of virology.

During the five days I was invited to make a lecture in the Chinese Academy of Medical Science and I made a presentation regarding the use of color in the healing arts from ancient times to the present. I am not sure that all of those in attendance understood my presentation in English, but I did have a very large and enthusiastic group.

At the end of the five days He Da-xun, Director of Medical Information of the Chinese Academy of Medical Science proposed a co-operation agreement between their Institute and the World Research Foundation. So, on May 9, 1987 we signed and opened up our information exchange with the People's Republic of China.

After our dinner celebration regarding our agreement, LaVerne and I were told that all arrangements had been made for our journey to Xian and Hangzhou.

In the city of Xian, we met with many officials in both standard medicine and the traditional Chinese medical practices. Another highlight of our visit was when we were taken to see the Terracotta Soldiers. A stone replica of an entire army that had been buried in the sand. It included the soldiers in full armor as well as their horses.

We left Xian and headed for the city of Hangzhou. It was here that we had our first introduction to the system called Qigong. We were taken to the Zhejiang Academy of Traditional Chinese Medicine and met with Fan Liang-qing, President of the Academy along with Ruan Shao Nan, Vice-Chairman and member of the Editorial Committee of the Zhejiang Journal of Traditional Chinese Medicine. Wang Guang-hua, who was Vice-President of the Zhejiang Academy, attended to our every wish.

On our first full day in Hangzhou we were taken to the special Qigong clinic. A woman who looked to be in her late 70s was brought into the room and was asked to lie down on a table. Our translator told us that the woman suffered from a paralyzed right arm and had not been able to move it for many years. In the next moments a doctor, dressed in a white gown, entered the room and proceeded to grasp the lady's wrist and feel her pulse. Dr. Huang Rui Sheng had a strong presence and there was something very unique about him. The translator then whispered to me and told me that the entire day is composed of people in this type of condition and that Dr. Huang would do something very special.

Dr. Huang then walked around the table where the woman was lying and stood behind her out of her visible sight. I watched as he took his right hand and pointed it at the woman's paralyzed arm. In moments her arm was almost hopping. Then as Dr. Huang raised his arm the woman's arm rose exactly at the same time and at the distance the doctor had raised his hand. In fact, the doctor moved his hand to the left, right, then back down and up and the woman raised her arm in perfect coordination to the direction and distance that the doctor desired. During all of this time the woman had absolutely no way of knowing what the doctor was doing because he was out of her line of sight. They also did not speak to each other. When the doctor was finished, the woman had regained complete control of her arm.

I was completely dumbfounded and was looking for mirrors or some type of explanation. For the rest of the day we watched patient after patient respond.

Next, I met Dr. Huang Guang Hua and Dr. Shen Ming Fang. Dr. Shen Ming Fang was our translator and told us we could call him Michael. It didn't take us long to ask Michael hundreds of questions about what we saw. Dr. Huang Guang Hua was also a Qigong Master, but we noticed that whenever he was together with the other Dr. Huang, he would become very silent.

Our first doctor, Dr. Huang Rui Sheng had been a Qigong master for nearly 40 years. The second Dr. Huang had been a Qigong master for about 25 years.

We were told that Qigong was the action of manipulating the energy of life called chi or qi. In other cultures, it might be called prana or life force. Dr. Huang Rui Sheng had been tested in Beijing and had received the status of being one of the most gifted Qigong doctors in all of China.

Our visit ended in Hangzhou and we were returning to Beijing to catch our flight home but I could not get the Qigong experience out of my mind. We had been talking about staging a second World Research Foundation Congress and wouldn't it be amazing I thought to have these Qigong Masters in the United States?

Fruits of this experience:

The energy known as Chi, Ki, Qi, prana and other terms is real with substantial medical and health benefits. While the energy itself cannot be seen, the affects and effects of the energy can be seen, evidence of the reality of its existence.

Chapter Thirty – Qi Gong Masters in Las Vegas

In everything there is a season; a time to reap and a time to sow, a time to laugh and a time to cry. Life tends to be filled with responsibilities. With work, with bills, children, spouses, jobs, obligations, obligations, obligations. But where do we find time for joy? For happiness? For foolishness? Our mental, physical and spiritual health comes from our wholeness; from the fullness of our expression.

Those who know me know that I am a loving, carefree and compassionate person. I am also passionate about my work, my family, my friends and my faith. To have lived as fully as I have, all of these are part and parcel of who I am. You need to discover this in yourself. Expand beyond two-dimension to three or four. From flat to a fullness; even expanding beyond this dimension into other dimensions. Many of the most joyful times of my life is when I have been able to participate in this with those whom I love.

The second World Research Foundation world congress was held in 1988 at the Sahara Hotel in Las Vegas. Among the 18 presenters from around the world were two Qigong masters and their translator from Hangzhou, People's Republic of China. In order for the three gentlemen to leave China we needed special clearance from the Central Government. We flew the three Chinese speakers to Los Angeles and in Los Angeles LaVerne met them and then caught an immediate flight to Las Vegas.

Dr. Huang Guang Hua, Dr. Huang Rui Sheng and Dr. Shen Ming Fang and never been outside of China. In fact, where they lived, they did not even have showers in their homes. They used communal showers at their Academy in Hangzhou.

They arrived at night and were driven down the Las Vegas strip to the Sahara Hotel. They were absolutely in chock! Dr. Shen Ming Fang (Michael) could not even find the words or do translating during the trip to the hotel.

We had arranged that each of the Chinese doctors would have their own room; but after showing them their rooms and trying to explain how the television remote worked and how to turn on the shower, we discovered that they all stayed together in one room for the entire five days they were there.

The literature from our congress brochure read; "The human body is composed of Qi, 'vital energy.' Qi energy is in all parts of the body. At optimum levels the Qi energy repulses pathogenic factors and balances the body forces. Qigong masters are able to control and direct Qi throughout their own body as well as direct Qi within a patient's body. Qi doctors can move the physical body of patients. Paralyzed limbs have been moved by Qi doctors without them touching the patient and without the patient being able to see the doctor. Two Qigong doctors from China, Dr. Huang Rui Sheng (40 years of external Qigong) and Dr. Huang Guang Hu (10 years of internal Qigong), along with Dr. Shen Ming Fang, will share their expertise and give demonstrations and interpretations of these effects. Also, there will be a discussion of a study in which a Qigong master fasted for 20 days while practicing Qigong. All of his vital signs were monitored and evaluated. Work with an actual patient will be done if time and conditions permit."

We had approximately 1500 attendees which included several hundred medical doctors and medical professionals. The majority of them had come to witness exhibitions of these Qigong doctors.

We decided to have some medical doctors bring their patients for consideration of being treated by the Chinese doctors. We finally decided on four people and included the wife of one of our speakers, Dr. Neubauer, who requested to be treated. Dr. Neubauer's wife was scheduled to have two knee replacements sometime after the Congress. The other subjects included a woman with Multiple Sclerosis, a man with a nerve condition.

When it came time for the Qigong doctors to make their presentation in front of our general assembly of attendees, a total of approximately 1500 people, I must admit I became a bit apprehensive. We had been advertising about the incredible affect that the Qigong practitioners had upon patients, but at the same time I had set up some pretty stringent testing. The Qigong doctors would not see any patients in advance and the patients that were used had no idea and never heard of Qigong.

This would be an extra tough test for the doctors because they had a substantial time change between China and Las Vegas, they had food they had never eaten before and the atmosphere was...it was LAS VEGAS. Not exactly where you would find Caine of the old Kung Fu television show!

With Michael translating, Dr. Huang Guang Hua and Dr. Huang Rui Sheng gave a brief background on the history, theory and practice of Qigong. Then they went into some practical demonstrations using the subjects that we provided. It was truly amazing. Dr. Nuebauer's wife had to be helped onto the stage due to her knee problems and she walked off on her own. It almost looked like a revival meeting! The other subjects showed enough change that the audience was completely in awe. Out of the 1500 attendees perhaps 450 were medical specialists. They witnessed the Qigong doctors standing over 30 feet away and still controlling the body of the subject that was lying on the table on the stage.

The day after their presentation I was approached by three doctors who were in the audience. They asked me if what they saw the Qigong doctors do was a put-on. Was this just a show that we had contrived? I told them that what they saw was a reality. I asked them what I might do to help them with what they saw. They asked me if I would set up a private demonstration with just a few people watching and they would supply a patient. I spoke with the Qigong doctors and they agreed that it would be fine. There exact words were, 'Mr. President, whatever you want us to do we will do it."

We arranged the personal demonstration in a mini conference room in the Sahara hotel and the demonstration began. Within minutes, the most powerful of the Qigong doctors, Dr. Dr. Huang Guang Hua, was standing behind the woman on the table, and different parts of her arms, legs, and head were moving in exact accord with where he would point. If he motioned toward her left arm and raised his hand three inches, the arm of the patient rose exactly three inches. He moved his hand to the left, right, up and down and without ever speaking or signaling the patient followed in complete accord even though he was three feet behind her head and out of her view.

Then the doctor completely left the room and went to an adjoining room. Because of the angle that we were at we could see the patient and the doctor on the other side of a wall. He maintained perfect control of the subject. Several times he left her arm or leg in an elevated condition and did not move. I know from my athletic background that it would be very difficult to hold some of these positions for the length of time that it was done. It just couldn't be done by the frail lady that was the test subject.

The western doctors that asked for the demonstration were absolutely satisfied. The overall effect of the Qigong doctors was quite profound on all the people who witnessed their exhibition in Las Vegas. Ever since that time whenever I have crossed paths with someone who attended that Congress, they will always remark on how their thoughts on life had been changed because of what they witnessed with the Qigong doctors.

On the last day before we would be leaving Las Vegas to return to Los Angeles I decided to try some experiments. Of course, my experiments were for science! I decided to take the doctors into the casino of the Sahara. We ventured toward the one-armed bandits in the quarter section. Through the translator I told them what we were looking for. We wanted to know if there was some machine they could point out to us that would drop money into the tray.

They agreed on a machine and I fed in 5 quarters. The next sound was money dropping down from a jackpot. We tried it two more times, for science, and two more large jackpots. We scooped it up and put it into plastic holders and gave it to the Qigong doctors. They wouldn't take it. They stepped back as if I had struck them in the face. It belonged to me and not to them. I told them that the $400 was a gift and was theirs. Michael told me that they were overwhelmed. Their salary was the U.S. equivalent of $19 per month.

We converted our quarters and I decided that we must proceed with our experimentation. We would go across the street to Circus Circus and find some dollar machines. All scientific!! We hit two jackpots on the dollar machines. I didn't need any more convincing of what the possibilities might be. My only thought was that someone would tap me on the shoulder and ask what was going on with these three men placing their hands on the machines.

We did get them to accept the cash and if I was more of a materialist, I should have seen what my new life might be.

The next day it was time to leave Las Vegas and the Qigong doctors said they would like to see the desert. I tried to tell them that they were already in the desert and they would get tired of seeing the desert over the three- and one-half-hour trip between Los Angeles and Las Vegas. Couldn't talk them out of it and they wanted to ride home with me in my car. After about one hour they became a bit fidgety and then I told them it would still be a little while.

While we were driving home, I had plenty of time to think and reflect on what I had seen them do. During this trip I also became inspired and had an idea. As we got very near my home in Granada Hills, California I asked Michael if any of the three men had ever heard of American Qigong. After talking together, he told me they had not. At that moment we came to my condo and I placed the car in park in front of my garage door. With my right hand I pointed to the garage door and with my left hand I touched my garage door opener that lie hidden out of their sight. I raised the heavy door up some inches and down some inches and up and down until I heard the three men speaking in excited tones.

They had never seen a television remote control, didn't know about showers and they never heard of a garage door opener. At that moment I was a Master. I was an American Qigong Master. They got out of the car and looked at the door…the door that I still had partially levitated as my hand was still poised holding it in space. They already held me in reference as Mr. President but now I was in an even greater status with them. I must also add that I never revealed how I did it. They left one week later and never knew my secret of American Qigong!

Fruits from this experience:
Even in the heights or depths of spiritual enlightenment, ordinary things can be marvels. The Qigong masters placed themselves at risk of persecution simply to encounter and experience the life we take for granted. We can find within the ordinary the extraordinary. Find sacred from the irreverent. Find beauty in the everyday.

Chapter Thirty-one – Czech on these Springs

I have been fortunate to have been of good health for most of my life. There are those though whose identities seem to be inextricably tied to their latest ailments, treatment or diagnosis. They seem to be fulfilled by going to the latest doctor, clinic or hospital. These individuals tend to seek only traditional medicines and healing modalities. Their proximity and investment in the establishment prevents them from finding true healing. Their symptoms are forever being addressed, usually through chemical/pharmaceutical intervention. Rarely do they stumble across a chance to permanently be resolved of their ailments.

My path to healing and health has been very different. While I certainly believe there is a time and place for traditional medicine, I more firmly believe that there are many more applications for "non-traditional" therapies. I have to smile to myself even writing "non-traditional" as these therapies are actually the most traditional, being handed down from generation to generation and culture to culture. My discovery of the healing powers of natural source hydrotherapies reinforced something I had already sensed to be true.

Providing therapeutic and medicinal modes of healthcare that are symbiotic with nature provide the greatest healing. With the traditional approach, the patient surrenders control to the physician. Unlike the traditional path of surgery, medication, rehabilitation, where the focus is on the process, the natural path engages the full participation of the patient. He or she alone possess the ownership of the outcome, including the permission to accept not just the possibility, but the likelihood of healing.

During a 1990 visit to Czechoslovakia I had the opportunity to visit the incredible springs that made up the spa city of Marienbad.

There are some 40 springs with an additional 130 wells in the neighboring area that comprise this unique and healing spa. The wells

in Marienbad reach different depths ranging from a few yards up to several hundred yards. The springs all have medicinal properties which are recommended by local physicians for a variety of health problems.

The gas-saturated water is acid, it decomposes and dissolves various minerals and then becomes enriched with mineral components of miscellaneous constitutions. After gushing forth to the earth's surface, the whole spa complex forms a medicinal mineral water.

I was told that the mineral waters of Marienbad were known before the establishment of the spa. The original site of the springs was a sparsely populated area with swamps and deep forests which were deliberately left untouched because of their vicinity to the border. According to preserved ancient documents, initial interest was aroused by the springs when attempts were made to extract salt from their waters. The salty flavor of the springs had been known for a long time. This is why King Ferdinand I had specimens of the water sent to Prague to be analyzed in the year 1528.

While the area had a remarkable beauty to it, I couldn't say the same for the air. Czechoslovakia, like most of the former Eastern Bloc countries, is so polluted that when you shower in the evening the tub is virtually black from the air pollution. Actually, the water at that time was also hard to shower in because of the coloring.

In the 18th century the fame of the waters spread to the surrounding areas and it was mostly village people visiting the springs on holidays and consuming unusually large quantities of water. It was in this manner, the proper indications for drinking cures were tested empirically. Eventually the proper quantities of water were determined.

The Abrose Spring, Ferdinand Spring, Cross Spring and Forest Spring were the ones mostly utilized as early as the first half of the 19th Century. The securing of the Rudolph Spring followed in the second half of the 19th Century. Due to the unique properties of the Rudolph Spring, the number of diseases treated in Marienbad increased with the ability to treat kidney disease and conditions of the urinary system.

What makes this whole area a real curiosity is due to the diversity of the composition and concentrations of various ions and compounds within the various springs of Marienbad. The temperatures range from 46 to 50 degrees F.

The specialty of the spa is kidney and urinary tract diseases. The local doctors will examine a patient and then prescribe the drinking from specific springs depending on the medical problem.

Fruits from this experience:
I was taken by the simplicity of treatment that nature provided. No prescriptions were necessary, no debilitating side effects, and no high cost deductibles, simply finding and using what nature provided. There never seems to be an end to the arrogance of man where we attempt to improve what God has provided. I was reminded of Paracelsus who stated in the 1500's who stated that when a health issue appears within a specific geographic area, God has provided the cure within the same locale.

Chapter Thirty-two – Spa City Bad Worishofen

Do you remember as a child how you felt going to the doctor or a hospital? If you were like me you probably felt a little frightened and certainly overwhelmed. There was a cold anger of the places. The people seemed otherworldly, almost frightening is their sternness. You waited on hard seats, only to wait even longer on a paper covered bed. When you enter into a healing world like this, angst at its highest how can you be expected to find healing.

There are places in our world where this is not the case. The healing environment is welcoming, serene, embracing. The "physicians" aren't only the schooled medical doctors, but the entire population who gather their energies to create a new meaning of hospital. This hospital is entwined with cities. Into their hotels, spas, clinics. You move from place to place, from healing to healing almost effortlessly. The treatment plan transforms from one attacking a single symptom, to a lifestyle where prevention displaces treatment. I've been blessed with finding and visiting some of the most profound of these places.

In 1987 I was taken to the incredible city of Bad Worishofen. Bad Worishofen literally means the 'Spa of Kings'. It is the birthplace of the famous Father Kneipp water therapy system. The entire city of almost 500 hotel/spas is dedicated to the Kneipp therapy.

I was met by Dr. Tassilo Albus who was the head physician who oversees all the physicians at the various spas. Tassilo was an outgoing, fun-loving, and high energy man who makes you feel good by just being around him. He told me that in a few hours we would meet Mr. Lothar Burghardt who was the head person over all of the individual spas throughout the city. So, I was very fortunate to be meeting with the chief of all the spas as well as the head physician in the city.

Tassilo told me that the Kneipp system of hydrotherapy and natural healing was actually practiced all over Europe. Father Sebastian Kneipp, who was born in Bavaria in 1821, was studying for the priesthood, when he contracted tuberculosis of the lungs. In those days that was considered a fatal disease. Father Kneipp treated himself and recovered by developing his own therapy.

Kneipp was ordained as a priest and his appointment to the Dominican Nunnery in Worishofen, Bavaria, determined the future of the present-day spa in Bad Worishofen.

Among Kneipp's patients were Pope Leo XIII; Prince of Wales, later King Edward VIII; Empress Fredericka of Germany; Baron Rothschild and of course, the poor and sick country-people who were so neglected and forsaken.

As we drove through the city it was comprised of hotels with Kneipp spas inside and parks and riding paths which had little turnouts offering Kneipp therapies.

Kneipp's program is a healing system with five principles: Hydrotherapy, Phythotherapy (plants), Therapeutic Exercise, Nutrition and Emotional Principles.

Kneipp's hydrotherapy utilizes the pure spring water from the Alpine foothills. It is not just a cold-water treatment but encompasses washings, gentle or strong showers, relaxing baths, compresses and steam. Many possible water temperature variations are used. Kneipp found that water, applied hot or cold, or alternatively, not only strengthens skin tissue but also influences the organs connected to skin areas.
The cardiovascular system is activated, the respiratory system, metabolism and digestion work in harmony, and even the hormonal balance is influenced in a positive way.

As Tassilo shared this aspect with me I became very excited and shared my story regarding my injury from stepping over the sprinkler head at my university. The therapy I used was a modified version of the Kneipp and I was alternating hot and cold temperatures almost 17 hours per day on my knee. I certainly understood the possibilities that were shared regarding Kneipp's therapy.

Tassilo explained that the power of plants or phytotherapy has been highly valued by medical experts for a long time. Father Sebastian Kneipp was one of the pioneers of ancient herb therapy. Herbal medication and remedies support the cleansing, strengthening and healing effect of the Kneipp therapy without any side effects.

We stopped and went over to one of the many walking paths that crisscrossed throughout the city. Tassilo pointed out that sufficient exercise is indispensable for healthy physical functions, a sound mind and strong nerves. Tassilo in his fun-loving style stated that even exercising should be fun!

The possibilities to keep fit in the city of Bad Worishofen is unlimited. We finally arrived at the central part of the city and the government offices of Mr. Lothar Burghardt. Lothar was a very matter of fact individual who would slip in little jokes when you would least expect it. I could also see that he and Tassilo had a good friendship.

Without missing a beat Lothar was discussing the emotional factors that are an aspect of the Kneipp therapy. He said that the saying, 'Order is heaven's first law', has a very deep meaning. The Kneipp cure itself entails order in the sense of biological rhythms and one's own attitude towards the solution of problems, conflicts and crisis. One person has simply to take a break, take a rest and let the 'inner clock' take over. Another needs new ways and experiences to actively combat stress. A third person tries to come to terms with himself, his environment and the universe. The fourth one finally has to express himself. The uncomplicated, serene atmosphere in Bad Worishofen, the individual care, the peacefulness and tranquility of the surroundings decisively contribute to restoring one's perfect equilibrium whatever that may be.

Lothar mentioned that the insurance companies actually reimbursed people one week every two years to come to Bad Worishofen even if they did not have a health problem. The preventive aspects made it cost effective.

The types of problems that are addressed in the city are circulatory disturbances, stroke, and recovery from heart attack, phlebitis, arteriosclerosis, rheumatoid, arthritis, gout, stress, nervous troubles, insomnia and more.

We checked into our spa hotel and it was a beautiful place and appeared to be like any other hotel except for the incredible Kneipp therapy area located in the basement area. What a beautiful place to be and certainly one of Europe's best kept secrets.

Fruits of this experience:
There are many healing approaches in addition to pharmaceutical protocols. The highest and best approach should be tailored to the individual and their particular temperament. The entire city is dedicated to a natural approach to health. When a visitor arrives for treatment, upon check-in to their hotel they are provided the opportunity to meet with a holistic physician. Based on their individual needs a tailored natural treatment plan is derived. The treatment engages the entirety of the city, its features, and its people. It moves beyond the "hospital" model and to an integrated living model.

Chapter Thirty-three – The Nobel Chairman is Ignored

In 2004, Chicago news anchor Bill Kurtis voiced the History Channel's "Investigating History" show on the assassination of John F Kennedy. The show examined the facts and evidence of the December day in 1963 in Dallas Texas. Kurtis drew out opportunities for new conclusions, new understanding of what may have happened. Despite the History Channel's stature and Kurtis' pedigree, the show was panned as another conspiracy theory. Unproven, and while entertaining unlikely to be true.

Now conspiracy theories aren't really my thing, but every once in a while, it's hard to deny that there are powers and interest who would interfere with the truth coming out. Typically, these conspiracies are the most powerful when fortunes can be made or lost, when the established players cling desperately to what they know and what they control. Very few places have the invested interest in being immovable as does healthcare. Doctors, hospitals, insurance companies, pharmaceutical companies, etc. all have millions, even billions to lose if their proprietary approaches are supplanted by treatments that are inexpensive and readily available.

Despite my own self-interest, I came to see a conspiracy in action in the mid-1980s. The established powers conspired not simply to silence a noisy outsider, but to silence one of the most respected physicians in the world. One of their own. The chairman of the world's most esteemed organization. His crime, to have the audacity to suggest that cancer could be healed apart from the 3 approved treatments – radiation, chemo-therapy, and surgery. The following story shows the lengths that organizations and individuals will go to stop such discoveries. I can't help but wonder, what other treatment discoveries have been silenced that came lesser known men or women.

Dr. Bjorn Nordenstrom was one of the featured speakers of the World Research Foundation 1986 World Congress. I became interested in Dr. Nordenstrom when I read the April issue of Discover Magazine.

It stated, 'Nordenstrom claims to have discovered a heretofore unknown universe of electrical activity in the human body – the biological equivalent of electric circuits…in the body electric, the circuits are switched on by an injury, an infection, or a tumor, or even my normal activity of the body's organs; voltages build and fluctuate; electric currents course through arteries and veins and across capillary walls, drawing white blood cells and metabolic compounds into and out of surrounding tissues. This electrical system works to balance the activity of internal organs and in the case of injuries, represents the very foundation of the healing process…it is as critical to the well-being of the human body as the flow of blood. Disturbances in this electric network, Nordenstrom suggests, may be involved in the development of cancer and other diseases."

Nordenstrom was working out of Karolinska Institute in Sweden, which is the home of the Nobel Assembly. In fact, Nordenstrom was a past chairman of the Nobel Assembly. He was the discoverer of needle biopsy and one of the top radiologists in the world. Yet, I had not heard of any cancer research money being sent to examine and determine if this was an effective answer to women's breast cancer. Nordenstrom had documented an incredible success rate with his unique and innovative approach to cancer.

We flew Nordenstrom into Los Angeles and he spoke at the conference and was one of two speakers who received a standing ovation. In front of approximately 1000 people, he presented his incredible research.

Before he arrived in Los Angeles, I received a call from the City of Hope Hospital asking if it might be possible for them to speak with Nordenstrom to arrange a presentation at their facility. I told them that I did not own him and of course they were free to make arrangements if they liked. My purpose for bringing Nordenstrom to American was to allow him to make direct presentations.

I had the opportunity to speak privately with the doctor and he told me about what he had been going through. While it was true that he had been very quiet about his work and did not allow others to know too much about it until he had further perfected his technique, when he did look to publish results of his work, the medical publishing companies did not want to publish because they said he would have a limited audience. Although he was a recognized surgeon, his use of electricity was not common for most physicians and the medical publishing companies would not take a chance on limited sales. Therefore, Nordenstrom self-published an incredible book of his research work. As a result, people in the medical profession said that his work had no validity because it was self-published. What a catch twenty-two!

If this was not bad enough, he was classified as an "alternative practitioner". Why? Because any person or technique that is not currently accepted as the recognized cancer therapy is classified as "alternative". Here is a valuable lesson, do not to accept a label that is placed on someone or some therapy that lessens its value. This is a practice that is very prevalent in the medical world.

When the Los Angeles Times called us to ask for an interview with Nordenstrom, he initially turned them down. This was very surprising for me, but he told me that he had received some pretty harsh press from some of the newspapers. In fact, the press was calling him an "alternative medical practitioner" although he was chairman of the Nobel Assembly. The papers liked to make references to Frankenstein and his work, which was condescending and belittling.

Nordenstrom was a tremendous surgeon and researcher. He was a physician's physician and his work should be in common usage all over the world.

The television program 20/20 interviewed Dr. Nordenstorm during our conference, however they did not air his interview until two years later in October of 1988. What stands out the most from that interview is the many reactions of the doctors interviewed from our leading medical institutions. Essentially, these doctors said that Nordenstrom's work was very interesting but they simply didn't have the time to look at something new. According to them, Nordenstrom's work was more in the realm of physics and not pharmaceutical/drug therapy and therefore did not warrant their attention. I guess that is easy for the men to say when they are not the ones getting breast cancer.

Fruits from this experience:
Therapies exist throughout the world that are from reputable and prestigious individuals that you may not be aware of. Those that go beyond the limitations and current medical practices can be too easily dismissed by the establishment. Your individual integrity, education, and advocacy are more important than the labels placed by others.

Chapter Thirty-four – Man is a Plant

Recently I was talking with a friend about her "new me." What she was talking about was that her life had transformed almost radically over the past 10 years, yet her longtime friends could only see the her from 10 years ago, not the her from today. She had been asking for their advice on the purchase of a new home. Invariably they offered her suggestions that seemed to be little about her aesthetics, and more about their own, or about what she may have liked 10 or 15 years ago. They failed to see her as she saw herself. These friends couldn't recognize the growth and change that had slowly but surely occurred.

Imagine now having a serious illness requiring radical treatment or intervention. Most doctors spend less than 5 minutes in a typical appointment with the patient. They have virtually no knowledge of the person. They may have seen the diagnostic reports, may have seen this in others before, and may have even successfully provided treatment. So what? Breast cancer in one woman is not the same in another, even if the cancer itself is of the same type. Each woman's life, lifestyle, and ability to heal can be vastly different. Approaching them as an assembly line of interchangeable parts can never be successful. To dehumanize the patient is to "kill" the patient. They may survive, but their individuality and spirit has been killed. Recidivism or return of the same malady serves as evidence to me that the necessary "cure" never happened, because the person wasn't treated, the "patient" may have been but only within the limited occurrence of their illness.

Although I was aware of the great German philosopher Rudolf Steiner, I was not aware that an entire university hospital and major government research center had been established upon his scientific and health philosophy. I journeyed to see the University of Witten/Herdecke. In 1991 I was met at the hospital by Dr. H.C. Kuemmell, Dr. Wolfgang Goebel and Dr. Kiene.

The hospitals basic underlying philosophy is that we don't just look at a tumor, we look at John or Mary or Bill's tumor. A second important philosophy is that the children's environment is compatible to health. A hospital should not look like a scary place but children should look forward to their visits.

Out of the 500 beds of the hospital there are generally 50 with children. The doctors said, 'we don't treat diseases, we treat people. We assist the body but don't ever force it. We attempt to understand the patient and help the patient bring harmony to all levels of the body.

I was told there were four levels which included;

Level 1 is to treat the patient with standard medicine if necessary.
Level 2 is to use homeopathy, herbs, mistletoe and etc.
Level 3 is to use artistic expression, drawing and music.
Level 4 is to reach the soul or I aspect of the patient. This is an aspect that needs to be heard.

There are over 70 medical doctors in the hospital and each of them will create a treatment that is as individual as the patient. They are involved with cancer, asthma, colitis, eczema and many other ailments. The doctors will use therapies that include:

- Mistletoe Therapy
- Fever Therapy
- Magnetic Field Therapy
- Intercellular Oxidation (Sieger)
- Color Therapy with Art
- Medical Herbs grown in gardens located on the hospital grounds
- Interaction of people with animals.

The German government publishes research projects through the university and the University of Witten/Herdecke has offered a full course for medical doctors.

Dr. Kuemmell, of the Department of Internal Medicine stressed that heart disease problems have been decreased through their specially designed dietary changes. We have stressed to our patients that if they follow our guidelines, we won't need to do a bypass. We are always trying to discover what possibilities might exist to help the healing process. What is the best way to treat this patient, we never try to figure out how to bend a patient to follow some general guidelines. We always take a non-dogmatic position with our patients.

Dr. Kuemmell went on to say that they had found a high correlation between the rhythmic relationship between the heart and the breath. We always look to use natural products whenever possible to enhance and not force the body into any activity. Our studies on humans have shown that there is a correlation between the heart, arteries, infection and the body attempting to mobilize itself. We are always studying the best therapies to have all the aspects working together within the body to solve the problem.

Dr. Wolfgang Goebel shared that the solutions in the hospital are totally individual and we might employ all forms of therapy. This means never do we force the body. We must help the patient to understand himself and all his parts of self. The patient is a self-contained individual. A doctor must first meet the patient at the patient's own level. As a doctor we must always strive to find the levels of vitality in each aspect of the patient. We must try to bring to harmony all levels of the patient for a better and more complete healing. There is a basic cognition or plant level a mineral, animal and higher part of each and every patient. While our solutions come from experience as discovered in the literature, we learn more from each patient we see. And further we are always open to use all therapies including all Western medicine and chemotherapy.

Dr. Kiene addressed us at the end of our visit and shared some of his work regarding mistletoe and cancer. He had conducted a three-year study with a government grant that showed the potential effectiveness of mistletoe. Along with mistletoe the University has been studying Fever therapy, thymus extracts, intercellular oxidation and magnetic field effects.

It was a great experience to see the mixture of western and non-traditional medicines. I was also impressed with the University's program with Hippo therapy. This was the use of horses as a therapeutic technique with children and people with psychological difficulties. All in all, a tremendous learning experience.

Fruits from this experience:
Never force the body - support, assist, and encourage. This philosophy works in all aspects of our interactions with all life on the planet.

Chapter Thirty-five– My Scientific Big Brother

I am greatly appreciative of the many important and caring people that I have encountered in my life. I have a single biological brother whom I love dearly, but there are others who have entered my life as brothers or sisters who seem as close to me as my biological brother. Like my "real" brother, this love and affection has little to do with what they bring but more about who they are, how our spirits resonate. I continue to encounter and discover new brothers and sisters. Pythagoras was right when he said my brothers and sisters are those of us who resonate within the same philosophy.

In 1985 I had my first meeting with Bernhard Muschlien of Germany. I will always consider myself so very fortunate to have met this man in my life. Bernhard combined an incredible intellect, a quiet and wonderful demeanor, an unquenchable desire to know the why of things and the perseverance to stay the course until he makes his discoveries. When I first met him in Wiesbaden, near Frankfurt, I had a feeling that I was meeting someone who had so very much to share with the world.

Bernhard had been working in the field of cancer and biological approaches for cancer therapy. Bernhard was a healing practitioner with a very long background in engineering. I had been told that he was the cancer specialists that other cancer practitioners went to when they had their own medical problems.

In 1985 Bernhard also was involved with an incredible new blood pressure measurement technique called Oscilleration Diagnosis by Boelger. This device was completely unknown in the United States but was utilized to measure other aspects of blood pressure that heretofore had not been measured or correctly understood. Here was a device that could pinpoint problems in blood pressure nearly 3 months earlier than standard measuring techniques.

Bernhard was also involved in nutrition and biological functioning; geopathic stress zones (frequency fields in the home and office); electromagnetic blood tests; mineral deficiency tests and various therapies for degenerative diseases.

Common acquaintances that we both knew told me that Bernhard was the ONE if they ever had health problems.

Bernhard was one of the featured speakers at the 1986 World Research Foundation Congress. Connie Chung interviewed Bernhard on her nightly news program after the Congress.

During Bernhard's stay in Los Angeles I was able to show him Rife's Universal Microscope which was at my home. Bernhard was completely overwhelmed by the device.

Bernhard's learning about the Rife Microscope would lead to the discovery of another microscope, the Ergonom 400 and Bernhard would eventually make several discoveries that would benefit mankind.

After his presentation at the congress Bernhard returned to his home in Germany and made a startling discovery. When he mentioned seeing a super microscope in Los Angeles, someone told him about a super microscope that was located in the town of Mossautal-Hiltersklingen in Germany.

Bernhard traveled to the location of the Ergonom 400 microscope and met its inventor, Kurt Olbrich. Mr. Olbrich had been using his super microscope for industrial research including finding flaws in computer chips. Olbrich had no idea that his microscope was a more powerful microscope than those being used in medical research. So, in 1987 Bernhard suggested to Olbrich that the Ergonom 400 should be tried in biological and medical applications as well. Muschlien became the head of a research team doing just that.

Muschlien began studying illnesses such as cancer, AIDS and Legionnaire's Disease His group's findings challenged long-held assumptions on the nature of disease itself. In medicine, the light-source research microscopes could reach magnification of about 2,000 times, allowing limited live observation of bacteria, but not smaller, virus-sized micro-organisms. While the electron microscopes were being utilized around 400,000 times, they work with x-rays and an evaporated vacuum and could not be used to view living cultures. The Ergonom 400, is a light-source microscope that magnifies 25,000 times, allows observers to view, for long periods, the development cycle of living micro-organisms as small as viruses.

It was interesting to learn that industry experts had told Olbrich that his goal of inventing a new super-microscope was 'impossible' because of the limitations in physics.

"Kurt Zanker, Head of the Institute of Immunology at Witten/Herdecke University, told a reporter for Capital Magazine, 'It is fantastic. I have never seen such things before.' A group of leading scientists in England have called the microscope a major development in the field.

I invited Bernhard to present videos taken through the Ergonom 400 at the 1990 World Research Foundation Congress in Woodland Hills, California. Muschlien presented video documentation of facts that are contrary to orthodox medicine, and completely contrary to orthodox research. However, his research proven through the Ergonom was not contrary to the research conducted over 100 years ago.

Antoine Bechamp, a French biochemist and toxicologist, discovered tiny, moving bodies in everything from human beings, animals, and plants, to soil, swamps, air and water. He called these microscopic forms 'microzymas', and believed they were one of the fundamental building blocks of life. Bechamp found that when a life-threatening trauma occurred in an organism, the microsymas could change form and begin destroying the body of their host. Similarly, these microbes could 'devolve' back into their previous benign state.

Bechamp concluded that certain conditions in an organism evoked the appearance of specific micro-organisms, and that such micro-organisms were, therefore, a symptom rather than a final cause of disease. Bechamp's theory of pleomorphism () the occurrence of more than one distinct form of an organism in a single life cycle) contradicted the 'germ' theory espoused by his more famous contemporary and rival, Louis Pasteur, who determined that germs from outside the body caused disease.

This microbe is present in all human beings. In its early stages of development, it is symbiotic, living friendly within the body, in harmony with the immune system. When a person becomes weakened, by surgery, infection, vaccination, stress, and so on, the microbe changes its cyclogenia (cycle of development). It becomes larger, aggressive, pathogenic and parasitic. These larger forms are found in the blood stream of people threatened by, or suffering from, cancer. With the Ergonom 400 one can observe at what stage this microbe exists.

By examining the stage of development of this micro-organism in the blood, Muschlein says, one can determine the state of health, or conversely, the level of pre-cancerous or cancerous conditions in the body.

Muschlein and his team made many discoveries but most important was his comment that his research confirmed the research that Royal Rife conducted decades ago.

The implications of this work with the Ergonom are very significant but unfortunately technologies and discoveries that are made outside of the 'ole boy' research groups that obtain public research money have a difficulty ever being seen.

I have always admired the efforts of Bernhard Muschlein. During the many years we have spoken together he has called me his little brother. I can't think of anyone I would rather have as my older brother!

Fruits from this experience:
Our brothers and sisters are those with whom we resonate; this was an ancient philosophical tenant. Distance, nationality, color…we are all family.

Chapter Thirty-six – The Rife Microscope

There is little in my life that has had the impact of my encounter with the Rife Microscope. I had been providing healing work and seeking the broadest possible spectrum of healing techniques. This work was by me, but not about me. It was the calling I felt in service to others. Service in which I knew that I too would be fulfilled. My "discovery" of the (existence of the) Rife Microscope not only expanded the healing work I would continue to do but became a seminal event in the founding of the World Research Foundation. My gratitude in the Divine guidance and cooperation I received in this discovery is beyond words.

For many years I had been looking for a particular book that had been out of print. It was my understanding that this book, "New Light on Therapeutic Energies", written by Mark Gallert, had information on several incredible healing devices and technologies. I had seen references to this book in many other books that I had been reading.

One night in 1983, I had the following dream. I saw myself driving in a car to the Bodhi Tree Bookstore that was located in Hollywood, California. I lived in the San Fernando Valley at that time and the bookstore was only a 45-minute drive from my home. In the dream I went to a particular book shelf and glanced at the books but none of them held any particular interest for me. I went closer to the books and then reached behind the books on the second shelf from the top. Behind the books I could feel another book. When I reached for it, I discovered it was the book I was seeking.

The table of contents listed the following persons and techniques; Dr. George Starr White, M.D. and natural energies from earth and sun; Dinshah Ghadiali and Spectro-Chrome Therapy; Royal Raymond Rife and the Rife Microscope; Dr. Wilhelm Reich, M.D. and Orgone Energy; Dr. Hahnemann and Homoepathic remedies; Dr. William Schussler, M.D. and the 12 Tissue Salts; Dr. Chas W. Littlefield, M.D.

and Vitalized Tissue Salts; Dr. W.E. Keesey, M.D. and Negative Galvanism; George Lakhovsky and the Multiple Wave Oscillator.

While I found virtually all of the above of great interest, I was especially overwhelmed by the information regarding Royal R. Rife and the Rife Microscopes.

Rife had apparently invented and constructed microscopes that exhibited unique properties. In fact, the following quote is from an article written for the 1944 edition of the Smithsonian Institute Publication and the Journal of The Franklin Institute regarding 'New Microscopes', written by R.E. Seidel, M.D. and M. Elizabeth Winter. "...a very successful and highly commendable achievement on the part of Dr. Royal Raymond Rife of San Diego, California, who, for many years, has built and worked with light microscopes which far surpass the theoretical limitations of the ordinary variety of instrument, all the Rife scopes possessing superior ability to attain high magnification with accompanying high resolution."

The first thing that jumped out at me was how do you surpass a limitation? Rife was using devices which went contrary to all laws of optics! Rife was doing this as early as 1922. His microscopes were ten times more powerful than the light source microscopes in use in his day and in our present time.

Although most people have heard of electron microscopes and the incredible magnifications that they are able to produce, most people are not aware that you cannot look at live specimens. An organism is placed in a vacuum and bombarded with electrons so it is impossible for it to survive. So, biomedical researchers were and are still using microscopes that magnify just under 2,000 diameters. Here comes Royal Rife with devices that magnified 30,000 – 60,000 diameters and did not hurt the specimens that were being viewed. Clearly this was unbelievable because this was violating all of the known laws of optics for light-sourced microscopes.

But what was even more astounding was that while viewing microbes and other organisms under the various Rife Microscopes they would 'glow' in their own particular color. Now I am being very simplistic here, but because of the unique aspects of the microscopes organisms would refract the same colors when stained by means of the monochromatic beam of illumination of the microscopes. "The virus of the Bacillus Typhosus is always a turquoise-blue, the Bacillus Coli always mahogany-colored, the Mycobacterium li prae always a ruby shade, the filter-passing form or virus of tuberculosis always an emerald green, the virus of cancer always a purplish-red, and so on."

So now every organism has its own particular color that is associated with it. A color is a rate of vibration. Different vibrations or vibratory rates make up our color spectrum. So, we know what the internal life vibratory rate is of the organism is that color that is being viewed.

Now what happens when a singer hits a particular note that resonates with particular types of glass? They can shatter the glass. Not every piece of glass that is nearby but only the glass that resonates at that same frequency that they have produced.

Looking again at what Rife found I read the following, "under the Rife Universal Microscope disease organisms such as those of tuberculosis, cancer, sarcoma, streptococcus, typhoid, staphylococcus, leprosy, hoof and mouth disease, and others may be observed to succumb when exposed to certain lethal frequencies, coordinated with the particular frequencies peculiar to each individual organism, and directed upon them by rays covering a wide range of waves. By means of a camera attachment and a motion picture camera not built into the instrument, many 'still' micrographs as well as hundreds of feet of motion picture film bear witness to the complete life cycles of numerous organisms."

Could this all possibly be true? Did Royal Rife and the scientists working with him actually have an understanding of cancer and a possible therapy so long ago?

This makes total sense. The question was is this real, true and where is the microscope and technology from the 1920s?

After reading all of this within the book I immediately thought of a medical friend of mine. Dr. Harry Lusk was a gynecologist and former president of Hollywood Presbyterian hospital in Los Angles. Harry was in his seventies at the time and had held positions at several medical institutions. I made contact with Harry and we met for lunch. Harry told me that when he was a young medical student that there were rumors about a very powerful microscope that was developed in San Diego, California. He had heard that it was being used but several prominent medical researches but was not being reported by the leading medical journals. Then he told me that approximately ten years earlier he actually attended a lecture by a man who had the Rife Microscope. I was in puppy heaven!

Dr. Lusk went on to say that after the lecture given by John Crane, he had tried to make contact for over one year but never could reach Crane. He had given up. I asked Harry if he had a contact number and Harry told me that he had no idea where it might be. I was somewhat disappointed at that news but elated that the Rife Microscope was real.

The next morning, I received a strange call from Dr. Lusk. He was stammering and stuttering and sounded very confused. He told me that when he had arisen in the morning that he found the piece of paper at the foot of his bed with John Crane's telephone number on it. He just didn't know what to think about his finding the information in that manner. I just accepted it and asked if I could have it. Harry gave it to me under the proviso that if I was going to San Diego to see it that he would come with me. No problem I told him.

Harry had told me that he had called the telephone number about fifty times over a one-year period and never reached anyone. When I called the number the first time, I reached John. He was very hesitant on the telephone and continually asked me if I was with any government agency or worked or consulted for any state agency. I assured him that I did not and that I was co-founder of a health information organization.

After approximately one hour of a conversation where John Crane seemed very evasive, hesitant and paranoid, he invited me to visit him in San Diego. We set up a meeting in four days and when I hung up, I called Dr. Lusk to give him the information that we were going to San Diego. Four days later when we were about to leave Harry was paged and one of his patients was going to be having her baby. Harry asked if I would reschedule. Oh, it was painful but I did call John and ask if we could come on another day. We arranged another meeting two days later.

Two days later when we were about to leave Dr. Lusk received a page that another one of his patients was ready for her baby. I told Harry that I appreciated that he was the one that helped me make the contact but I was going to San Diego. One year later I was given the Universal Rife Microscope for a two-year period.[1]

Fruits from this experience:
The Rife Microscope surpassed the accepted theoretical limits. But what are limits? Limits are often just artificial constructs we impose on ourselves. When we fail to dream, we limit ourselves; and when we limit ourselves, we fail to dream.

---

[1] For a complete history of my experience with this incredible microscope that was ten times more powerful than other light source microscopes, as well as the history and impact in the medical world, see my book *And Nothing Happened, But You Can Make it Happen*, ISBN 978-0-578-01687-0.

Chapter Thirty-seven – Getting Insurance

In December 1986 LaVerne and I were interviewed on a KABC radio show about the Rife Microscope. A month or two later I received a call from Bob Maver about the show and about the Rife Microscope. I had never met Bob but he told me that he was completely enthralled with what he heard and wondered if I would be open to meeting with him. He was calling from Kansas City and wanted to meet as quickly as my schedule permitted. We set up a meeting the following week in my office in Sherman Oaks, California.

Bob Maver was the head actuary for Mutual Benefit Life Insurance Company (MBL). When I met Bob, he was in his 30s having started with MBL when he was 18 years old. Although he had come only seeking more information about the Rife Universal Microscope, he was surprised that we had almost 20,000 books dating to the 1400s on a variety of health topics.

About thirty minutes into our conversation he asked me if I would mind if he audiotaped our conversations. Bob would tape over 8 hours of information over two days.

Bob had no idea that there were so many health therapies that he hadn't heard of to treat cancer, arthritis, diabetes, Parkinson's, multiple sclerosis and several other conditions. As I continued sharing with him, Bob was very perplexed and confused at not only the techniques and practitioners I was sharing but how successful each seemed to be in treating the health problem. After all, he was in the health field and in his actuarial position he was exposed to a great number of therapeutic approaches (some experimental) that were both paid or denied. I was presenting new therapies and practitioners that he had never heard of.

Bob showed so much interest and enthusiasm regarding the information that I presented that I kept sharing from early in the morning until late in the evening. At the end of the second day he made an interesting proposal to me. He told me that he had originally come to learn more about the Rife Universal Microscope but he had received so much more than he had imagined and he wondered if World Research Foundation might we interested in working together with Mutual Benefit Life. I told him that we would be very interested and I would like to know what he had in mind.

Bob had an idea of forming a research division within MBL. This research division would go around the world to discover technologies, techniques, individuals, clinics and practitioners that were getting results in the health field. He turned to me and smiled and said, you will be that research division. Now all Bob had to do was to talk with the president of MBL and convince him of the idea. An idea that was totally unique and not done by any other insurance company in the world. Bob told me that instead of flying home to Kansas City he would fly to the MBL's main headquarters and speak with Hank Kates the president of MBL.

Within a week I received a call from Bob telling me that he had tentative approval to begin the MBL Research Division. Mr. Kates was impressed with the information that Bob had shared and felt that he should explore the possibilities of therapies that might assist MBL's cost containment strategies.

Three weeks later Bob called and told me that not only had the MBL Research Division been officially approved but also, he had been given a new title and position as head of the Research Division of Mutual Benefit Life. Bob invited me to the corporate headquarters to meet Mr. Kates and have further discussions regarding our direction and what potential results might be garnered.

I flew to New Jersey and spent several hours with Bob and Mr. Kates I knew that Kates was looking to get some type of feeling for who I was and how reliable the information was going to be.

The most interesting words from Kates and directed to Bob and me was, Mutual Benefit Life is a 146-year-old company and I don't want MBL to be embarrassed by what the two of you are doing!
Bob set up WRF, and me, as consultants for the MBL Research Division. I believed one of my first priorities was to establish our credibility with Bob and MBL.

I began our cooperation by taking Bob to visit two medical doctors in the United States, Dr. Stanislaus Burzynski who was utilizing a therapy called Antineoplastons and Dr. Nicholas Gonzalez who was using a special enzyme program, both doctors addressing various forms of cancer.

Dr. Burzynski's research is based on his discovery that the body itself has a treatment for cancer, a separate biochemical defense system completely different from our immune system. One of the components of this system is growth-inhibiting peptides, which actually control some types of cancer, not by destroying cancer cells but by correcting them. He named these peptides 'Antineoplastons,' due to their activity in inhibiting neoplastic or cancerous cell growth.

Before we visited Dr. Burzynski I asked Bob to check with the medical consultants that MBL had been using and see what type of information they had provided regarding Dr. Burzynski's work. The information he received from the group who claims they uncover the questionable cancer therapies as well as the American Cancer Society was that this was a doctor with no published medical papers and it was an unapproved medical therapy.

The information World Research Foundation supplied was that Dr. Burzynski had received special awards in two countries for his innovative therapy. In addition, he had over 50 peer-reviewed studies. Clearly MBL had received bad information from there so-called experts. In fact, when Bob re-contacted the American Cancer Society, they said that they were very sorry but they hadn't updated their records because they are so short on funds. And, oh by the way, would MBL like to make a donation so they could update their records? This is not the place to say more regarding the American Cancer Society but only that Mutual Benefit Life no longer contacted them for any information regarding cancer.

When I took Bob to the office of Dr. Burzynski Bob asked if he could randomly choose 15 out of the thousands of case files Dr. Burzynski had in his office and see what results he was obtaining with patients. I thought this was a good examination since Dr. Burzynski could not just hand pick what he wanted us to see. Amazingly four of those 15 files were insureds with MBL. Several of the cases were over six years old and the patients were told before coming to Burzynski that they had only months to live. Their diagnosis came from the top cancer hospital in the U.S. The patients had decided not to go the orthodox route but chose Burzynski.

All of the patients were still alive and well after six years. Also, Bob saw that MBL had denied the claims of all four because Antineoplastons was not a recognized therapy. MBL had denied the claims without checking what was done because they did not want to pay for unauthorized therapies that their experts said they didn't have to pay for. Surprisingly MBL would have authorized more expensive therapies at the time because those therapies were approved. Bob Maver made it a point to call the four patients and verify they were still alive. All of the patients were still alive and cancer free. In addition, Bob authorized MBL to reimburse the four individuals.

Our next visit was to Dr. Nicholas Gonzalez who was located in New York. Dr. Gonzalez was offering an intensive nutritional approach to the problems of cancer, multiple sclerosis and other degenerative diseases. Dr. Gonzalez was utilizing an approach that he had researched which had proven itself with a patient base of over ten thousand patients. Joining Bob and I was Dr. Anthony Taresenko, the head physician for MBL. Dr. Taresenko asked if he could choose 15 cases at random from the files of Dr. Gonzalez, exactly as we had done with Dr. Burzynksi. Within this group of 15 people were found several insureds of MBL. Once again, they were all still alive many years beyond what they had been diagnosed by the leading cancer hospitals. MBL again reimbursed those individuals who were their insureds.

As an additional note, Dr. Gonzalez has proved his cancer therapy and it ranks as one of the best in the world. Finally, after many years the NCI has placed his therapy in clinical trials. Year after year he proves that his therapy is more effective than any other therapy in use. Year after year the NCI has him conduct further studies and it never hits the mainstream nor do you hear about it. His therapies do not have side effects that cause the patient harm.

Mutual Benefit Life was to make an even larger commitment to discovering what type of medical therapies were not making it into mainstream medicine in the U.S. I asked for and received money for the World Research Foundation to fully establish a European office in Stuttgart, Germany. MBL provided the money, with no strings attached, and Prof. Karl Walter and Heide Kleber began operating out of the WRF European Headquarters. The WRF European Headquarters in Stuttgart provided our launching point for all our European journeys.

Virtually all of Bob's contacts throughout the industry were trying to figure out how he was able to identify therapies and techniques that no other company was able to find. In answer to the numerous questions he published the following article in the Spring 1991 issue of *Discoveries in Medicine* from Mutual Benefit Life Insurance Company.

"The Tip of the Iceberg"
Readers of Discoveries have asked the obvious question, how is it that an actuary from Kansas City is able to locate such diverse and recondite medical technologies and therapies from so many countries around the world.

When the Research Division was initially conceived, the vision was to ultimately build worldwide network of open-minded scientists and physicians representing literally every medical modality in use around the world. The data would be collected in an unbiased manner and stored in documentation centers on the major continents.

I saw that a critical key to this research effort would be on-site evaluations by advisors with the appropriate scientific background, who also spoke the native language of the innovator. In this way, geographical as well as language barriers to innovation would be overcome. Additionally, this preliminary screen would go far in separating the 'wheat from the chaff,' thereby maximizing the probability that my own site visits would be worthwhile.

This research network would have to interface comfortably with all levels of scientific and governmental hierarchy, from the isolated innovator in rural Germany to the Chinese government's Institute of Traditional Medicine, to the Pasteur Institute in Paris, France, to the British Parliament. Moreover, in order to be truly effective, it would have to develop relationships with innovators and enjoy a reputation for integrity that would allow these innovators to be comfortable making rare or privileged information and data available to the network.

Finally, the network would need to be instantly linked via computer and facsimile machines, affording timely analysis of research that might be simultaneously occurring on different continents and, at the same time, facilitating the natural synergy that occurs when brilliant scientists in different disciplines with different cultural backgrounds interact.

In other words, I was looking to create something that was either impossible or that would take too many years and too much money. The Mutual Benefit Life Research Division manifested much sooner than expected when an organization was discovered that already had built such a network. It is this organization [World Research Foundation], working as consultant to the Research Division that has enabled us to monitor research all over the world and to continually uncover some of the most promising, yet little known innovations.

The main documentation centers are located in Germany, China and the USA, with secondary centers in England and India. An integral part of the research network is libraries that contain medical texts dating to the 1600s in Europe and to 600 BC in Asia. Research from the 1920s through the 1950s, by innovators far ahead of their time, has been preserved in its entirety.

Over one hundred medical and scientific advisors in countries around the world represent some of the leading thinkers in a variety of disciplines. As an example of the wide range of the advisory board, it includes a past-president of the Nobel Assembly, the president of the Chinese Academy of Medical Science, and the consultants to Who and NATO medical sections. Cooperative data exchange agreements are in place in a number of countries.

Key contacts in government, especially in Europe and Asia, have yielded access to research that is otherwise difficult to uncover, for example, from East Germany and the Soviet Union.

These consultants have been able to arrange meetings for us with the innovative scientists. Thus, when we reported in the last issue on the imaging of acupuncture meridians in the Neckar Hospital in Paris, this was after a meeting with the developer, Dr. Jean-Claude Darras. Similarly, when we reported on the Russian MRT, this was just after a series of meetings with the inventors Dr. Sitko and Dr. Zhukovsky.

We have not even begun to explore this vast and largely untapped network and its information capabilities. There is a limit to the amount of research we can work on at any time. It is interesting to contemplate the breakthroughs that might occur if a number of insurance companies were to pool their resources and study cost containment opportunities." Robert W. Maver, Discoveries in Medicine, spring 1991, pg. 1.

Our project with MBL would remain active for another two years enabling WRF to introduce them to an incredible AIDS therapy in Belgium; and African herb that eliminates the need for heart-by-pass surgery in almost 90% of cases; an electromagnetic therapy that accelerates wound healing over twice normal speed and many other innovative therapies from around the world. Mutual Benefit Life paid more than

Maver

$1,500,000 dollars in two years. The research project ended because Mutual Benefit Life was forced out of business by the Insurance Commission. MBL had made poor real estate investments leaving them with financial resources lower than what was allowed by law for them to have on hand to take care of their insureds. I found it interesting that the president had mentioned that he didn't want the research division to embarrass the company…they did it on their own.

Fruits from this experience:
Hold fast to your dreams. Believe, trust and keep alive the knowledge that all things are possible. I believe my life to be an example of that. Earlier I mentioned that my father asked me how we would fund the worldwide health network that I had dreamed of. I couldn't provide him a definitive answer, but I knew what had been revealed to me in my dreams, and what I had had dreamed of building.

Chapter Thirty-eight – The Clinic Tour

Starting out from the World Research Foundation office in Stuttgart we had an ambitious plan to visit some of the premier healing clinics throughout Germany. In late 1989 we would visit the Habichtswald Klinik, Werner-Wicker Klinik, Veramed Klinik, Silvaticum Klinik, Schwarzwald Klinik and the Rhea Klinik.

The **Habichtswald Klinic** is located in Kassel-Wilhelmshohe in Germany. Heide was good friends with the owner and director, Mr. Wicker. This clinic was a unique blend of both traditional and non-traditional medicine. The philosophy of the clinic is that the hospital environment is an integral part of the healing process. Mr. Wicker told us that he took great care in all facets of the clinic including the choice of building materials and the geometric construction of the building. Wicker believes that the physical, mental and spiritual aspects of the patient must be addressed, not only by the medical professionals that are involved with the patient, but also by the actual building in which the therapy and recuperation takes place.

Another underlying concept of the hospital is that patients must learn how to develop their own healing power or capability. They shouldn't just come and expect some outer agency to heal them.

The medical doctors in the clinic are trained in Western allopathic medicine which gives them a truly balanced approach to the healing art. Some of the interesting features of the clinic which would have an influence in the healing process included;

- All the rooms are made from natural woods with no metals found in the room.
- There is no synthetic filling in the mattresses
- All wiring is specially insulated to guard against detrimental electromagnetic fields
- All room carpeting is made without synthetic materials
- Each hospital room has live plants and foliage.
- Heating is done by the utilization of underground natural thermal pools.
- Every room is checked for geopathic stress zones
- Special colors, believed to help in the healing process, are used in all the rooms and hallways.
- There are 3 special meditation rooms, each with its own mandala.
- There is a special emotional room (sound proofed) where one can yell, scream or beat the walls.
- There are specially created waterfalls producing soothing musical sounds and beautiful pictures adorn the walls throughout the hallways.
- Therapies include; Ozone Therapy, Kneipp Water Therapy, Electromagnetic Field Therapy, Music Therapy, Showerhead Therapy, Schielbader (foot baths).

There is a main concert hall in the clinic where live musical performances are held. Each room in the clinic is connected and bed-ridden patients can hear the musicals in their rooms. The clinic handles almost all degenerative diseases along with cancer, heart and circulation problems, diabetes, multiple sclerosis and psychosomatic problems.

In addition to the above the clinic is attached to one of the premier spas in all of Europe. Patients that are not a risk are able to go through an underground tunnel system and reach the spa. The spa is one of the main financial drive-wheels of the clinic.

We next visited a second clinic that was owned by Mr. Wicker called the **Werner-Wicker-Klinik** which is located in Bad Wildungen-Reinhardshausen, in Germany. This massive structure is as large as any of our hospitals in the U.S. It was the only clinic in Europe especially dedicated to spinal problems. The clinic specializes in scoliosis conditions along with paraplegics and quadriplegics. While we were visiting the clinic a siren rang and we were told by our host that we needed to wait in the waiting room. At that moment a helicopter was landing on the roof with a patient whom at been injured while skiing. It was an extremely serious spinal injury where the patient was paralyzed. Even though it had happened in a nearby country, this is the premier clinic for these types of injuries.

The Werner-Wicker Klinik has over a 90% success rate for severe disc problems. In 1989 the staff consisted of two of the foremost spinal surgical specialists in the world. Their unique surgical procedure for scoliosis has attracted top surgeons from around the world who come to view the surgeons during operations.

What was unique about the clinic was that the lobby was like a little city street. There were shops and the setting was more like a hotel than a hospital. Everywhere you looked you felt very uplifted and energized. I noticed that they were very clever with their positioning of plants and the coloring that was part of the motif was unlike any other hospital I have ever seen.

The basic philosophy of the hospital is that the 'patient is king'. The Director of the clinic said, 'here, everything is individualized and specialized for each patient.' Everything in the hospital is oversized to help the patient. This 320 bed hospital had patients ranging in age from 3 years old to 80 years old. There are three main departments including paralysis, scoliosis and urology. Other unique features included;

- Meals prepared to order based on the food preference of the patient. Including various specialties of different countries. Asian, European, Middle East cuisines were all available.
- Space is provided within the clinic for family members who need to be present while their loved one is rehabilitating.
- Special wheel chairs are manufactured directly on the premises and are completely custom made. They are modified as the patient's needs and capabilities change.
- Gymnastic and sport facility is second to none. All of the sport and exercise facilities were the highest standard equipment.
- A beauty shop is located on the premises.

The special Ergo Therapy for the handicapped patient includes;

- What can you do as a handicapped person
- Muscle training
- How to communicate with others
- Learning how to do one's own tasks in the kitchen
- Full training for independence at home
- Starting preparation for a new profession in the future.

At a certain point on our tour we were told we were going to the fourth floor and we headed for one of the elevators that we say. The Director laughed and said it is forbidden for any walking person to use an elevator; you must always use the stairs.

Up to 1989 the Werner-Wicker Klinik had produced over 20 gold medal winners in the paraplegic Olympics.

The success rate of the clinic is extremely high. At that time the cost per day, which included food, surgery, room and more was lower than a daily hotel rate in the United States.

The **Veramed Klinik** is located in Inzell, Germany. We were greeted by Dr. Friedrichsen who was an expert in clinical ecology and environmental effects on health. The department we visited was involved with ortho-molecular medicine as it pertains to rheumatoid arthritis.

We were told that chronic forms of allergies transmitted into problems with the autoimmune system. In 1989 over 50 % of the children in Munich had allergies of one type or another.

The research at the Veramed Klinic had determined that diet had a profound influence on several major diseases including arthritis and multiple sclerosis. There were ten Western trained medical doctors utilizing 138 beds in the hospital with some of the doctors working with special diets, homeopathic remedies, ozone therapy, and special electromagnetic therapy equipment.

Their studies had shown that if you do not stop the allergic reactions taking place in the body that you will begin to see the onset of various degenerative diseases taking hold. They told us that they had been rectifying the problems of the majority of their patients within six weeks. When I asked why six weeks they told me that this was the only period that insurance was paying for.

The Silvaticum Klinik is located in Horn-Bad Meinberg in Germany. This is a gigantic hospital facility with a department specializing in electromagnetic and other holistic therapies. We were given a tour by Dr. Klaus Marzahl as he related that there were nine medical doctors within the department. They were specializing in rheumatism, arthritis and the difficulties with the general immune system.

We were told that there are over 200 offshoots of rheumatism and arthritis which leads to chronic pain all over the body. The doctors in this department had begun to investigate other possibilities when they realized that biochemistry was not working. They have been utilizing special electromagnetic field therapy (Mora Device) along with Japanese Cryotherapy, Kneipp Therapy, Acupuncture and Homeopathic remedies.

The doctors in the department had started with electric currents and water, and then went into cryo-therapy then impulsed electromagnetic fields and then acupuncture. They found all of these rather tedious and time consuming and eventually discovered an electromagnetic device called a Mora Machine that worked effectively.

The doctor told me that the cause of rheumatism is unknown but that treating the patient several times over a two to four week period seemed to last for between one and two years.

Their research work has been pointing to the fact that the leading causes of the degenerative problems was metals in the dental work, amalgam fillings, bridge work, false teeth and that patients lived or worked in electromagnetic interference fields or what is called geopathic stress zones.

Another medical doctor of the group told me that they were having up to a 60% effective rate without using any medications. Interestingly he noted that children seem to respond almost immediately.

Finally, I was told that the doctors would use special mud packs with sulfur that pulled out toxins. There were special treatment rooms for the mud packs were they rapped the patient in plastic and mud. The mud was coming from a nearby town where it had been proven that the mud had certain characteristics that helped the healing process. Also, they doctors used inhalation therapy, galvanic treatments, underwater message and special oil messages.

Despite their good success the insurance industry would not pay for the therapy because it did not appear to be scientific enough. That is a shame because you would think that results would be the most important criteria over someone's belief system.

Next, we visited the **Rhea Klinik** located in Klausenbach, Germany. The main therapy in this large facility is Hyperbaric Oxygen Therapy or HBO. The clinic had 210 beds and the patients came with problems of stroke, M.S., lung problems and hyperthermia. The Director told us that the clinic was financially supported by the pension insurance companies. This was due to the documented successfulness of HBO.

In one three year study it was found that over 75 % of patients returned to work within 5-6 weeks after a stroke. I was told that this was compared to 5 percent in the United States.

When the Director turned to me and asked how many articles I believed had been written on HBO I told him I didn't know. He told me over 10,000 articles have been written. In Russia I was told there was one HBO unit for every 50 people.

At the Rhea Klinic over 80,000 treatment sessions had been given and documented. The Rhea also provides special diets that they have discovered helps increase the mental functioning in elderly persons. They have also invented a machine called Brain-Jogging. This increases mental sharpness. So the clinic's basic strategy is to use HBO, diet, physical exercise and brain-jogging.

The conditions addressed are angina pectoris, tinnitus, stroke and coronary problems. Through the use of the basic strategy of the Rhea Klinic, brain jogging increases speed of information transfer in the brain, the physical exercise which includes bicycle riding increases the blood flow and the effectiveness of medications are increased.

Finally, we visited the **Schwarzwald Klinik** in the Black Forest region of Germany. The main focus for the clinic was all types of skin disorders especially neurodermatitis. We were greeted by Wolfgang Spiller, who was the founder of the clinic and the Head Physician, Dr. Sawatzki.

It is the belief of the doctors that the majority of problems stem from environmental toxins, unhealthy diets, vitamin and mineral deficiency and adverse effects of pharmaceutical products.

The clinic does not believe in merely an external therapy to solve the patient's difficulties. Their model consists of three aspects; treatment of the causes, a holistic view of man and nourishment as medicine. The youngest patient at the clinic was 8 and a half months and the oldest patient is 90.

The detoxification process is very important and included the use of homeopathy, acupuncture, Baunhtscheidt and personalized diets.

The basis of the dietary program is formed by a raw food diet devoid of animal proteins, which is later changed into whole food. The experience of the clinic had shown that a whole food, or raw food diet, without animal protein is more successful with most patients than a whole food diet containing protein. In addition to the dietary program plant therapies and homeopathic preparations are prescribed depending on the patient's constitution and the healing process.

It was not easy taking a tour of the facility and looking at the skin problems of the patients. I believe that this was one of the most difficult tours that I have taken. There is no hiding when the skin on the face has these problems. But, we were shown so many successful before and after photos that we felt very good about the work that was being done at the clinic. From the Stuttgart office we conducted follow ups with some patients and found a very high success level.

Fruits from this experience:
The first thing one notices about these clinics is their sheer size. I learned from this experience that what orthodox medicine would call alternative in our country can be mainstream in other parts of the world.

I found highly regarded and credentialed medical doctors utilizing sound, color and light, herbs, diet, electricity, magnetism, acupuncture, homeopathy and so many other regimes with high rates of success. In all of these clinics treatments were geared specifically to the individual who had the medical challenge.

I would go from this tour and begin sharing and helping various medical and health practitioners in the United States to integrate more of these regimes in their practices because I showed them just how profound these techniques could be.

Chapter Thirty-nine – Dowsing and Chocolate Cake

Not all things in the modern spiritual movement are created equal, and certainly not all practitioners are created equal. When we first encounter someone or something that is outside the ordinary, we can have a tendency to dismiss them. I have not been immune to this jump to judgement. I had to learn that the skill of the practitioner makes all the difference. The distance from the novice to the expert can be a long one, but patience from the novice to the master can be even longer.

In his book *The Outliers: The Story of Success*, Malcolm Gladwell writes of the 10,000 hour mastery threshold. His study has shown that it is around this time when any practice becomes second nature, it becomes internalized, and it becomes mastered. I'll amend Gladwell's observation by offering that we need to observe those 10,000 hour practitioners before we either accept or reject the practice they show. Here we can more easily distinguish the master from the novice, those who most fully represent the practice not simply someone playing in the space. We should be both open, yet cautious. Observing and adapting when we seek to supplement our own practices, before we jump to judgement.

While attending a philosophical lecture in 1979 I had my first experience with dowsing. During a break, I was at a buffet table watching a woman spinning an object over various dishes. I asked her what she was doing and she shared that she was determining which foods were good for her by using a pendulum.

I thought it was strange because it appeared that her entire hand was moving the pendulum, in the direction that she said was positive, and it happened over all the deserts, especially the chocolate cake. With this being my first introduction to this type of activity, I wasn't very impressed, even though I did like the chocolate cake.

For several years I never paid much attention to dowsing because I didn't have a very good first impression of it. In 1986 while visiting one of our foundation advisors in Germany, Dr. Wolfgang Ludwig, I was surprised when he and his wife, Gisela, both reached into their pockets for a pendulum while looking at a dinner menu. I was dumbfounded and asked them what they were doing and why.

Dr. Wolfgang Ludwig was a world renowned physicist with more than 100 peer reviewed papers on the effects of magnetic fields on biological systems. Wolfgang told me that very often when he arrived at a critical point in calculations he would utilize his pendulum. He would draw a graph on a paper and then allow the pendulum to guide him to the correct percentage or number. He said the pendulum was an extension of his own inner consciousness.

Wolfgang motioned to me to turn around in my chair and look at one of the booths at the back of the restaurant. The man in another booth was dowsing his menu. Unbelievable!

I became more amazed after my meeting with Karl Milde (long since deceased), a healing practitioner in the city of Kornwestheim, Germany. He didn't speak any English and I didn't speak enough German to carry on a conversation. He was very intense, not unfriendly, but a no-nonsense type of person.

Prof. Dr. Walter, who was in charge of our World Research Foundation Stuttgart office, had known Milde for many years and told me that Milde was a master dowser. Milde had done everything from dowsing for underground springs, finding raw materials, discovering underground cables and springs, finding unexploded bombs after WWII, and diagnosing people's health.

During our drive to meet Milde, Dr. Walter had shared that soon after WWII, Karl Milde and his colleague Mr. Eckardt were asked to find unexploded bombs in several cities throughout Germany. At another time, one of the largest companies in Stuttgart, had used Milde to help find underground springs and cables, while the company was repairing airfields in Germany.

As Karl Milde's fame spread throughout Germany, he caught the attention of some medical people in Stuttgart who had heard of his abilities to diagnose people without disrobing them. Prof. Walter met Karl Milde along with Prof. Dr. med S. Rilling in the Katharinen Hospital in Stuttgart. Dr. Walter and several other medical specialists decided to test Milde.

The test was made by blindfolding Karl Milde and then bringing before him 8 corpses from the hospital morgue. The corpses were covered with a blanket and Milde, who was still blindfolded, was asked to describe the locations of any surgery performed on each body. Milde told them exactly, without any error, each of the spots and types of operations performed on each body. Karl Milde never used any device except for his two hands. One hand would scan the body and his other hand would be moving back and forth at different speeds.

In 1991, Prof. Walter and Karl Milde conducted an experiment with a company, which claimed their special electromagnetic equipment cleared water of harmful materials, while at the same time magnetizing the water for healing purposes. Prof. Walter told me that he was skeptical of this claim, due to the substances in the water, so he asked Milde to go with him to the manufacturer to test out their device.

10 glasses of water were placed on a table. Some of the glasses had normal water and some with the special magnetized water. It took only seconds for Milde to point out which of the glasses contained treated water. Then Prof. Walter and Milde left the room and the company's personnel changed the positions of the glasses. Milde was again able to point out the magnetized glasses. The company was so grateful about the results that they made a donation of their machine to our Stuttgart office.

While touring Karl Milde's office he suddenly stopped and ran over to someone in our group. He then proceeded to tell her about specific operations she had as well as explaining an unsolved medical difficulty. He had dowsed her from across the room.

Everyone is familiar with a dowsing rod or some type of pendulum that his held in the hands, I was impressed how Karl Milde just used his body. As he scanned the body with one hand, his other hand was moving rhythmically from side to side until it would violently shake, and he would stop, and begin sharing what he had discovered in the individual's body.

Fruits from this experience:
My experience was important to me for two reasons. The first was that it is an example of another ability that we all possess. The far more important thing that I learned was not to form quick judgments about people, techniques, clinics or products. I needed to remember this when I was introduced to cow dung therapy. I've come a long way since experiencing the woman dowsing the chocolate cake.

Chapter Forty – Baubiologie

Have you ever stepped into a space and was simply overwhelmed with a sense of peace or calmness. It might not have been immediately apparent why, but you just knew that there was something about this space. Similarly, I'm sure you've experienced the opposite; that hair standing up on your neck where the place just didn't feel right. Far too often we either take for granted or ignore the environments in which we work and live. We see a house as a house and not necessarily as a home. We see our offices as a place to work, not the place we spend most of our adult lives. Living in consciousness and living in purpose means to be living acutely aware of the power and impact of my surroundings.

While at the World Research Foundation office in Stuttgart, I came across a very interesting reference to a subject called Baubiologie. The loose translation is bau which means building and biologie which means the knowledge of the living world. So baubiologie deals with the subject of the health of buildings and homes.

Prof. Dr. Walter brought me to meet Wolfgang Maes who was formerly a journalist for an important magazine and was now a practicing baubiologist.

How safe are our home and working environments and is our current health system addressing these considerations? I can address these questions in the following manner.

If you are walking with a pebble in your shoe, is it possible to walk comfortably unless you stop to remove the stone?

When you are carrying an extremely heavy bag of groceries, does the pain you are experiencing go away as long as the bag remains in your arms? Someone could address the pain but wouldn't it still remain when the weight is still being carried? In fact a lighter weight if held with your arms outstretched becomes harder and harder to bear. Even the lightest weight can seem like a ton.

Imagine now that there is a beehive next to your bedroom window and a bee from the hive stings you. You proceed to the hospital because you are having an allergic reaction. Even though you are given the appropriate therapy from the doctor, if you return to your home and subject yourself to the same hazard, will the therapy you received at the hospital protect you?

Imagine you rare cleaning your garage and beginning to sneeze from the dust being stirred up. You might stop your reaction by leaving the dusty area, showering, and changing your clothes. But if you return to the garage with your clean clothes and bathed body and kick up more dust, will you once again begin sneezing?

When we become ill we usually make our way to our health practitioners for solutions to our health problem. But have we really addressed the causes of our problems or only the effects that have manifested in our bodies? Numerous studies demonstrate that major diseases or illnesses can be a direct result of our diets and environments, two factors that are generally around us all the time except when we are being diagnosed by our medical or health practitioners in their office.

As simplistic as my previous examples might seem, every day we may be exposing ourselves to potentially harmful situations which may be affecting us physically, mentally and/or emotionally. The factors that might have the greatest influence upon us might not be recognized by our health practitioners.

Wolfgang Maes shared his own personal health experiences which included major health problems in which the medical doctors could not discover the cause. The problems continued year after year as he would go to have his problem looked after but upon returning to his home the problems would soon start again.

After thoroughly investigating his own life situations, Wolfgang determined that he was reacting to effects from his own home, office and buildings that he visited.

When a house, apartment, office, stable or other structure is constructed, we must have care as to dangerous and damaging influences which might be present in the structure as well as the objects placed within. We must consider electromagnetic fields from wires and electronic equipment (including clocks by our night stands); the effects of heating blankets; toxic paints; wall coverings; lacquers on woods; asbestos; radon; cork, bricks, stones, clay and insulation fibers; geopathic stress zones and underground water flows.

I was very impressed with what Wolfgang was sharing. I wondered to what degree we all suffer from sick homes and offices? Is it possible that we are placing ourselves into electric and magnetic beehives which are literally stinging us over and over again? Do we return again and again into the dusty garage in the form of our new synthetic carpet? Do we carry a pebble in our shoe as we move from our home environment to office environment and back again?

Wolfgang went on to say, 'Computer supply rooms, photo studios, measuring places for electro-encephalograms and other medical departments for diagnosis and therapy have to be totally free from electrostatic elements. Look at computer rooms, operation theaters and manufacturing places for sensitive devices: the air humidity has to be perfect no interference of electro-magnetic fields is allowed, temperature is kept on an ideal middle level. The Japanese worker is not even allowed to wear a synthetic blouse when she assembles her Nikon camera. She is grounded with a chain from her copper wrist bracelet. Why is it not also self-evident for the living and sleeping room? That is the place of the most sensible and vulnerable computer in the world. His name is human being!'"

All of what he shared seemed to make sense. More importantly, if any of these environmental factors adversely affect our vitality is our health practitioner aware of these causes or do we receive an examination and treatment outside the true 'causal area'? Our systems may be cleansed of the foreign substances that the doctors find while we are being examined (or at least our symptoms masked by one prescription or another), but do we then return home or immerse ourselves into the same environmental conditions without even a helpful word or advice?

We know that we can induce reactions by subjecting people or animals to various frequencies of sound or color. We can even render someone unconscious or cause death by releasing certain fumes. Some elements in our environment are so dangerous that we can recognize their effects immediately. But other elements may be affecting us so subtly that they could be causing sickness or death without our realizing it.

There is very interesting evidence that there are sick houses and sick offices which may lead to sick guests. Visitors to these locations may find themselves with problems ranging from slightly negative reactions to severe medial problems, even death. I believe that the science of Baubiologie from Germany should be an important area to consider for any diagnostician. Our homes and offices may have the appearances of castles but may render the effects of dungeons.

It is something to consider when someone has a health problem in which they just can't seem to figure out what to do.

It is fascinating to see the results of investigative work that has been done to determine how residents of certain living places have all ended up with the same physical health problems. As new families moved into a specific residence, the occupants of certain rooms within the home would end up with the same catastrophic health problems. The negative influences within the room where not visible obvious but through testing it was discovered that highly dangerous electromagnetic fields were present. These were finally identified and corrected through Baubiologie.

Fruits from this experience:

The important of our environment cannot be underestimated. However, environment means more than the physical aspect. Our mental, spiritual and political environments have equally profound influence on our well-being.

Chapter Forty-one – The Alchemical Castle

We seem to be living in a digital culture. Not simply digital with respect to our gadgets but living digitally in our understanding of the world. Science and alchemy are an example like this. Most learned people dismiss alchemy out of hand because they see it supplanted by science. Science not in the scientific practice or research, but a compromised idea of science where only the "proven" is held to be true. We seem to have lost the appreciation and value of those things we observe, sense and feel, but have yet to be proven.

Digital here means that we have been pushed to accepting one or the other. I have learned that while some things are best held in a digital world, most of life, creation, and reality are analog. That is, they exist within a varying spectrum of reality and truth. From unknown, to fully known. From intuition to fact. This was my experience when I had to the opportunity to explore the science in addition to the facts of discovery. The chance to experience both the rational and super-rational modes of discovery side by side enriched my understanding and healing practice.

In 1989 I was back to my office in Stuttgart. Heide, Karl and I had set up an itinerary to visit several clinics in Southern Germany, Italy, Austria and Switzerland.

As we left Stuttgart to begin our journey, Heide asked me if I would like to visit a castle that was very near where she had grown up. It was in fact the castle of a very famous alchemist. We would travel to Donaumunster in Germany. I was very excited about visiting a castle. Didn't have too many castles where I grew up in the San Fernando Valley outside of Los Angeles!

When we arrived I had a great feeling of anticipation but couldn't quite determine why I was feeling the way that I was. We had turned onto the street, Alexander-von-Bernus Strasse and at number 4 we came to the castle.

We knocked at the door and a wonderful older lady appeared at the door. It was the Baroness von Bernus. Her forename was Isa and she greeted Heide and Karl. Isa was 95 years old. When Heide was a young girl she came several times to the castle and knew the family. Isa then  turned to me and said, 'I have expected you.' I assumed that she had been told that I would be coming with Karl and Heide but Heide told me that they had not mentioned that I was coming. They were just paying their respects and only asked if they might visit for some cakes. Isa spoke little English but I was told she understood many words. We would look at each other and smile. She had such a wonderful smile and appeared to be such a very kind person.

Alexander von Bernus was a remarkable man. He was born in 1880 and was a poet and alchemist. At a very early age he became a publisher of a literary magazine, Die Freistatt, for which several renowned authors wrote articles at the turn of the century. A few of the authors included, Hermann Hesse, Maria Rilke, Thomas Mann, Karl Wolfskehl and many others. Von Bernus had very friendly relationships with Herman Hesse and until 1926 von Bernus kept open his country residence for all of his writing friends to meet and work during the summer months. At 23 years old von Bernus went public with his own literary works and met immediate success. From 1907 to 1912 von Bernus with several friends ran his own little theatre called Schwabinger Schattenspiele. In 1912 von Bernus met Rudolf Steiner and a close friendship developed between both of them until Steiner's death. Over the course of his life von Bernus published over twenty volumes of poetry, shadow plays, mystery plays, prose texts and an important work in the fields of alchemy and healing.

Beside his literary work von Bernus focused his life on alchemy and the natural sciences. He founded his own alchemical laboratory in 1921 and developed more than thirty healing substances. Von Bernus continued the ancient tradition of alchemy and placed it in a more practical standing and he was very instrumental in helping to prove to our current century that alchemy was more than a superstition from the middle-ages.

I was told of some interesting experiences that took place during WW11 and the Nazi regime having orders that they were not to confront this alchemist and the castle. The Castle von Bernus would become a safe haven for many people during the war because of the fear that the Nazi's had of confronting von Bernus.

Isa and her husband worked closely together for 35 years until his death in 1965. There were many other important facts dealing with von Bernus's life especially a close relationship with the Goethe family. This however is private and a part of the family history.

As we walked through the castle I was overwhelmed by the incredible books, art work, sculptures and furniture. Many of the rooms had floor to ceiling bookcases. I looked at a coffee table and there was a book of Paracelsus dated in the 1600s. I glanced at some titles in the bookcases and found some extremely rare titles that I was familiar with. I was so tempted to take books out of the shelves but kept my hands behind me and continued to look at the books on the various shelves.

I heard my name mentioned several times as the conversation was only in German but when I would look up Heide or Karl would let me know that I wasn't needed but they were telling Isa about me and some of the experiences that the three of us had together on our last journey in Europe.

I settled over to the group and found a luscious slice of cake and watched as they spoke. Heide then said that Isa would like me to stay some days with her in the castle. They didn't have to twist my arm. Karl and Heide would return to Stuttgart for several days and then come back to pick me up.

Staying in the house with Isa was a house-keeper who spoke good English and Marino who continued the alchemical work in the castle.

The Baroness told Heide to tell me that I was free to look at any books or scrolls that were in the castle.
The first night I slept in an upper
floor of the castle and noticed a
trunk in the corner of the room.
I opened up the trunk and found
it full of parchments and scrolls.
All were hand written in various
languages, unfortunately none in
English. I noticed parchments with dates several hundred years old.

The next morning, I was up at first light and with the sun shining in the rooms was exactly like a kid in a candy shop. I couldn't read any book for more than ten minutes without glancing around the bookshelves and finding another book of interest.

I was told that many libraries had visited the castle and tried to convince the Baroness to place some of the materials in climate-controlled places and not leave some of the great artwork so exposed to the environment. Wherever I turned there were such beauty, light and wisdom.

On my first full day I met Marino and he took me to one of the alchemical laboratories. It was enclosed in an octagon shaped glass room. I had very strange feelings as soon as I entered the octagon. I noted that there was an automatic change in my breathing rhythm. I also felt as if I had known something but couldn't remember it because

I was asleep. I couldn't draw some recognition from out of my consciousness. I found that I was getting mad at myself because I was not able to remember some process that I had spent so much time with before. In all the other rooms of the castle I was always so calm and relaxed.

Three days later Karl and Heide returned to Donaumunster to pick me up. We were about to leave when Isa grabbed my arm and motioned me to follow her. Heide told me to go. We went down a hallway and took two turns and came upon a closed door. Isa reached into her pocked and pulled out a long key. We entered the room and I knew it was a special room of the house. Later I found out that it was her husband's study and she did not allow anyone in the room. The room had remained completely unchanged since her husband's death. We sat quietly for about ten minutes and then I heard Isa stand up. She glanced at me and smiled and we returned to Karl and Heide.

When we were in the car returning to Stuttgart Heide told me that the baroness never allowed anyone into that room.

That evening I slept in the attic at Karl's home. I was awoken during the night as I slept. There was the sound of someone walking on the floor next to my bed. I asked who was there and did not hear a physical voice but I knew it was Alexander von Bernus. I heard within my head that all was alright and I should go back to sleep. I couldn't wait for morning and at an appropriate hour I placed a call to Heide to explain what had happened during the night. She promised to call Isa.

An hour later Heide called and was laughing. She told me that when she called Isa, the baroness asked if I liked that her husband had visited me during the night. Heide had not even had the chance to ask her about it. Isa said that her husband enjoyed my visiting him and he wanted to visit me!

Several months later I received the following note from Heide:

Dear Steve,

I had a long telephone call with the Baronesse and at first she told me, how often you have been in her thoughts! She asked me to tell you of her feelings and that you come back to her soon. So she is looking forward to see you again. You can stay in one of the guestrooms for as long as you want and she would enjoy very much that once again you are near to her. In this way you can study all that you want. She never forgets about the special dream you shared with her and your warm wishes when you left. So, I bring you the kindest regards from her.

Yours, Heide

Fruits from this experience:
I spent three days within the Castle von Bernus and since the Baroness did not speak English I spent much of my time in quiet contemplation. At no time in my life did I have the opportunity to be surrounded by such wisdom and at the same time have virtually no distractions.

I understood from this experience the importance of quietude as well as the importance of having a good atmosphere or environment. My experience with Alexander von Bernus coming to me even though he had been deceased for several decades convinced me of the **continuity of existence beyond the physical realm.**

Chapter Forty-two – A Friend of Lakes

While in Germany during 1991 I met a fascinating man who had developed a new and innovative system of revitalizing dead and dying lakes and waterways. I had been told that Mr. P. had taken lakes that have been classified as dead for up to ten years and has brought them back to a healthy state where they once again are teaming with life. In addition, he has been able to reverse the growth of algae and remove many pollutants from lakes without chemicals.

When I met Mr. P. the first thing that I noticed was the unique coloring of his blue eyes. He didn't have a hair upon his head so his eyes really stood out and showed that there was something very unique about this man.

Mr. P. had been working on lakes in Switzerland, Germany, Italy, Czechoslovakia and Austria. There were numerous newspaper accounts as well as testimonial letters from the managers and directors of the various lakes he had helped, all attesting to his success.

What is most remarkable is that he uses no chemicals, no radiation, no electric currents, no magnetic fields and does not physically pump oxygen into the waterway. He is able to significantly increase the amount of oxygen in the lake by placing special containers, throughout the lake, which include a vibratory frequency of oxygen encoded on information panels.

Mr. P. has been working under the auspices of government officials who have signed declarations as to his effectiveness and success. One of the lakes, Kleinen Arbersee, near the German and Czechoslovakia border was considered an absolutely dead sea. Six European universities including the renowned Institute of Ecology of Munich were using it as a test facility.

The research groups were using the lake to document the plight of dead lakes. Starting with a pH of 2.5, and a condition where fish placed in the water died within hours; within four weeks, Mr. P., the 'friend of the lakes,' had the pH at 5.7 and the fish population was thriving. No research body or scientists anywhere in the world were able to achieve what Roland did or even explain how he had accomplished this feat.

Other lakes that Roland worked with included the Lake of Sudtirol, a lake in Boson and the lake in the city of Bad Laer.

Through World Research Foundation we followed up on some of the testimony letters and contacted the spa director in Bad Laer. The director of the town told us that the lake, which is called Glockensee, is about 8,000 square meters and had been overgrown for ten years with algae called Fadenalge Zannichellia-balustris. No treatment that had been tried ever proved to have even the slightest success. From 1988 until the spring of 1989, when he made his testimony, all the algae had disappeared. Now as we spoke with him in 1991, in one of the warmest periods they could recall, the algae could not be found.

The canisters that Mr. P. places in the waterways are extremely light. When they are opened they are virtually empty except for a small piece of wood that is about the size of a small matchbook. The thickness is less than a quarter of an inch. Upon these small pieces of wood are imprinted a code of the substance of element that Mr. P. is using in the treatment. In the case of the lakes it is the code for oxygen. Again, we are speaking of a symbol or vibration on a piece of wood and not actually the substance that is being applied.

The machine that imprinted the coding was designed by Mr. P. and was based upon the experimental work conducted by Wilhelm Reich. Sometimes Mr. P. would use wood and sometimes other metals. He told me that there is a continuous flow of the energy pattern that he has imprinted upon the medium or carrier, as he explained it.

Mr. P. has not limited himself to only lakes and seas. In an experiment that he performed at the Wicker Institute in the city of Essen, the researchers watched a sample of blood through a microscope, as Mr.

P. placed one of his imprinted substances one foot from the slide. Microorganisms and parasites dissolved after ten seconds. In fifteen minutes the oxygen content continued to increase and the reactions on the blood were noted.

Mr. P. was able to work on the blood as he did with the lakes.

The more technical description of the system is as follows;

The technique for rehabilitating rivers and lakes involves the use of a physical process to transmit bio-energetic effects. Special energy carriers installed in tubes and buoys are connected to form energy systems for energizing water. In addition to other materials, certain specially selected silicates are used for these energy carriers.

The properties of the energy in a system of this type are akin to those of other forms of physical energy or their respective fields, such as already known with electricity, magnetism and gravitation. This energy form can only be detected to a limited extent with known scientific measurement methods (i.e. by measuring the emission photons), but direct measurement processes are being developed.

Every quantum of mass in a gravitational field possesses a certain amount of energy. The latter can be measured as the potential of the gravitational field, its magnitude being dependent upon the mass concerned. Every discrete particle of mass thus influences its surroundings by a certain potential.

Electromagnetic fields act upon their surroundings as oscillations at a certain frequency. This basic principle can be traced right down to the structure of the atom; the electron can thus be considered as an oscillation at a certain frequency and with a corresponding energy content.

By transmitting energy, the material receiving or carrying it has additional effects or properties modulated upon it, which do not however destroy or disturb its existing properties. The equipment specifically developed for the energy transmission system described here enables certain properties of substances (i.e. oxygen) to be modulated. Although the substance concerned is led into the transmission instrument, it does not come directly into contact with the receiver/carrier material itself. Specifically selected silicates, etc., and other empirically evaluated substances are used as receiver/carrier material, which is then sealed into buoys, tubes, etc.

These energy systems then act permanently upon the water in which they are installed, its oxygen content being increased by measurable amounts. This oxygen enrichment process reduces the growth of algae to natural levels or even stops it altogether, in addition to other beneficial effects. Due to this as yet inexhaustible oxygen activation/formation method, decomposition of the toxins largely present in polluted river or lake mud, and even decomposed mud itself, have been observed.

Approximately two decades before Schumann waves were physically recorded, the Austrian philosopher Dr. Wilhelm Reich discovered that the atmosphere is filled with oscillations which contain enormous energies.

Reich describes harmonious oscillating energy fields filling the entire cosmos and accordingly its presence in the earth's atmosphere constitutes the background of all life processes. Orthodox scientists regarded it as a mystical fairy tales because even to this day there are no instruments to measure and prove its existence.

Reich found a way to collect and concentrate this life giving energy, which he gave the name 'Orgon'.

An energy collector transmitted the energy into the so-called Orgon box. Patients were treated for various illnesses simply by entraining the body in Orgon energy. The orthodox medical world treated his work with great suspicion and called him a charlatan. Reich died in 1957 before his life's work could ever be accepted.

Mr. P., who is an engineer, became interested in Reich's work in 1980 and developed an energy collector. Mr. P. discovered that Orgon energy can be 'programmed' on to any material, which then becomes an energy carrier material, which he refers to as PENAC = programmed energy accumulator. Especially suitable are organic materials such as wood, wool or cotton. Energized cotton cloth is used to alleviate pain. Energized wooden trays are used to enrich food value.

Fruits from this experience:
Everything is vibratory and an important approach to problems in the environment as well as our physical bodies can be addressed successfully through the use of the electromagnetic spectrum. Seeing in a most dramatic manner that polluted lakes could be rectified through just a piece of wood and a vibratory code again demonstrated to me that there is more than what we accept as our physical laws.

Chapter Forty-three – Bypassing Heart Bypass

What a bold statement this is, bypassing heart bypass!

Karl and Heide took me to visit Berthold Kern who was a medical doctor living in Stuttgart. They had shared with me that Dr. Kern had been involved with a remarkable discovery. As a young medical doctor during the war it was his job to do autopsy on the soldiers that died. Even if the cause of death seemed obvious, he must do a medical examination.

Dr. Kern was very surprised to notice that a high majority of the very young soldiers had very dramatic blockages of the main arteries leading to their heart. However, none of these young men died of a heart attack. None of these young men ever complained of heart and chest pains. As we all know you hardly ever hear of any young person dying of a heart attack.

His theory and work dealing with coronary blockages was unique but very heavily proven through studies and testing.

Dr. Kern had developed a therapy using a product called Strophanthin. Karl told me that he had been personally using the product for many years and he was a member of a group of doctors that had been compiling information and studies on the effectiveness of strophanthin. It appeared to be a truly a remarkable product.

When I met Dr. Kern he was very advanced in years. He was still able to communicate but I did note that he was very frail. His daughter, who is also a medical doctor, was at his side.

Karl and Heide translated for me as Dr. Kern shared some of his experiences. What stood out most was his story regarding the introduction of Strophanthin to the United States many years ago. This should have been a wonderful story of how one of the major factors of death had been met and defeated by use of a little-known herb from Africa. That would not be how the story emerged in the United States due to a mistranslation.

The individual who translated the information regarding Strophanthin from German to English mis-translated the dosage at that time. In those early days, Strophanthin was used in an injectable form and because of the translation it was used at hundreds of times the correct dose. As result of this error and its effect, Strophanthin was stopped and never looked at again in the United States.

Dr. Kern went on to say how the current model of the heart and the concept of heart blockage was not correctly understood by modern medicine and that heart bypass was not always the correct approach. Dr. Kern told me that his theory had also been validated through studies conducted by several prestigious groups in the United States but because of financial interests associated with bypass surgery, Strophanthin was not known or even allowed in the U.S.

I was very shocked when I asked what the cost of his therapy would be. When he mentioned that it was about $30 per month I didn't have to think too much regarding why it was not available in the U.S. The cost of heart bypass is in the multiple tens of thousands of dollars.

Today Strophanthin is given orally and has virtually no side effects. One individual attempted suicide by taking an entire container of Strophanthin pills. The individual ended up with an upset stomach. In 1990 the Strophanthin association gave all of its many hundreds of double-blind studies to the World Research Foundation in Stuttgart, Germany. Having all of these studies within our own organization just confirmed how truly effective this little herb was in helping to bypass surgery.

The following is from our World Research Foundation news:

G-Strophanthin: A "New" Approach for the Heart

Coronary artery disease is currently the leading cause of death in the United States. Despite the increasing sophistication of surgical techniques, the introduction of new techniques such as balloon angioplasty, and a number of new drugs (e.g. beta blockers, calcium antagonists), it is estimated that over 1 million heart attacks will occur this year, resulting in 500,000 deaths. In short, we do not have an adequate therapeutic solution to the problem of myocardial infarction (heart attack).

The cornerstone of therapy for treatment and prevention of myocardial infarction is to remove blockages in coronary arteries that are thought to be the cause of the infarction. This adheres to the widely accepted coronary artery thrombosis theory of infarction; that is, arteries become clogged with plaque, damaged from such things as smoking or high cholesterol. A clot forms a fissure in the plaque. The clot may shut off the blood flow of the coronary artery, causing a heart attack. It is deceptively simple: The coronary arteries are clogged. No blood can flow, so the muscles of the heart cannot be supported, and heart metabolism stops, leading to death.

In Germany, another theory of myocardial infarction has been proposed by Dr. Berthold Kern (1911-1995). Dr. Kern, while performing autopsies in Germany in the 1930's and 1940's, observed that the findings of these autopsies did not corroborate the coronary obstruction hypothesis. He began researching the literature, looking for clues as to an alternative etiology. What he found was not only a new theory that may provide the missing piece of the coronary obstruction theory, but a therapy now being used by over 5000 physicians in Germany with reportedly remarkable success.

Dr. Kern's claims, as set forth in his 1971 informational paper, *Three Ways to Cardiac Infarction*, can be summarized as follows:

1. The coronary obstruction theory cannot adequately explain observed facts.

2. The major etiologic factor underlying myocardial infarction is a primary chemical destructive process, cause by unchecked metabolic acidosis

(accumulation of acid) in the left ventricular tissue and substantially unrelated to coronary artery disease.

3. The regular, clinical use of oral g-strophathin (a cardiac glycoside derived from the West African plant strophanthus gratus):

    a. Prevents lethal myocardial tissue acidosis, and thereby

    b. Substantially reduces the incidence of myocardial infarction and completely prevents infarction deaths.

Dr. Kern's observations that most myocardial infarctions occur in patients without significant obstruction of the coronary artery supplying the infracted tissue finds great support in the American peer-reviewed literature. Since 1948, over a dozen reports of post-mortem examination of infracted hearts have consistently failed to corroborate the coronary artery thrombosis theory of myocardial infarction. That is, victims of fatal heart attacks have had no evidence whatsoever of coronary occlusion.

An example of the degree of non-confirmation can be ascertained by the following quote from a 1980 article on *Circulation*:

"These data support the concept that an occlusive coronary thrombus has no primary role in the pathogenesis of a myocardial infarct." The reviewer went on to note, *"These reports also present clear refutation of the most common explanation used today to dismiss autopsy findings which detect no coronary thrombi, i.e. that thrombi existed at infarction but have since lysed, embolized or washed away."*

There does not appear to be any literature that effectively refutes these autopsy findings.

Another source of inconsistent data are the many reports in the literature of myocardial infarction in patients without coronary artery disease, as deduced by normal coronary angiograms. Other autopsy data has revealed widely scattered areas of necrotic tissue that produces a substantial incongruence between the area of infarction and the arterial supply.

In a 1988 editorial published in the *New England Journal of Medicine* titled "Twenty years of coronary bypass surgery," Thomas Killip observed that *"Neither the VA [Veterans' Administration] nor CASS [the National Institute of Health's Coronary Artery Surgery Study] has detected a significant difference in long-term survival between the two assigned treatment groups [surgical vs. medical] when all patients have been included..."*

More recent work with coronary angioplasty and anti-thrombolytic agents has also failed to demonstrate any clear cut improvements in survival.

Dr. Kern went a step further. In his review of the literature, he came across the notion of collaterals (or anastomoses), a finely-meshed network of small blood vessels that act as natural bypass channels in the heart muscle. These collaterals have been made visible by Professor Giorgio Baroldi in studies at the Armed Forces Institute of Pathology.

Baroldi developed a technique for filling the arteries of the heart with artificial blood, a chemical substance that thickens in the blood vessels. When later the tissues were dissolved in acid, the entire structure of blood vessels in the heart was revealed. Kern hypothesized that bypass grafts were created naturally by the body via the collaterals whenever a coronary artery became blocked. Therefore, heart bypass would be redundant to a large degree.

A study by Rentrop *et al* in the April 1, 1988 issue of *The American Journal of Cardiology* has produced results completely at odds with the coronary artery blockage theory, and consistent with Kern's hypothesis. In an accompanying editorial, Dr. Stephen Epstein of the National Heart, Lung and Blood Institute summarizes Rentrop and colleagues' 'extremely important observations." They found that in an advanced state of the narrowing of the coronary arteries, the supply of blood to the heart muscles is fully assured via collaterals that enlarge naturally in response to the blockage. Interestingly, they observed that the more the coronaries narrow, the less danger there is of heart infraction.

Dr. Kern's second claim, i.e. his proposed new theory of metabolic acidosis, can be summarized as follows: Metabolic conditions in the most healthy of hearts are, at best, marginal in the constantly beating left ventricle. This is the part of the heart responsible for pumping blood to most of the body, the right ventricle merely supplying the lungs. Oxygen and energy requirements are always perilously close to available supplies, and any of the several stressors may cause an oxygen/energy deficit, with deterioration in oxidative metabolism, and consequent development of acidosis. Lack of oxygen sets off the process of zymosis or fermentation metabolism, an anaerobic process, in order to produce energy in the cells. This, in turn, lowers the pH.

This lowering of the pH sets off a destructive chemical process, literally a suicide reaction of the cell. Lysozymal enzymes are released, causing cell self-digestion. This starts as a single point in the muscle, then many points, which eventually join to form a small area of necrotic tissue. Finally, a critical mass is reached, no bigger than the head of a pin, which triggers larger and larger areas of damaged tissue, resulting in infarction (heart attack).

Ideally then, the remedy to address infarction would be a restoration of pH balance to the heart muscle, thereby preventing tissue damage and fatal infarction. The problem Kern faced was how to accomplish this without causing positive inotropy [increasing the strength of the muscular contraction], i.e. without putting further stress on the contracting heart muscle itself. The cardiac glycosides, including digitalis and the strophanthin byproduct known as *ouabain*, are known to produce such a deleterious effect, and this is why they are not effective against infarction.

This is where Kern made an important *re*discovery. In reviewing the literature, he came across the work of Dr. Edens, who in the 1920's had reported on a qualitatively different effect of strophanthin given intravenously versus orally. Specifically, the positive inotropic effects [that is, increasing contraction] that accompanied intravenous administration were not observed with oral administration.

This important observation has been confirmed in a study by Belz published in the *European Journal of Clinical Pharmacology* in 1984. Utilizing a randomized, placebo-controlled, double blind methodology, the researchers found that the intravenous *ouabain* (strophanthin) produced the expected increase in cardiac inotropy. However, the investigators stated quite definitely that, *"... the single sublingual (oral) dose of ouabain did not exert a positive inotropic effect."*

The postulated mechanism of action, based on animal research done by Adams, Powell and Erdmann, is that there are two receptors in the heart: "High affinity" and "Low affinity." It is thought that intravenous administration triggers low affinity receptors, and thus positive inotropy. High affinity receptors, on the other hand, react to small concentrations of g-strophanthin via oral administration, thereby avoiding the dangerous effect of positive inotropy.

Dr. Kern reported results of his clinical practice in Stuttgart over the period 1947-1968 involving over 15,000 patients. His patients treated with oral g-strophanthin experienced no fatal infarcts and only 20 non-fatal heart infarcts. These patients included many suffering infarction prior to entering the study. In contrast with these results, government statistics for the same time period would have predicted over 120 fatal heart attacks and over 400 non-fatal infarctions in a group of patients this size.

Currently, there are approximately 5000 M.D.s in Germany using and prescribing oral g-strophanthin. The booklet *Eine Dokumentation ambulanz-kardiologischer Therapie Ergebnisse nach Anwendung oralen g-strophanthin* represents the results of a survey wherein 3645 medical doctors made statements on use of this remedy in their practices from 1976 to 1983. Of these, 3552 gave exclusively positive testimony with no reservations. No one gave a negative response.

In addition to accumulating clinical experience, a number of studies have demonstrated excellent results with oral g-strophanthin. One fascinating report in a real-life setting took place at a German coal mine. During the period 1972-1974, miners suffered episodes of acute chest pain 229 times. Medical help was a two-hour ride away, and 11 miners died during this period. From 1975-1980, all miners who experienced acute chest pain (280 episodes) were immediately given oral g-strophanthin. During this period, which was twice as long as the comparison period, no miners died after the onset of symptoms. No toxic side effects were observed. Many variables were studied, i.e. age better access to treatment, different working conditions, etc. to ensure comparability of observation periods.

A rigorous, double blind, randomized control study of oral g-strophanthin in the treatment of angina showed impressive results at statistically different levels. After fourteen days, 81% of patients in the treated group experienced a reduction in attacks, while in the control group, 72% receiving placebos registered an increase in attacks.

In a study of 150 seriously ill heart patients, who altogether had 254 heart attacks, oral g-strophanthin was successful in 85% of the cases. Dr. Dohrmann, who conducted the study, observed, *"A positive result was registered when the severe heart attack abated at least five minutes after the g-strophanthin capsule was bitten through, and after ten minutes at the latest, they disappeared completely."*

A consistent feature of clinical reports using oral g-strophanthin is the absence of side effects. The cost of this remedy, which is currently available to German physicians and their patients, is approximately $30 per month for typical use.

At this point, every indication suggests that oral g-strophanthin may be a significant breakthrough in the treatment and prevention of myocardial infarction. What is needed is a definitive American clinical trial.

At an annual meeting of the American College of Cardiology in New Orleans, it was mentioned that every year one million US citizens suffer a heart attack. Of these, about 60 percent get to the hospital alive. About 16 percent never leave the hospital, and a further 10 percent die within a year. This should be keen motivation for a complete and intensive investigation of the benefits of g-strophanthin.

The prospect of replacing heart bypass surgery with a safer, more effective, and less expensive treatment may be another reason to interest other parties in funding American research on oral g-strophanthin.

Fruits from this experience:

Although the accepted medical model for the causes of heart attack and the accepted protocol for heart bypass are steeply engrained within the allopathic community in the United States does not necessarily mean that it is accurate and the highest and best approach. Dr. Kern is representative of someone who looks at facts and doesn't just accepted theory, and because of his desire to learn more made a discovery that was validated by one of the leading journals in the United States that hadn't received its proper recognition. Never accept something because experts say it so if they have not sufficiently proved it to your satisfaction.

Chapter Forty-four – Early Warning Plants

In 1991 I came across a very unique and interesting pollution monitoring system called Bioindikation. Bioindikation is a monitoring system using living plants and micro-organisms to indicate effects of pollution on people and animals. This technique, which is used by governmental agencies in some parts of Europe, has aided environmental scientists in determining the effects of various levels of ground, air and water pollution.

Often a standard analysis of air, water or soil will determine that a certain level of poison exists. However, researchers are not always sure of the biological consequences. With Bioindikation, plants can show you what is happening. Plants give the answer or signals through their functioning.

Plant specimens are place at monitoring locations for 3-4 weeks, 8 weeks or longer depending on species and specific testing requirements. Each plant has a very definite biological reaction to specific chemicals and polluting poisons.

Plants are placed near new settlements or developments to monitor the impact on environment. In the case of over-pollution of the environment during construction, the building or new development will be temporarily suspended until the environment has settled down.

Plants are also placed near industrial companies, trash and dump sites, as well as the freeway system to monitor exactly the effects of dispersed pollutants. In several places in Europe, Bioindikation is written into the law. Numerous plants are used including lichens, grass, tobacco and cabbage. Plants are also helpful in analyzing soil. Specimens are photographed and analyzed in laboratories to compare tolerance levels. Full reports are generated with diagrams and calculations.

It is truly a plant early warning system which can help protect the life and health of humans and animals.

Fruits from this experience:
Here was a novel idea to protect the health and well-being of people through the use of an aspect of nature that had not been utilized anywhere else in the world. While all life is sacred, I was impressed by the use of plants rather than animals or people.

Chapter Forty-five – Going to Hale

I had a very eventful European trip in the early part of 1989. The trip included meetings with the Royal Society of Medicine; the Research Council for Complementary Medicine, the Chief Executive for BUPA (the leading provider of private health care in the UK), along with meetings with Members of Parliament and Denis Haviland and Peter Rost. I had the opportunity to speak with some group members of the Parliamentary All Party Group on Alternative and Complementary Medicine.

The Parliamentary All Party Group was a body of Members of Parliament, Peers and some external members that had significant potential to act as a very effective lobby on Ministers and other policy-makers. I had the opportunity to make a presentation as well as hear the state of alternative and complementary medicine in the United Kingdom.

Included in this great trip was my meeting with a wonderful and energetic lady named Teresa Hale. Teresa Hale is the founder and guiding light of the Hale Clinic, which is located on four floors in the prestigious Nash Terrace in London.

The Hale Clinic is a very large, beautiful and unique concept that blends the best of holistic medicine with orthodox medicine.

Teresa shared the following with me, 'the original idea of the Hale Clinic grew out of the fact that I was a yoga teacher and I often referred my students to an osteopath or an acupuncturist before they started yoga, and it struck me that it would be a good idea to open a center for yoga and any other holistic therapy under one roof.

I started in a very small way in my flat with one osteopath and one acupuncturist around 1982. The Clinic gradually grew to its present size of 40 consulting rooms, a lecture hall and a restaurant.

The philosophy behind the Clinic is that it is possible for orthodox and holistic medicine to work closely together and complement each other. This is borne out by the fact that at the Hale Clinic we have 20 medical doctors working alongside 100 complementary practitioners. Due to the situation in England under Common Law (anyone is able to practice complementary medicine, they do not have to be a medical doctor), we feel it is necessary to insist on high standards of training.

The Hale Clinic, therefore, insists that any complementary practitioner involved in diagnosis, have at least three to four years full-time training, and we only accept people from certain colleges. We try to eliminate the danger that unscrupulous people may try to practice, thereby giving complementary medicine a bad reputation. In addition, some medical doctors were taking very short courses to learn some complementary therapies. We don't consider a weekend course for acupuncture as adequate training for a medical professional.'

We stopped for a bit and Teresa gave me a full tour of the Clinic and then we had a meal in the restaurant. Everything about the Hale Clinic was professional and very stately. Stately is the only way I can describe the incredible building with its pillars at the front entrance and the sparkling condition within.

Teresa continued, 'all the practitioners at the Hale Clinic are self-employed and are allowed to freely practice their specialty as long as they cause no harm to their patient. We find many of the therapists cross reference between one another. During an initial consultation we have three practitioners meet the patient. Although only one practitioner works with the patient, the patient's case is discussed at a weekly meeting of the three practitioners to monitor progress, and perhaps, at some point, have another practitioner of the team begin a new therapy. We wish to encourage co-operation between therapists but, at the same time, give them freedom to express their healing regime.

When the patients begin, we find some are ready to embrace the philosophy of holistic medicine and look at their illness from a spiritual, mental and physical perspective, whereas, other patients just have an ache or pain and have tried everything else. We do not try to force any particular perspective on the patient but try to see what the most appropriate form of treatment for them is.

An advisory service is provided for those patients who need advice and seek medical guidance concerning holistic treatments available at the Hale Clinic. The advisory service is provided by a medical doctor who is trained in complementary medicine.

A patient is examined from an orthodox and holistic perspective and advised of the most appropriate form of treatment for their condition. The initial doctor will also try to refer the patient to a practitioner with whom they are likely to have a good rapport."

I asked Teresa what the political climate was like regarding the acceptance in England of holistic medicine in general and her clinic in particular.

Teresa told me that she was working with a Parliamentary Committee in England which was supporting holistic medicine.

The Hale Clinic has seen up to 4,000 people a month. It is such a treat just entering the Clinic and I believe it is because it is totally based on the concept of Feng Shui, or the concept of the placement of objects in a space.

Over the years the Hale Clinic as boasted some very interesting clients including Linda McCartney, Tina Turner, Richard Gere and Arnold Schwarzenegger. The Clinic was officially opened by The Prince of Wales.

A listing of the therapies that have been performed at the clinic included; Acupressure, Acupuncture, Alexander Technique,

Aromatherapy, Auditory Integration Training, Ayurveda, Bio-Energy Healing, Body Harmonics, Buteyko Method, Chinese Herbal Medicine, Chiropody, Chiropractic, Colon Hydrotherapy, Deep Tissue Message, Ear Acupuncture, EMDR, Flower Remedies, Hellerwork, Homeopathy, Hypnotherapy, Iridology, Kinesiology, Light Therapy, Lymphatic drainage, Marma Massage, Medical Herbalism, Naturopathy, Neurotherapy, NLP, Paanchakarma, Physiotherapy, Polarity Therapy, Psychotherapy, Qigong, Reflexology, Reiki, Shiatsu, Stress Management, T'ai-Chi and Yoga.

I believe that the Hale Clinic concept is so very important in medicine. The concept is that all avenues for the improvement of one's condition are explored. The orthodox medical doctors at the Hale Clinic have just as fine credentials as other doctors both in Europe and the United States. Their belief is that you start with the least invasive procedures first. If they are not working then you continue with more aggressive and invasive approaches.

I have often used the analogy of a fly landing on a table. In order to get that fly you could use one of those gigantic wrecking balls that bring down buildings. Now you will get the fly but you will also destroy the table. You might consider a bowling ball to get that fly. You'll get that fly but you will certainly damage that table. What about the fly swatter? You got the fly and you did not destroy the table. In my analogy your body is the table and the fly is the temporary condition that has affected you.

Fruits from this experience:
There has long been animosity between allopathic[xxiv] medicine and complementary or 'alternative medicine.' The health model at the Hale Clinic has allopathic medical doctors working closely with complementary practitioners. The joining of these two approaches, each aspect being used when necessary, proves that the best approach is to start with the least intrusive regime and go to more drastic or invasive techniques if necessary. From my experience at the Hale Clinic I came up with the analogy of…if a fly lands on a table and you

use a wrecking ball, you might get the fly but you will destroy the table (human body}. You might also use a baseball bat, you might get the fly but you will chip or break the table. Another approach is to use a fly swatter, you will get the fly and save the table.

Chapter Forty-six – Visualizing Acupuncture

I was always fascinated with the concept of acupuncture. Here was a 5,000-year-old system of therapy that was still in use. It seems hard for me to believe that something that didn't work could have that type of longevity.

There has always been a lot of controversy and certainly negativity in the medical community when it came to acupuncture. Most doctors that I was aware of viewed it as something that was more in people's mind than having any reality. After all doctors hadn't found any meridians or acupuncture points while doing surgery.

Through a contact I learned that there were two doctors in Paris, France that were doing some unusual research regarding acupuncture. Dr. Jean-Claude Darras, M.D. and Prof. Dr. P. DeVernejoul, M.D., were working out of a prestigious hospital in Paris to discover if the Chinese meridian systems really existed.

Prof. DeVernejoul was a doctor of medicine and science and Head of the Dept. of Biophysics of Necker Hospital in Paris. He was also Chief of the Department of Biophysics and Nuclear Medicine at Public Hospital in Paris. In addition he was a member of the French Nuclear Regulatory Board.

Dr. Darrass was a doctor of Aerospace Medicine and a medical doctor at Hospital Necker and Hospital Henri Nonmondor.

I traveled to Paris to meet the doctors and learn more of their work. They were very gracious, open and eager to share their research. In fact, I was present in their research center as they conducted studies for their project.

The two doctors devised an experiment to test the validity of a postulated mechanism of energy transport, along the acupuncture meridians. Experiments consisted of injecting various supposed acupuncture points with a solution of isotope (te99) while doing high-speed catscan   Their experiments proved that the acupuncture meridian transport system existed and it was not the nervous or circulatory system but a unique transport system where energy flows could be measured and documented in a visible manner.

There work was so profound and documented that it was accepted in the French Academy of Science. There presentations had the WRF Congress were extremely well received and virtually none of the acupuncture practitioners that we met had ever heard of their work.

Before I left on my trip, I was able to find some information regarding the background of the doctors. Both doctors had very impressive medical backgrounds. Dr. Pierre de Vernejoul, M.D., is the Chairman of the Biophysical Medical Department for Necker Hospital in Paris. He was chief of the Nuclear Medicine section of Infant Maladies at Necker. Dr. de Vernejoul was also the Chief of Service of Public Service Medicine in Paris. In addition, Dr. de Vernejoul was a member of the French Commission on Atomic Energy and held numerous positions with other groups involved with biophysical and nuclear imaging.

Dr. Jean-Claude Darras, M.D., is a nuclear medical doctor as well as President of the World Union of Scientific Acupuncture Society. Dr. Darras was working under Dr. de Vernejoul when Darras devised a unique experiment to test the validity of specific acupuncture points and whether or not there is a mechanism of energy transport along the purported acupuncture meridians. Dr. Darras wanted to devise accurate experiments that could be recreated in other laboratories in case his experimentations yielded any tangible results.

Dr. Darras, working with his colleague Dr. de Vernejoul, decided to experiment by injecting various acupuncture points with a solution using a radioactive trace mineral while doing a high-speed cat scan. The doctors chose Te99 as their solution. The results showed that the actual molecules of radioactive material, as well as the carrier agent, rapidly moved along the meridian directly to the organ that corresponded, according to classical Chinese acupuncture literature, to the point injected. They found that 40% of the solution was transferred within 12 seconds.

Working with 70 patients in a hospital renal ward and 50 subjects with healthy kidneys, the doctors found that the isotope consistently migrated along the same pathways. There are reportedly 12 bilateral meridian pairs and 2 medial meridians.

In their main study, Darras and de Vernejoul simultaneously injected Te99 at the point "kidney 7" on both ankles and scanned the flow up the legs. They tested the rate of flow in the kidney meridian, which was symmetrical in both legs of normal subjects. For patients with degenerative kidney problems the flow in the leg on the unhealthy side showed a scattered pattern of the Te99. (See following pictures).

The doctors also discovered that laser stimulation of the kidney points distal to the point of injection caused the flow rate to increase in both normal and degenerative conditions. The stimulation responses from the laser showed the doctors that this aspect could lead to new diagnostic techniques.

Dr. Darras

An interesting experiment showed that if a person had had a kidney removed, the flow of the kidney meridian was blocked, and the flow migrated to the nearest "healthy" meridian.

Dr. De Verneioul

While I was visiting their research area in Necker Hospital, these fine doctors performed several experiments for me to see. What was very interesting was when they injected the body with the Te99, and it was not on an acupuncture point, the substance just pooled up and remained at that spot. When they injected at any acupuncture point, the isotope then migrated in lines corresponding 100% to the ancient Chinese meridian drawings.

The doctors were able to prove that the substance was not moving in the lymphatic, nervous or circulatory systems. When laser stimulation was used on non-acupuncture points, there were no measured isotope movements. The doctors found that the isotope moved about 3 centimeters per second along the meridian lines.

I believe that this work is very exciting. First, the doctors have been able to make visible a subtle energy that courses through the body. What other subtle energies might also be present that we are not aware of? Second, for too long, aspects of acupuncture have been ridiculed by standard medical doctors. In addition, these two doctors found that the meridians follow the same pathways as laid out by the ancient Chinese texts several thousand years ago. How did ancient Chinese writers see and understand these points and meridians?

Dr. Darras and Dr. de Vernejoul also used their research to help ascertain the effectiveness of some of the standard operations that took place in hospitals. When someone had surgery on a particular organ, the doctors were able to test the patient to see if the flow of energy was re-established in the organ that was operated upon. This would be very difficult using standard methods. The surgery might appear to have been successful from the visual standpoint of the organ being repaired, but that would not necessarily correlate with how effective the organ was working.

Although the findings of Darras and de Vernejoul have been accepted by the French Academy of Medicine, in the last twenty years I have met only a few acupuncturists who were aware of this landmark research. For that matter, I haven't met any doctors who heard of the experiments. What I still find at the time of this writing are comments from some of our leading medical information services that claim that acupuncture is a fringe medical technique that has not been proved to be effective.

Two respected doctors proved that acupuncture is effective and that meridians exist, but is this ancient method used as often as it could be—as a safe modality for healing?

Bull. Acad. Natie Méd., 1985, 169, n° 7, 1071-1075, séance du 22 octobre 1985

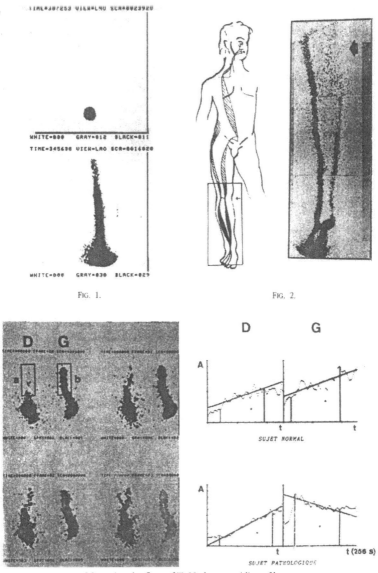

FIG. 1.   FIG. 2.

Measuring the flow of Te99 along meridian of legs

Fruits from this experience:

As we seek to protect ourselves from the unproven, a protection that can be detrimental, we may lose the opportunity to benefit from well-established and highly effective treatments.

It wasn't necessary for physicians in China to know for 5 millennium the effectiveness of acupuncture, yet our western medicine refused to accept its value until it could be "proven" to their scientific expectations. So while, it took thousands of years for Western science to develop and construct devices that could measure this subtle energy, half of the world's population had been using the subtle energy sources for healing.

Chapter Forty-seven – Diapulse Twice Normal Speed

I have discovered that I never know where and when I might come across some important health information. In 1976 I was watching the Olympic Games broadcast on ABC's Wide World of Sports. As a former track and field athlete I was very interested in the running events and turned on the television as Jim McKay was talking about Lasse Viren. Viren was running the 10,000 meters at that moment and McKay was sharing that Viren had slightly injured himself when he won the 5,000 meter race a few days previously. Then McKay began talking about a therapy device called a Diapulse Machine. Viren had taken several treatments after finishing the 5,000 and here he was running a dramatic 10,000 meter race in which he would win.

This was not a television commercial and McKay was sharing how this machine accelerates the healing process.

Several weeks later I decided to see what other information I could find about the Diapulse because I had never heard of it. To my amazement I found out that it was currently banned in the United States. This was very curious because it was being manufactured in the United States but could not be sold in our country.

I must share with you that I believe the full story of Diapulse should be told. I know that the owners and directors of Diapulse Corporation are happy with what is happening now in the present and do not want to dwell on the past, but I believe you should know something about the history of the Diapulse and the tenacity of the principals of the company that have made it possible that it is still available today.

The Diapulse is a remarkable machine that uses pulsed electromagnetic frequencies to accelerate the healing process. Not only that but it has such a dramatic effect on medicine and medical costs.

The Diapulse has repeatedly shown in double blind studies to accelerate the healing process to almost twice normal speed. Also, wounds that never healed in the control groups were successfully treated with Diapulse. In one double blind study of hand injuries, 29 out of 30 patients had been discharged in seven days versus 3 out of 30 in the control group. In a 1962 study, clearly ten years before the FDA ban, the average hospital stay was reduced from 13.5 days to 7.4 days with Diapulse therapy.

Based on earlier studies demonstrating regeneration of nerves in rats, a study was performed on cats who had their spinal cord crushed causing paralysis. Half the cats were ambulatory within 2 months with Diapulse therapy versus none in the control group.

Another study covered a period of 9 years and over 2,000 burn victims. Diapulse was used to prevent the development of edema and pain as well as to reduce local post-aggressive phenomena in burns. Results were described as 'significantly positive.'

This was some of the information I had learned upon my first introduction to Diapulse. Needless to say, I was very confused when I learned that the FDA claimed that Diapulse was a fraud and a quack device.

Further I learned that as early as 1940, animal studies were performed at Columbia University to prove the efficacy and safety of the Diapulse. In the 1950s the Director of the Tri-State Research Program for the U.S. Government concluded Diapulse was safe and effective. The Mayo Clinic and the New England Institute for Medical Research confirmed Ginsberg's earlier studies.

Tracing back, I found that the Diapulse prototype machine was developed in 1932 by Abraham J. Ginsberg, M.D. and Arthur Milinowski, physicist. Dr. Ginsberg had received medals from the U.S. Government for his invention of the 'sniperscope' used on the M1 rifle. He also worked with Albert Einstein on the application of electromagnetism to medicine.

Confirmation of safety and efficacy continued throughout the 1960s, 1970, and 1980s at University of Montreal, Baylor University School of Medicine, University of California, Royal College of Surgeons in London, University of Toronto, Georgetown University, Virginia Medical College, Leeds University, just to name a few. Virtually all of these studies were conducted before the FDA banned the sale of the Diapulse.

During the 1950s, the driving force behind Diapulse shifted from Ginsburg to Dr. Jesse Ross, (no relation to the author) a biophysicist, whose impressive background includes professional associations with Einstein and being one of the founders of the prestigious Bioelectromagnetic Society and a NASA consultant. Ross created the Diapulse Corporation of America (Great Neck, NY), developing a collaboration with Remington Rand to produce the device. To further assess the device's healing potential, Ross then launched ambitious research with universities and clinicians around the world.

One famous customer was former President Harry Truman, who rented the device in 1966. The Olympic Organizing Committee, in 1967, requested Diapulse to make available 30 machines for use by Olympic athletes at the Mexico City games. They had been used at every Olympics through the 1980s.

This is truly an incredible device and the validation came from numerous sources from throughout the world. So what was the problem?

FDA took the Diapulse Corporation to court in 1972 after a decade of fighting and had Diapulse banned, seizing the 1500 machines then in use. The FDA also wrote to Ministers of Health in other countries in an attempt to prevent Diapulse from selling machines overseas. This tactic was not successful by the FDA. In fact, the London Times reported the following on November 22, 1977; "Mrs. Callaghan, the Prime Minister's Wife along with Lady Hamilton and Princess Helena Moutafian watched a child being treated by Sister Mary Wallis with a

Diapulse electromagnetic therapy instrument at Great Ormond Street Hospital for children, in London. The machine is used to accelerate healing after surgery.

It took 15 years of fighting by the Diapulse Corporation before the courts finally agreed that FDA had been 'arbitrary and capricious' and the Diapulse was finally allowed to sell its machines in the United States. Interestingly, soon after the approval by the FDA, Diapulse's president, Jess Ross, gave a lecture at a conference of 'Emerging Electromagnetic Medical Technology', which was partially sponsored by the FDA Center for Devices and Radiological Health. The FDA has sanctioned use of the Diapulse in the treatment of post-operative swelling and pain in superficial soft tissue.

In 2005 the Diapulse was approved for Medicare patients. I am very pleased for the Diapulse Corporation but even more pleased that this wonderful device will be more readily available to those who are in need.

What happened in this situation? We had developers with incredible credentials and continuous studies and validation and yet it was withheld from those in need for so many years. The people at the Diapulse Corporation won't talk about this period because they would rather let the sleeping dog lie and they are happy to be moving forward. In my mind it is very simple. The FDA is influenced by the pharmaceutical industry and has maintained a continuous program of stifling and restricting all aspects of the therapies coming from the electromagnetic spectrum.

Fruits from this experience:
Despite the validation of this approach by several of the most prestigious universities and research groups throughout the world, an agency of the United States decided to shut it down and attempted to force it into bankruptcy. In taking the time to do my own research and gather all the information that I could find, including going directly to the Diapulse Company, I learned that truth could still be covered up through vested interests. I learned that one must always research to a

greater depth than just accepting someone's opinion on the surface of things.

Chapter Forty-eight – Thoughts do Heal

It is somewhat sad to me that we seem to live in a world where any means to an end has become the standard. The world that I would like to see is the opposite of this, where the intention we hold during the action becomes the result we want to see. If we have questionable means, the ends are always questionable. If we hold good intentions, act with noble purpose, the outcomes will always be good, even if they are not the outcomes we hoped to achieve.

In my journeys and my own personal healing experiences, I have found that healing does begin with thoughts. But perhaps they are not simply thoughts alone. Thought becomes the starting point (the mind); it animates the healing through the physical (the body); and culminates in outcome aligned with its intention (the spirit). There are many profound examples of this in all of our lives. My life has held many of these experiences that has left me utterly amazed. All of our abilities intermesh in a complex and beautifully synergistic harmony.

In 1993 I met Hubert Schweizer during a trip to Switzerland. I was told that he had information regarding an Italian doctor who had made some amazing and very profound discoveries in the early 1900s. Hubert was to tell me an amazing story about Dr. Giuseppe Joseph Calligaris. But before he started he jumped forward in his story and mentioned that upon Calligaris death in 1944, all of his papers were seized by a group from the Soviet Union and Calligaris' work forms a basis of research at twenty-three Soviet academies.

Calligaris was born in 1876 in Forni di Sotto, in Northern Italy, where his father was the doctor. Forni di Sotto means 'stoves from below'. There were always indications that there are some unusual magnetic influences in that area. Calligaris decided to study medicine and received his medical degree in 1901, 'summa cum laude'. His dissertation was titled, Thoughts Do Heal.

In 1902 he went to Rome to work as an assistant to professor Mingazzini, the director of the Institute of Neuropathology at the medical faculty of the Royal University. Professor Mingazzini became his spiritual mentor for the next twenty-five years.

In 1909 Calligaris was asked to be the secretary of the first Italian Congress of Neuropathology. In that same year he edited a scientific book of neuropathology and moved to Udine where he set up a hospital for nervous diseases together with his father. During World War I, Calligaris had to enter the army as a surgeon and received honors of his medical skills. Eventually Calligaris did become a full professor and lectured until 1939.

What he ended up discovering was what he called a body-mind skin-reflex-chain. He published about twenty books comprising about 20,000 pages. Most of these were taken when the Soviet Union took his materials. Calligaris discovered that certain lines and points, on the skin, were related to the conscious and the subconscious portions of the mind and even to the enhancing of paranormal abilities. Calligaris called this, 'linear chains of the body mind.' He discovered experimentally a network of lines, a grid of longitudinal meridians and parallels of latitude on the skin that have less electrical resistance, are hyperesthesia and form geometrical patterns.

I was completely captivated with what Hubert was sharing. With all of the research I had done I had never come across any reference to Calligaris. I asked if these lines were the nerves or acupuncture meridians. Hubert said they were not.

For more than 30 years Calligaris examined thousands of individuals and discovered that the system of coordinates and points, on the skin of the human body, evoked reproducible effects. He proved that everybody could be stimulated to enhance their clairvoyance, clairaudience, precognition and retro cognition, the same way that we learn writing or mathematical calculations. Calligaris discovered points of intersections, or cosmic energies, which acted as mirrors, collectors and accumulators. He found that these points could be pressed or forced by metal cylinders, stimulated to better reflect the higher intelligence and to produce an echo of the vital vibrations of the body.

Sound crazy? Why did the Soviet Union not only go after these materials but set up research institutes? Could this be the reason that the former Soviet Union seemed to be so far ahead in researching these fields?

Calligaris believed that our brain just may be a concave mirror for the Universal Consciousness. Calligaris thought he was presenting something of great value to the world but others thought differently. He was excommunicated by the Church and in 1928 he was repudiated in the Academy of Science of Udine. He ended up losing his professional seat in the University, his title of medical doctor was taken away and his professional license for his hospital.

In his own memoirs he wrote that he did not quit or lose courage 'even for five minutes.'

The more I head the more confused I became. If it was quackery than why was so much research being conducted following his lead? If it had some basis in truth than why had I not heard one single word or seen anything on the internet?

Hubert mentioned that all books by Calligaris were extremely rare and that according to a government decree the Italian libraries were not allowed to lend or copy his books.

In 1995 I published a brief article on Calligaris in the third quarter of the World Research Foundation News. Several weeks later I received a note from a man in Santa Monica, California who stated that he was very familiar with Calligaris and he wanted to talk with me. He was born in Italy; he was a psychologist and had closely followed Calligaris' work. Most times I would have contacted this man immediately but ending up delaying for over a year.

As I mentioned there was virtually nothing written about Calligaris. Hubert delivered a lecture in England in 1987 and that was the extent of information on Calligaris, or was it? While in my library at the beginning of 1996 and before I attempted the contact with the man from Santa Monica, I was drawn to a book I had read about twenty-five years before. The book was written by Yogananda and was titled, *Autobiography of a Yogi* and was originally written in 1946. I  picked up the book and glanced at the index. To my surprise there was a reference to a footnote within the book dealing with Calligaris. The footnote from Autobiography of a Yogi read, "In its own way, physical science is affirming the validity of laws discovered by yogis through mental science.

For example, a demonstration that man has television powers was given on Nov. 26, 1934 at the Royal University of Rome. 'Dr. Giuseppe Calligaris, professor of neuro-psychology, pressed certain parts of a subject's body and the subject responded with minute descriptions of persons and objects on the opposite side of a wall. Dr. Calligaris told the professors that if certain areas on the skin are agitated, the subject is given super-sensorial impressions enabling him to see objects that he could not otherwise perceive. To enable his subject to discern things on the other side of a wall, Professor Calligaris pressed a spot to the right of the thorax for fifteen minut4es. Dr. Calligaris said that when certain spots of the body are agitated, the subjects can see objects at any distance, regardless of whether they have ever before seen those objects." Autobiography of a Yogi by Paramahansa Yogananda, 1959, pg. 26.

This was the only reference to Calligaris in English before Hubert's lecture. At the time I read the book I did not even give it a thought.

About ten months later I tried to contact the man who had written to me only to learn that he had moved to Italy. I continued to see if I could find the man but eventually learned that he had passed away. I was very disappointed. I continued to do some sleuthing and eventually contacted a relative of the man who had passed away.

She told me that before he had passed the gentleman had crated up some books and given them to a bookstore in Los Angles called the Bodhi Tree. I was in shock! This was and is my favorite bookstore. This is where I found the book that led me to the Rife Microscope. This is the bookstore that I would spend at least one day every other weekend searching through its used book section.

I was able to contact one of the owners of the Bodhi Tree and explained who I was and what we did at World Research Foundation. He invited me to come to the bookstore and he would look in one of the rooms that held books that were still in crates. He believed he remembered the delivery but hadn't had any chance to look at what was in the box.

We went through the various crates of books and then found the box that contained books from the gentleman who contacted me. Inside the box were five books about Calligaris. I had told the owner of the Bodhi Tree about the work and he just handed me the books. I asked him how much he wanted and he didn't take any money. Do the best you can with them, he told me. They were of course in Italian but you have read how difficult it is to have any Calligaris materials.

Later I would contact the university where Calligaris studied and ask if they could find the dissertation of Calligaris. The staff at the university sent me a copy of the hand-written dissertation of Calligaris, titled *Thoughts Do Heal.*

Fruits from this experience:
The biggest fruits from this experience is that "There are more things in heaven and earth, Horatio, then are dreamt of in your philosophy".

The possibilities of this research are unimaginable regarding human potential and that the Russians took everything that they could find and established so many research Institutes should be an indication of the reality of the possibilities that were mentioned by Calligaris.

Chapter Forty-nine – A Title Entitles

In 1994 I had the opportunity to appear on a national program on NBC called, The Other Side. As a result of the program the World Research Foundation received approximately 20,000 telephone calls from viewers. I had the opportunity to speak with many people from throughout the United States. Since the program was dealing with aspects of complementary or what might be called alternative medicine, it allowed me to get a feeling for the type of person that was interested in this field.

I was very impressed with the demeanor, personality and warmth of the people that I spoke with. They were intelligent, caring, thoughtful, appreciative people; all seeking, searching, hunting, praying and hopeful that some answer exists for their health care concerns.

Many of the people, when I introduced myself as Steve, called me Steve until they realized that I was the fellow from the television show, then they called me 'Mr. Ross.' They couldn't believe that I was personally speaking with them and spending the time with them. I was even laughing and joking with them.

What has become of people helping and caring for each other? Why do we find it so hard to relate to medical and health authority figures who seem to place themselves on a pedestal and act in such a manner that they have closed off the meaningful exchanges between us. I believe that when you use anything other than your first name you lose the intimacy and bond that people can share with each other. This distance eliminates the healing balms of love, compassion and caring. Perhaps the reason it is done is because some of our medical and health professionals don't want to be close because they do not have an answer and they choose to stay distant.

I believe that life is a schoolroom where we learn through lessons, to move outside of our own ego-ness and to come into harmony with the people and nature that is about us.

I noticed an even greater reaction from people when they realized that I had a Ph.D. Immediately they became apologetic and hoped that I hadn't been offended. Why?

Is it a sin that we don't relate to someone's title? Is it a matter of respect or a carryover of 'those who would be king.'? How has a group of people been able to place so much importance and emphasis upon a grouping of letters behind a name? Perhaps some of these people who are into their letters, should consider the farmer who provides their food. How about the people who stitch and sew the clothing that we wear? Are these two professions any less important than the medical and health care professionals? Take away the food which is available for doctors to eat and the clothing that they wear and how visible would the person be?

Why am I stressing this point? Almost without exception their medical doctor has treated the people that I spoke to with little respect, warmth or compassion. They have been treated with contempt if they asked questions and with disgust if they wanted explanations. For the hard earned money they have paid, they have received virtually no satisfaction.

I was not speaking with the sour grapes, negative group of people who are down on everything. I spoke with people from all walks of life around this country; in every sort of occupation from farmer to insurance salesman, from homemaker to civil service worker.

People are not receiving what they need from our current medical system and many who perform services within it. I am not speaking of the well-meaning medical professionals, who do communicate well with their patients and often use their first name; I am speaking about those professionals who act like pompous....

One reason why our medicine is failing, AND IT IS FAILING IN VIRTUALLY ALL THE DEGENERATIVE CONDITIONS, and for many other medical conditions, is that we have lost the humanness of interaction. We have lost our capacity of love and sharing and then when it comes time for the assistance of the medical profession, they reinforce this even more.

No doctor has ever healed a patient. They can cut, saw, hack and sew, but the healing comes from within the patient. In days of old, one of the greatest reasons that medical professionals had success, was because the patient believed they would be helped. A person believed in the doctor and just the sight of 'ole doc' coming was already the start of the healing process from within the individual.

Today, visiting the doctor is an ordeal. It is as if you are attending a coronation. When you ask for more detail, you are often placed in a position of being considered a pest and someone who is taking too much time.

Greatness and respect should be earned as a result of service and deed, not from a title. We have too many fair weather practitioners that fill the airwaves of radio and especially television that are full of babble. It is doctor this and doctor that and yet if you check beyond the television monitors these people cannot even run their own lives effectively. They are just as ill as those patients they counsel and they need as much psychological counseling as those who come to them.

Who is great? All of you who serve others with love and care, who live in beauty and walk in beauty.

Fruits from this experience:
Through my interaction with several thousand individuals throughout my 40 plus years of work, I have heard the constant complaint that the medical professionals that the patients met did not treat them with respect or truly make them believe that the medical or health practitioner really cared about them as an individual. For me the fruit of this experience is to never forget that I am interacting with a person with a body, heart and soul. We are all people living experiences on

this earth and as the old saying goes, we all put on our pants one leg at a time.

Chapter Fifty – Not Just a Riddle

Some of the poems that I have received during the night have been both prophetic as well as a commentary on current events.

I received a call at my office in early January of 1994 from a woman I had never had contact with previously. It was a Tuesday and she had asked if we might meet two days later on Thursday. Her name was Carole and she said she wanted to discuss a particular health technology.

On Wednesday evening the day before our meeting I awoke from a dream and then heard the following poem:

> Carole passes, through the gate
> On this course, will she be tempting fate
> The flight will leave, following the plan
> Where she will confront, a dangerous man
>
> Salvadorian, he appears to be
> In the company of another three
> Take heed, be cautious, and take a close look
> Don't initially make haste, to complete the whole book
>
> Your guides will sing, into your ear
> When danger appears, to be coming near
> Columbia gold, takes many lives
> As many people with the letter B, enter the hive
>
> It takes one sting, to put you away
> You must be cautious, throughout each day
> Ticket changes, might provide a key
> Follow the sequence back, and you will see
>
> Following your guidance, the pathway you will find
> Watch each step, with this kind

Others with you, watch from the United States
You're the one however, that tempts the fates

Glory be, the prize that's found
Only if you still walk, upon the ground
It's not just a riddle, that we send
It is a warning, that we pen.

When I awoke I really did not know what I should do. I didn't know the slightest thing about Carole or why she was coming to see me. I did feel the lines seemed very specific and I thought of the easiest manner in which to present the poem.

Carole M. met me at 10 am and I told her that at times I receive various insights for other people. I asked her if she would mind if I shared something with her. She told me it would be all right and I gave her the poem and she settled down on a sofa that was in my office.

I will never forget the look on her face as she was reading the lines and then when she finished. She was stuttering and trying to figure out what was happening at the moment.

Carole shared with me that she had come to talk about the Rife microscope but that she was in the television and motion picture business. Carole later would have a wonderful television series called The Marshal. At this time Carole was working independently with a partner and they had some interesting information regarding Pablo Escobar, a Columbian drug lord. They were working toward a possible collaboration with ABC News. Carole was literally on her way to Columbia to get background information and work with people affiliated with the Columbian police.

Now the poem made great sense to me as it did for Carole. Carole was so overwhelmed at the moment that we never discussed the Rife Microscope but she wanted to know more about how this information came to me and what she might want to do. I mentioned to her that she needed to just think about it and she left my office soon after. It was also interesting to me that in the dream I saw her named spelled Carole instead of Carol.

The next morning Carole called me and told me that she had read the poem perhaps over one hundred times. She had called many of her friends for their opinions and possible explanations.

Carole's final decision was not to tempt fate and she passed on the project.

Carole and I became very good friends and have shared several other interesting connections since our first meeting. Carole gave her approval for me to share this experience.

Fruits from this experience:
When we interact with the spiritual side of our existence we find that all things are possible. I never met Carole nor did I have any knowledge of who she was or what she did in life. To receive such exact and profound information through a means other than my own intellect provided me the assurance that there is more guidance and support surrounding all of us beyond what our physical awareness assumes.

End of Part II

Part III – Poetic Nights

Chapter Fifty-one   Poetic Nights

"But all art is sensual and poetry particularly so. It is directly, that is, of the senses, and since the senses do not exist without an object for their employment all art is necessarily objective. It doesn't declaim or explain, it presents."

– William Carlos Williams

As we come to the end of Steve's theophanies we depart from the normal dream sequences and move into poetic dreams. While we have seen dreams as part of the "words" in previous chapters, here we share dreams that have come solely as poems. Poetry in the spiritual life is often very common. The classic *Dark Night of the Soul*, by Juan de la Cruz (John of the Cross), a spiritual classic, is perhaps one of the most emblematic examples of poetic revelation.

Almost from the beginning of his awareness of revelations in his dreaming, Steve found that he was receiving more than just an increased amount of dreams. He would often wake six or seven times a night and "hear" poems. The poems would have themes that were about beauty, love, philosophy, spiritual subjects and sometimes commentaries regarding something taking place in the world or something or someone from past history. Over the years these poems now number in the hundreds.

We include the "poetic nights" in that mystical tradition, where words convey more than just information, they convey images, and ideas, and transcendence. Poetic nights create a picture, draw out emotion, and connect in a deeper more meaningful way. We present these dreams just as they came to Steve, without interpretation or explanation.

A message of time

Come hither to find,
The message of time
You live and react,
With all of the pack
When once you do soar
Your feet leave the floor
Your spirit takes flight
You disappear from physical sight.

The master plan

To raise above, the field of action
To place yourself, above reaction,
These lessons are, the work of Man,
It is all a part, of a Master Plan
Obtuse we are, we previously did state
But it is our plan, to help you reach the Divine Estate,
Listen to our words, and please take note,
It is intended to help, your spiritual float,
You must have the heart, to carry forward and see,
All of your future, pos-si-bil-i-ties.

An open book

Climbing or building, they all try to make,
A very big pile, of the material estate,
But a closer look, at the things in the stack,
Brings most people, to an unhappy fact,
The mountain of baubles, which carries such weight,
Cannot be carried, beyond this world we make,

These things are not carried, by spiritual hand,
For they have no real value, in the Promised Land,
Better to pile, the qualities of mind,
Which leads one into, a spiritual find,

On closer inspection, if you take the time to look,

The reality of your world, is like an open book,
The drama at hand, which trouble or pleased,
Is in reality, nothing more than a tease,

Some chase after bounties, which momentarily give pleasure,
But then they discover, there short of the measure,
Others are hounded, by troubles each day,
It is their own actions, which hold them in sway.

Upward it soars
The words in these messages, which we do send,
Cross time and space, to be written by your pen,
We hope that you find, as you write down each line,
That we have helped, to broaden your mind,

Not just the mind, which you use every day,
But the spiritual mind, which shall never decay,
The physical one, will end in a time,
But the spiritual one, will continue to climb,

Upward it soars, on its way to its home,
Plenty of guidance, so it's never alone,
Your Father will welcome, his child with much love,
He patiently waits, as a state of awareness above,

There was never any distance, wherever you roam,
Just opening your awareness, brings you instantly home,
Imagine a world, where true love you will see,
You become such a place, if you desire to be.

Greetings from Pythagoras
The creases in my robe, like the never-ending sea,
Roll back and forth, in eternity,
Time is a stead, which races fast,
From anywhere in the future, to anywhere in the past,
Imagine where, you want to be,

Ride her stoutly, and you will see,

The concept held, about the life,
Can be minutely dissected, cut sharply like a knife,
Slice it up, and you will see,
It's all a piece of eternity,

Crossing the great void, will bring you home,
You will find, you were never alone,
Another soul, has sat by your side,
Whenever you had, much to decide,
A provision of God, has placed them near,
So you should never, have any fear.

Soul takes its flight
The wings of Pegasus, flap in the night,
As the soul within, looks to take its flight,
While mired in the earthplane, it does not see,
The part it plays, in eternity,

With grace and beauty, the soul takes its flight to see,
The past or present, where it desires to be,
Now come leave your bed, and fly with me,
And we will traverse, the endless sea,

The sea that stretches, from shore to shore,
Or like the actions, of a revolving door,
The cycles of life, which seem so real,
Are shuffled like cards, on each new deal,
You play your hand, that you have found,
Until the time, to lay the hand down.

The master plan
She laid in bed, not making a sound,
Hoping her mate, might be profound,
He worked his pen, through the night,

Jotting the words, which might provide insight,

The thing which means, the most you see,
Is do your best, in all you be,
Live your life, and learn all you can,
To bring out the meaning, of your Master Plan,
Look deep within, and you will see,
The returning glance, of eternity.

Spirit light

People work, at what they do,
Some try to even, smile with you,
Trying just, to pass their day,
There quite unhappy, in their way,

They have not found, the little light,
Which can give them guidance, day or night,
From spirit does, this light come lit,
Then they and life, make a better fit.

The spiritual seed

Visiting far off, lands and times,
Find the meaning, in the rhyme,
To help each fellow, in their need,
Is an important part, of our creed,

To come to aid, those in need,
Helps to activate, the spiritual seed,
To love and help, that follows God's Plan,
To lift the spiritual, that resides in Man.

Child of spirit

Let the bells, of Wisdom ring,
Listen to the choir, of Angels sing,
They found the soul, which resides inside,
Transcending all, their earthly pride,

It is the Father's, wish you see,
That you become, all you can be,
A Child of Spirit, You'll soon discover,
When you remove, your earthly cover.

Climbing the mountain

To climb up, to the mountain top,
You must proceed, and learn when to stop,
A double meaning, we try to set,
Which will bring you wisdom, so don't get upset.

There is a key, we try to deliver,
It isn't our intention, to make you quiver,
You halt on your climb, when certain actions appear,
This will elevate your thinking, and bring you near,

Climbing the mountain, you do have the choice,
To follow the physical, or your inner voice,
It takes full attention, to bring you near,
Do not remain idle, in neutral gear,

You must make the choice, to change your state,
Always remember, it's never too late,
To your higher self, you make the request,
But don't allow the physical, to indulge in protest,

Don't make noise, and bemoan your fate,
It generates anger, and residual hate,
Carry reverence along, with you each day,
Be grateful for your journey, don't get stuck in the play.

Finding the course

Come hither to find,
A higher state of mind,
The earth's sandy state,
Is not your estate,

For something greater to see,
When you come up to Me,
So stay on this track,
And establish the fact.

The winds blow, in each direction,
Allowing all to reach, true perfection,
No right or wrong, effects your course,
A seeming mistake, should bring no remorse,
For each reaction is a lesson, for you to see,
To bring you on, a course to Me.

Promise to keep

The action within anyone's act,
Will give you keys, to an important fact,
So continue to walk,
Purify your talk,
Live the right plan,
Find the greater in Man,
Relax, but be true,
Forget what others, think about you,
It is true wisdom you seek,
God's promise to keep.

The spiritual quest

You made it this night,
The soul took its flight,
It quickened to see,
A brief glimpse of Me,

I AM here inside,
A real state of mind,
A friend to recover
Which you'll soon discover,

Some take much time,
To finally find,
I am their true self,
Who is placed on the shelf,

So take a firm grip,
Bring me along for your trip,
You're not alone,
When we finally come home,

We both take a ride,
As you seek to discover Me inside,
A spiritual quest,
With lessons that do test,

Life is the way,
To prove what you say,
The world is your stage,
Where you act out each play.

Return to your home

The crux in the head, provides the key,
The spiritual pathway, that brings you to Me,
Placed by God, to give you the chance,
The return to Eden, is not happenstance,

The lights on the line (chakras),
Are activated in time,
Gifts you discover,
As each light is uncovered,

Steer in the lost ship,
To return to its slip,
On earth voyage you roamed,
Soon you will return to your home.

Out of the deep

Listen, for the words we speak,
Brought forth through you, from out of the deep,
From the land, of the Unknown,
It comforts those, who long to come home,

The messages, are loud and clear,
About the guidance, which is ever near,
So walk the streets, and give the words,
That lift and help, and do encourage,

We guide your steps, upon spirit's lake,
Which help others with, the decisions they make,
Wisdoms words, are kept in trust,
For those who climb, they are a must,
Let not your worry, shorten your step,
Begin to move forward, your journey is set.

Transcend the mean

Listen closely, and you will hear,
The voices from Spirit, which are quite near,
Words of wisdom, we do send,
You'll provide guidance, for women and men,

It comes at a time, which needs to know,
That this world you live in, is really a show,
From birth to death, your struggle to find,
The things that will bring you, peace of mind,

But lo the things, that this earth be,
You never possess, but are just pleasing to see,
Greater victory, is to be found,
By the inner spirit, which is more profound,

Your greater part, remains unseen,
Until you learn, to Transcend the Mean,

Working, playing, it's all right,
Serious work, is done through dreams at night,

And when you finally, leave this physical land,
You will discover, it was but shifting sand,
True substance was always, a breath away,
But you'll discover it, upon another earth day.

Words from up high

Cross the river,
You don't need a boat,
Work on the self,
You'll be able to float,

Currents are present,
But all is not lost,
With Spiritual guidance,
There isn't a cost,

Your body must follow,
The words from up high,
So keep on the pathway,
You'll arrive by and by.

Elevate your thinking

You walk the land,
To try to see,
If you can arrive,
At what God, intended you to be,

The trials and worries,
Which surrounded your walk,
Have largely been caused,
By your erroneous thoughts,

So elevate your thinking,
And you will see,
How easy It Is,
To receive guidance from Me.

Poets visit

Poets visit, from time to time,
Passing wisdom, across the line,
Leap across, the woven spell,
You will find, you still do well,

Illusions seem, to find their way,
They keep your course, through games you play,
Life is just, a flow of time,
The idle drifting, of your earthly mind.

Receive your guidance

The vulgar is the heavy,
The spirit is the light,
Learn to receive your guidance,
During the day as you do at night.

The spot on high

Deliver to us, Oh God, the Father in our heaven,
To come to the resting place from all our woes,
The spot on high that holds the key of immortality,
The furies carry on in man
As long as you allow yourself to ride upon these grounds.

The journey home

The land of Canaan, holds the key,
Of the journey home, towards immortality,
Your struggles are noted, but it's no matter,
Life on earth, just makes you sadder,

Bring your thoughts, to higher levels,
You then experience, in higher trebles,

Look up the Ganges, from where the river flows,
The source of which, is God you know.

Harken upon the new

Let swing the change of pattern,
Make haste to come up new,
Cleave not to things of old actions,
But harken upon the new.

Trifles of life

Climb the steps that lead you higher,
Out of the source, of earthly fire,
The loving arms, of spirits wait,
To help you pass, through Heaven's Gate,

It all depends, on your state of mind,
An important truth, you're sure to find,
Trifles of life, kept you spinning,
Causing you to forget, your spiritual beginning,

At all times, you've been looking for your home,
Through many experiences, you've wandered and roamed,
Keep your thoughts fixed, and head toward Heaven's Gate,
Where you will find, your Heavenly Father awaits.

The divine mind

To the center of Being, you travel to find,
Your connection to, the all-knowing Divine Mind,
Messages delivered, from a wisdom you see,
Which passes understanding, but comes directly from Me.

Our vision is higher, learned from many go arounds,
Our solutions for problems, will seem quite profound,
We are not affected, by hunger or thirst,
Our input can guide you, from experiencing the worst,
Lessons are handled, with spiritual gloss,

Victory is achieved, with little loss.

Distinguish the spirit
Kindness and charity, are more than just words,
They distinguish the spirit, from the masses of herds,
Each spirit is clouded, in its view,
Due to its covering, it knows not the true,

The herd is a group, of spirits you see,
Who have lost their sight, of whom they might be,
True spirit is Godly, of substance so fine,
A part of the Creator, the Ultimate Divine,

Lessons bring clarity, to each in the pack,
Giving some recognition, of their spiritual fact,
Some learn truths, from meeting one that does shine,
Whose radiance and love, shine forth from the Divine.
Peace and comfort
Divest yourself, of weary thoughts,
True happiness comes, it is not bought,
For help is always, a breath away,
It matters not, the time of day,

Attunement is possible, by a thought,
Conceive of the Supreme Intelligence, you've been taught,
God provides, through His Plan,
Peace and comfort, for every Man.

The spiritual dance
Come my child, and follow our steps,
Not south, north, east or west,
A journey inward, to a wonderful land,
Of greater beauty, and a Master Plan,

All do too, it isn't by chance,
You finally reach, the spiritual dance,

There the orchestra plays, a special tune,
Written for all, from the Creator's plume.

Grace and ease

Carry your weight, with grace and ease,
T'is only your God, not man to please.

A whirl of energy, sings with light,
For God has created, another delight,
A touch of the Master, remains in the clay,
As the wings outstretch, to fly away,

But into the darkness, each does file,
To pass on earth, for a little while,
To learn, to grow, it's a part of Man,
Continuing on, in the master plan,

It's dusty cover, allows all to see,
It is combined of atoms, and of earth it be,
But under the cover, the spirit be,
A whirl of loving energy.

Come to see

The stars are placed, in the sky,
By the Creator, from up high,
They do twinkle, with a light,
Which can be seen, in day or night,

The path of light, can be found,
You can find it, from the ground,
Think how happy, you can be,
Once you finally, come to see.

A heavenly key

Words of wisdom, quite profound,
We deliver, without a sound,

Coming to you, from far but near,
Just relax, and you will hear,

Riding closely, with each breath,
Always speaking, we need no rest,
Life's a test, so make the grade,
By love and will, you'll find the way,

For each is provided, a heavenly key,
Available to all, through eternity,
We can speak, if you will listen,
Helpful guidance, is our mission.

Clothed in light

High and straight, be sure to face,
Compete with none, it's not a race,
Born to flesh, that is a cover,
That is sparse, you'll soon discover,

Your Mother clothed your light, with a gentle hand,
Built with substance, of the earth land,
It melts away, upon your death,
Flowing back to clothe, someone who comes next,
Then once again, spirit you be,
Traveling on the road, of eternity.

The inner land

Listen closely, to this story,
To find inner peace, and outer glory,
Life's a journey, with a plan,
Leading each, toward an inner land,
Wrought with hardships, to help you discover,
An inner land, you must uncover.

Created by thought

Courage to dare, thoughts do create,
Begin through desire, then have patience to wait,
Elements find, their pattern from mind,
Then the clusters form, into different kinds,

Frequency acts, as a band of glue,
To produce a form, which is new,
But what you see, exists before your time,
For only now you see it, with the earthly mind.

Acquire the key

Fettered brow, waits at the gate,
Hoping the Father, will not be late,
Bringing us wisdom, and guidance so near,
To handle the stress, and ease our fear,

Rumble and tumble, off goes the quake,
It is a message, to get you awake,
You must understand, what matters to see,
True life is not baubles, but spirit it be,

What has true value, in life's great plan?
Is it money, or your piece of earth land?
Is it the trinkets, or car that you drive?
Or is it the spiritual, which resides deep inside?

Extending your hand, to help those in need,
Remember this schoolroom, provides lessons to see,
Be not worried, or panic as you live,
Only the earth shell, will eventually you'll give,
For grander you are, and always shall be,
Go within, to acquire the key.

Love of God

Carrying forward, on through the night,
The love of the Deity, enlivens the sight,

Turmoil and stress, the plight of the lost,
Turn inward and upward, for this there's no cost,

The heartbeat of matter, is spirit you see,
To reach this awareness, just use this key,
Look for the inner, the driving force,
T'is the handiwork of God, your spirit of course,

For each there's a pathway,
So seek it each day,
It might become visible,
At work or at play,

Life is a schoolroom, lessons to learn,
Competing with others, should not be your concern,
Locate the pathway, and you will find,
Your journey homeward, leads to greater peace of mind.

Concealing the promise
Curtains of stars, draped in the night,
Concealing the promise, just out of sight
Our awareness is limited, but we can still see
Trusting our vision, used in-tu-i-tive-ly.

The wise path
A little journey, you do make,
To help your soul, to Heaven's Gate,
A state of mind, is what it be,
Surrender the gross, to find the key,

The Subtle One guides, your every step,
Its gentle urging, helps you on your quest,
Completion is, a state of mind,
Force won't work, as you will find,

You'll finally come, upon a room a glow,

Then you'll awaken, and you will know,
Two great paths, your choice to walk,
One by insight, and one by talk.

Clothed in the spirit
The dross is burned, through your inspection,
Of this earthly world, which is a reflection,
You don the clothes, of this world,
For lessons to learn, which do unfurl,

Although they hurt, and seem quite real,
T'is just the illusion, that you feel,
So try to discern, what's real to take
And worry not, about the fake,

Look beneath, that which comes,
Is it illusion, or spirit from?
Dance the steps, that you must,
But realize the part, which will turn to dust.

Dreams of wisdom
Life's a struggle, yes indeed,
Don't you worry, or try to please,
Wisdom is gained, from dusk to dawn,
Dreams of wisdom, quite profound,
T'is a game, but you can't hide,
We will chide you, from inside.

Masks of illusion
Masks of illusion, quite profound,
It's a part of life, during each go round,
That which is behind, each personality,
Is invisible, from most to see,

Life is not as real, as you might think,
Helpful corrections, come during sleep,

Let us not, make haste and worry,
The inner lights glow, but do not hurry,
You will finally, learn to depend,
On your inner self, your wisest friend.

Tide of emotion

Consider this, upon your side,
Your emotions, move as does the tide,
Sweeping in, to cause a flurry,
Then out again, without a hurry,
The wrath is great, the storm is high,
And moments later, a clear blue sky.

Trail of tears

Trails of tears, our brother's walk,
Proud once, but now with little talk,
Herded and pushed, along the way,
Little hope and not to say,

Weeping tears, that stained the land,
The hardened fist, of the White man,
Braves did drop, with all hope lost,
Our sacred heritage, was the cost,

Oh Great Spirit, hear our plea,
Can you come, and let us see,
Your great power, we do need,
Your great wise guidance, we will heed,

On we marched, no food to eat,
Along the trail, losing inner heat,
At last our walk, came to an end,
Back to Great Spirit, we now depend.

Guidance from on high

Concentrate, on the task at hand,

As you traverse, across the land,
Paying attention, and taking heed,
To all your neighbors, who are in need,

You'll draw wisdom, from our side,
Bringing down guidance, from up high,
Walk your path daily, and you will see,
The loving help, we provide to thee.

Ask and you will receive

Elementals, are a key,
Learn to command, then let it be,
Direct the wish, in some direction,
They can move, the earthly reflection,

Swift as wind and hard as a rock,
Elements of nature, controlled through thought,
Vibrations of wish, are held in mind,
You can manipulate, most any kind,

But the move, must be to make,
A healing effect, for others sake,
Direct the force and then give thanks,
For the Great Spirit's Guidance, is what it takes.

Spiritual Senses

Words of power, day or night,
Begin the inner, in its flight,
Keying on, the desired goal.
Fulfillment managed, by the soul,

Medicine, to ease the pain,
Words do emanate, from the brain,
The level of action, that you believe,
Is a factor, toward what you achieve.

A special key, you will discover,
Releases force, you do uncover,
Direct your wish, towards its end,
Learn on elementals, to depend.

Set an image, in your mind,
Its accomplished, you will find,
Look to help, those in need,
We will support, and water the seed.

A shining star

The plight of Man, through earthly course,
To find the key, throughout his course,
A shining star, in each there be,
When rightly aligned, its light all see,

Each action taken, has greater force,
As the inner star, makes bright its course,
For all who perceive and allow it to be,
They bask in love, truth and harmony.

The loving home

Rounds of lives, continues to turn,
It is the vehicle, to help us learn,
Birth, death, like a wheel,
Continues to turn, as you search out the real,

Some see death, as a final end,
Others recognize, it's only a bend,
You cross the boundary and leave the earth,
But what you find, is a kind of rebirth,

Some are sad, as a friend departs,
It feels as if, we have a broken heart,
But it is loneliness, that we feel,

We are left alone, with struggles so real,

But eventually, you do see,
That living on earth, is just a key,
To put in practice and to discern,
Those principles in spirit, you have to learn,

And finally now, you might want to know,
Where that loved one, had to go,
Back to beauty, light and love,
Our spiritual birthplace, high above,
It is not a place, or time of pain,
But the loving home, of our Parent's Domain.

The yellow stone

Where did it go,
The land of our home,
Selfish desire,
Greed on fire,

The yellow stone (gold),
Brought them to our home,
There is never enough,
As you gather the stuff,

It excites the mind,
With each nugget you find,
Steal what you can,
Maybe kill the next man,

Look at your life,
Is filled with much strife,
Have you excited a fire,
With a craving desire?

What planted the seed,

That fired your need,
Must have hold,
Of some earthly gold?

Take a good look,
Learn from life's books,
Following the spiritual inside,
Would be a good guide.

The signature of God

The signature of God, is in all you see,
In every life, and object it be
In each act of nature, it does show,
Behind each emotion, it's the awareness that knows,

The sky, the sea, the mountain range,
It is His Hand, that fashions the change,
He creates the time, where you experience lessons,
Learning what is important, spirit or possessions,

Take the middle road, spiritual balance to gain,
From too high or too low, you must refrain,
The Witness watches, from up high,
A part of God, your spirit inside,

You learn your lessons, through your reaction,
No matter what, your physical action,
Learn of God, who fashioned the plan,
Who created the object, that you call Man,

As this earthly schoolroom, runs its course,
You will learn the subtle, from the course,
At times you study, at times you play,
And finally then, Graduation day.

From Mother earth

Buffalo stretched, for many miles,
They clothed and fed us, through many trials,
As they left, our heart was taken,
Our trust in Whites, was also shaken,

For here came people, who didn't care,
They took the buffalo, and didn't share,
From Mother Earth, they took her love,
But gave no thanks, to Spirit above,

And finally they, will come to discuss,
That they took it away, from all of us,
But then the Mother, may not give again,
And them from whom, will they depend?

The three bodies

Your family had, much to see,
Forced to learn, an important key,
These are lessons, used to teach,
Greater precepts, which must be reached,

For in each shell, a greater stirs,
A soul must learn, for growth to occur,
For each in time, will finally see,
The goal is, a spiritual unity,

You blend your three bodies, to function as One,
A balanced Being, you do become,
Manage the spiritual, the gifts you possess,
This will lead you, to greater happiness,

The experiences of emotion, may bring you pain,
Higher awareness, is yours to gain,
Does it matter, the face you project,
Or is it materiality that, you do protect,

Discover yourself, and learn the plan,
Express your true Spirit, when you can,
Love and humor, Is the key,
Then the inner spirit, becomes easier to see,

Your Heavenly Parents, do await,
But do not worry, about being late,
Keep your faith, and allow all to be,
For you are a part, of eternity.

Energy of love

Spinning balls, of light you all be,
Created from God's, loving energy,
Placed on earth, to walk the land,
A greater awareness, is the plan,

Trials occur, to make you see,
More than physical, that you be,
Can you walk, with peace and love,
Living those precepts, learned from above?

Your path may bring you, face to face,
Deeper understanding, of the human race,
Beyond the physical, can you see,
You're a living spirit, of eternity.

Objects of desire

Conquest of self, is an important goal,
It's an aspect of life, to teach the soul,
Continued lessons, during the day,
To learn what is real, and what is play,

Loosen the grip, of things you call matter,
Objects of desire, which can make you grow sadder,
Be conscious of things, which start up your fire,
Then build and increase, into a quenchless desire.

Look to uncover, the light from inside,
The flow of the spirit, which always resides,
This spotlight of wisdom, which God did impart,
Given to you, right from your start.

The song of nature

Sing the song of nature,
Winds and thunder in the band,
The symphony of ocean waves,
Orchestrated by the Creator's Hand,

The gentle mist of dewdrops,
The spray of waves so great,
The mighty power of currents,
The many patterns of snowflakes,

The sky which goes forever,
Dark clouds of a storm so near,
The lightning which brings the message,
The voice of nature sound so clear,

The hills which roll so gently,
The walls of granite which stands so tall,
The peaks that wear the snowy caps,
The canyons where echoes call,

The gifts of Mother Nature,
Provides everything that we need,
So love, respect and keep her safe,
Don't act as just you please.

Create the moment

The song of life, like a record plays,
As each rotates, through their days,
A groove is followed, as the record spins,

Originally recorded, as each begins,

Imagine that you, can replay,
The thoughts or actions, of any day,
Travel forward or backward, without any risk,
You locate the period, then play the disk,

Think of a time, or place to see,
Create the moment, and let it be,
The song remains, as a great imprint,
In the record player, of God's firmament,

Voices, actions, smells and thoughts,
Can all be found, if that is what's sought,
The Masters of Time, will see you through,
Come quite humbly, to seek what is true.

Live in the light
Drifting sands of time release,
Greater awareness and inner peace,
Long for beauty, truth and love,
The greater virtues, learned from above,

Above is not, a place or direction,
But the greater awareness, which is not the reflection,
Rekindle the flame, from an earthly spark,
Live in the light, dispel the dark.

A robe of stars
A robe of stars, adorn the sky,
The twinkle of light, informs the eye,
That greater wisdom, and good prevails,
No matter what, your earthly trails,

Spiritual matter, behind the scenes,
A closer touch, you make in dreams,

The play of life, you dance and sing,
Further enlightenment, you hope it brings,

Tune into the stars, and behold their light,
It brings you guidance, through the darkest night,
Seek for messages and guidance true,
Provided by beings, with greater wisdom than you,

The tides, whirlpools and currents of life,
May guide you to harmony, or bring you much strife,
Look to Nature, to provide a helping hand,
Spirit's guiding signs, appear across the land.

The eternal flame
Become one with the object, you see today,
The barrier of division, will fade away,
Cross your eyes, and do not stare,
Colors of light, will float in the air,

Send the self, to overlay,
Watch the feeling, that we say,
Bodily reactions, you will feel,
There just reactions, but are not real,

Cross the Jordan, on your quest,
Place the mind, in conscious rest,
Higher awareness, is yours to gain,
As you become one, with the Eternal Flame,

From a higher state, the vision clears,
Past or Present, comes quite near,
Actions, dramas, the steps you take,
Higher learning is at stake.

Illumination
Imagination, holds the key,

To transverse the gap, through eternity,
Leap the void, by using thought,
Your tool to travel, is not bought,

Illumination, is just a word,
A goal to reach, which you head toward,
But it is more, a state of mind,
Which you can become, with this key to find,

Go forth in life, come what may,
Use your life, in a spiritual way,
No right or wrong, is in your choice,
Honesty and truth, should be your voice,

Magic comes, to save your day,
The gift of spirit, in all you say,
Align yourself, with speech and action,
You'll be guided, in each reaction.

Glory comes

Many think, that life is a gamble,
No rhyme or reason, you just slide and ramble,
But I do believe, that there is a plan,
For all the people, both woman and man,

For your best, to help those in need,
Follow your spirit, rather than greed,
Yet following the path, at times seem rough,
You seem to struggle, as times get tough,

But glory comes, to those who wait,
As the grace of God, throws open the gate,
Life is good, and the bounty becomes great,
For those who work hard and have the patience to wait.

The music of life

The music of life, the continuing song,

Plays its melody, your whole life long,
Some notes are high and others are low,
But the melody continues, as long as you go,

So pick up the tune and sing with each stride,
Your choice is the movement and your feelings inside,
Lively or slow, it's your choice to make,
Don't rush or be hasty, it's your time to take.

Move in harmony
Don't hurry through life, as if it's a race,
Meet each challenge, with beauty and grace,
There is no winner, at a finish line,
As you come to the end, of your allotted time,

The swan or the cockatoo, to glide or to squawk,
Do you move in harmony, or is bitterness your talk,
It was all in the journey, each step that you made,
Did you plant flowers, or bring others pain?
Glance back at your pathway, look where you've crept
Did you flow in harmony, or were you heavy in step?

Life is a mirror
Your life is a mirror, that you will find,
Shows you the image, you carry in your mind,
A subtle reflection, of each thought that you make,
Your world becomes solid, in each step that you take,

Project out, what you desire, it takes form in your life,
An act of creating, bringing harmony or strife,
Always your choice, a lesson in the Great Plan,
Your Spiritual Parents, provide to each woman and man,

Decisions are made, by each in their way,
You always create, at work or at play,
How do you move, with harmony or strife,

Did you seek your own glories, or assist others in their life,
Each are together, not separate as it might seem,
You will someday awake, from life's slumbering dream.

Simple acts of kindness

Simple acts of kindness, toward your fellow Man,
Move the soul toward greater heights and you will learn the plan,
Bring to each the gift of love, the mystery becomes quite clear,
That all are not so really distant, but come to you so near,
The pull of matter brings us close, to actions that we fear,
But the heavenly bodies that we see, bring love and guidance clear.

Set your course

Listen well, to the voice,
That now must make, a difficult choice,
The teacher in each, guides our hand,
As we move through the shadows, of this land,

In this world, our facets turn near,
They act their parts, to make us clear,
To be a complete soul, in the light,
As we move toward, greater spiritual sight,

Keep yourself, in your upper mode,
Your actions guided, from your higher abode,
Live as an angel, in your choice,
Or follow the earthlings, little voice,

No right or wrong, in any action,
Your soul catalogs, each reaction,
You learn to see, your greater side,
Not the little, earthly pride,

This end of the road, is not what you physically see,
But the choices you made, is an important key,

Lessons give you, a chance to show,
To what aspect, your soul does grow,

Can you see, the soul's shining light,
Through life's choices, the soul can burn bright,
Illusions melt, as you discover,
The greater you, that must be uncovered,

Set your course, with the wind YOU blow,
Don't let others push you, to make you go,
On a course, which they have set,
But follow your inner, toward your quest.

Spiritual essence

Mists of shadows, float in the air,
Moving quite freely, as you pass by them there,
They travel on pathways, chosen from above,
Some looking for happiness, some giving out love,

Crossing each other, and mingling their mists,
Some giving off kisses, others raising their fists,
Meeting together, to learn of the plan,
What are these mists, we call woman and man,

Are we made of solid matter, so hard and so firm,
Or are we just dust, to the earth we return,
Does all just end, when the mist we no longer see,
Or is there more, than we must be.

Can there be more, than this shadow does show,
Can there be more, than to dust we must go,
Can the Creator of stars, the rivers and trees,
Have more in His Mind, for you and for me,

Nothing is lost, our scientists say,
As energy and matter, convert everyday,

And what of the experience, we gather in our head,
Do they turn into dust, when the mists appear dead?
Could it be this I AM, that I know,
Will go onward forever, for many earth shows?

Living water

Rivers flowing, toward the source,
A journey home, upon the course,
A new beginning, a body you see,
A continuation, of your destiny,

Choices in spirit, a definite plan,
The life to be lived, as either woman or man,
Each has lessons, which are to be gained,
The growth of the soul, is what is obtained,

Round after round, your soul does make,
Throughout eternity, your travels take,
So does the river, flow back to the source,
Back to the Creator, more perfected of course.

The source of life

The source of life, the building plan,
The creation of, the earthly Man,
The path of atoms, the planets clear,
Every part, of the earthly sphere,

The force of gravity, the sting of the bee,
All the landscape, your eye can see,
The ocean tide, the mountain range,
The passing of seasons, which constantly change,

The power of laughter, the sting of fear,
The feeling of ecstasy, the vision of the seer,
From when it comes, not by man,
Yet all the workings, of a Master Plan,

Direct your gaze, toward the light that glows,
Deep inside and you'll begin to know.

The stamp of divinity

Those who wish, to see the plan,
Which God ordains, for the mortal Man,
Need to glance, upon the Source,
The Mighty Hand, which sets the course,

Not by mortal, eyes to see,
But deep within, yourself it be,
The finger print, of your creation,
The soul which learns, from each relation,

The stamp, of your divinity,
That part of God, which in you be,
That indestructible, part of self,
Which guides your course, toward spiritual wealth,

Whisper softly, in my ear,
To guide my course, and make it clear,
How I can serve, my fellow man,
And be the best, example I can,

Of the Creator's, work of art,
Of which I have, my place and part,
Let me be guided, through the perils and strife,
To add my strongest thread, to the tapestry of life.

The mighty hand

The Mighty Hand, that moves the sea,
The Creator of the Ideal, of you and me,

The Landscape Artist, of all you see,
The Hand that fashioned, all the trees,

Who keeps the stars, within their path,
Holds the orbits of particles, that spin so fast,
Daily raises the sun, so we have no fear,
Provides all the sustenance, in this earthly sphere,

All is beyond the mortal Man,
Who acts like God, but never can,
Create the things, that last through life,
Man's creations wear down, under earthly strife,

What lasts longer, an object or a thought,
A builder's stone, or what a philosopher taught,
Our earthly hands, which mold in clay,
Create many things, that seem to fade away,

But rising within self, to a precept clear,
Entering into, the Idea Sphere,
We come upon, a state of mind,
That produces a solid, of another kind,
And if inside, we strive further to see,
We will touch the forever objects, of eternity

Spiritual wealth

Service to others, rather than self,
Brings you a bounty, of spiritual wealth,
Giving yourself, to offer a hand,
This you must do, as you cross over the land,

Keep your demeanor, on an even keel,
Though the wind blow contrary, to how you might feel,
The journey is really, the trials that you face,
The goal is not the arrival, at any particular place,

Life is the journey, so keep a good pace,
Don't push or shove, as if in a race,
Keep true your heading, to gain all that you can,
T'is the experience for the soul, that is the plan.

Inner sense

The mind is clear, of drifting thoughts,
As you bring through the spirit, that is sought,
Attune your frequency, to what is taught,
It is not by money, or by favor bought,
Tune your dial, until you feel,
By inner sense, you have reached the Real.

Lessons were taught

Sight unseen, as in a dream,
By intuition, do you glean,
Many facts, to give to Man,
About their future, destiny and plan,

Not to interfere, do we give,
But to help each one, to better live,
Watch your step, Oh earthly man,
Live by spirit, if you can,

While in Spirit, your lessons were taught,
Then for demonstration, to earth you were brought,
Have you learned, your lessons clear,
From Spirit realm, to earthly sphere.

Soar with eagles

Soar with eagles, when you can,
Or suffer with the body of the earthly Man,
Attached to body, of earthly make,
Which by illusion, you do take,
Place yourself, in a state of mind,
You really are, of an angelic kind,

Look away, from that body that you use
Dwell as an angel, if you choose.

Write a new scene
You do act, upon your stage,
With your higher energies, caught in a cage,
The actor works, through each scene,
Moving endlessly, as in a dream,

The drama moves, along its course
Driven onward, by a higher force,
Wisdom gleaned in your acts,
By how you move, and by your choice to react,

But you can write, a new scene that is clear,
Or follow the lines, with apprehension and fear,
The acting coach, which is the soul,
Has spiritual perfection, as its goal.

The imagery, the beauty, the simplicity and even the complexity borne in poetic dreams speak to us of possibilities. Possibilities of more. More of who we have been. More of who we are. More of who we will become. More of what we have experienced. More of what we are experiencing. More of what we will experience.

To see the world (both visible and invisible) through the creativity of poem ignites our mind, enlivens our spirit, and refreshes our soul. The words of poetry open the mind's eye, the spirit's eye, and the soul's eye; seeing divinity in the world, in ourselves and in the cosmos. Allow poetic dreams to wake you, refresh you and inspire you.

"Poetry is ordinary language raised to the Nth power. Poetry is boned with ideas, nerved and blooded with emotions, all held together by the delicate, tough skin of words."

– Paul Engle

End of Part III

Afterword – The call to more

By Steven A. Russ, Ph.D.

About 40 years ago I read an interesting article in a magazine regarding how to utilize your dreams. The article went on to say that if you want to have dreams regarding your favorite subject then spend your day reading books, thinking and talking about your favorite subject and then you will have a wonderful evening of dreams. The topic that was used in the article had to do with skiing. I have no doubt that this would happen and someone could spend evening after evening having dreams on their favorite subject.

I have learned through my experiences and reading on the subject of dreams and dreaming that there is so much more to this channel that we possess. There have been many books written on what the ancient philosophers, teachers and mystics have stated regarding dreams. The temples of Aesculapius were predicated upon patients having dreams regarding their health problems and potential cures. Dream incubations, environments that were established to foster ones connections to the Divine through dreams, were established several thousand years ago.

Perhaps a good analogy of what could happen with your dreams might be surfing the internet. If you desire one specific approach to a situation you might just type in what you imagine to be the answer to your particular query. If I am desiring to find out if substance A will be the best for my project, I will generally receive lots of information regarding the positive or negative effects regarding that substance. If I type in what might be the best substances and materials to use in my project, I will receive a vast amount of additional information regarding what might be beneficial for my project. I will receive many more substances and aspects that I might not have considered.

My point is to be as open as possible yet know that answers, solutions and directions will come. "If you ask for bread, you are not given a stone." I know from experience that the channel of dreams is much more profound then you can imagine. Another example might be that you've grown up with a special friend who has moved away from your area. You would like to remain in contact. You buy a phone so that the two of you can communicate. This is a wonderful tool for the both of you. But, you discover that you can also use that phone to get into contact with other people. I like this analogy because the telephone allows you to get into contact with others who have telephones. Your dreams allow you to come into contact with everyone else on the planet as well as energy patterns in other realities and dimensions. The frequencies available in the dream state are your portal to everywhere. In my dreams I've had dinner with presidents & politicians, kings & other royalty, movie stars, philosophers and my friends, relatives and many other people who I don't know in this lifetime.

In my dreams I've flown in all sizes of planes, rocket ships and other types of flying devices. I've watched myself in actions in places all over the earth as well as what seemed to be other planets or dimensions. Were these activities real? It depends on what we consider real. If reality is an experience then yes these were experiences and they appeared very real to me.

In 1977 while participating in two-man competitive beach volleyball tournaments, I had a profound experience. I had been playing in a weekend tournament in Santa Barbara, California and was gone from my home. When I returned I found five messages on my telephone answering machines. Remember, no cell-phones in those days. A young woman had tried to reach me because she was having emotional difficulties. She was told by someone that I might be able to help her during her depression. As I continued through her messages something stirred within me that someone was reaching out to me and I was not hearing her.

I then heard a voice say to me, "What is more important, your place in the universe or smelly gym socks?" It was definitely outside of me. I voiced within myself, "What am I to do to be of service?" I heard, "By desiring to align yourself with the Deity, by going within yourself and finding your link to the Creator and becoming a servant thereof." In my dreams I received telephone numbers or was told to visit a certain location in order to receive something that was waiting for me. When I called the telephone numbers I heard the same thing. In several recurring dreams I was standing in a line within a library. At the front of the line was a raised podium with a seemingly important man behind the podium address the person who was at the front of the line.

In every dream that I had in that manner, when I reached the front of the line the man would say, "We would now like you to learn about person (X). Always the name given to me was a person I did not recognize and when I read the following morning what I had written during the night, I immediately began research what I could find on the person. My research would include finding out-of-print and rare books concerning the individual and actually traveling to Europe or Asia to the site where the individual lived hundreds or thousands of years previously.

How real is all of this? It is as real as the information, artifacts and rare materials that I found and received upon following the 'leads' I was provided. In some of my dreams I was directed exactly to what store, bookcase and bookshelf to find what I was seeking.

Along with my dreams in which I was seeing or involved with the action, I would hear a commentary given to me regarding the meaning and purpose of the dream I had just had. The procedure would be that I would go to sleep with a large yellow legal sized tablet placed next to me in the bed. I would wake up from a dream, locate the tablet and pencil, place the table straight up and begin writing, all of this without opening my eyes. I taught myself how to write each line beneath the previous line by slowly moving the tablet upwards. I could feel when I was near the bottom of the tablet and I would then turn to the next page. Again, never opening my eyes. When I was completely through writing the dream, I would immediately hear a voice speaking directly to what the dream was about or what philosophical or spiritual principle was important for me to understand at that moment.

I did recognize that there were several different energies that were providing the commentary. I also found that as I heard the commentary, I had the ability to ask questions regarding what I was being told. I would get an immediate response. Sometimes I would go to sleep with several questions on my mind and they would be answered that night through my hearing a voice or some action scene I would be shown.

The most dreams that I actually recorded without opening my eyes was 11 dreams. Interestingly enough I recorded 9 the next evening followed by 7 on the third evening. I would generally average 3 dreams that I would recall and write down.

I had many prophetic dreams where I received information concerning donations coming into the World Research Foundation. These would be exact numbers and I was not given a specific name at the time but only the dollar amount that appeared as a check or donation that was wired. I received notification in this manner of $5,000, $25,000, a million and $3,500,000.

People who know me or hear my stories believe that I have a magical life. They tell me I am blessed, lucky, and so spiritual that I deserve it or whatnot. I do believe that I am blessed but I don't believe that I am unique or lucky. I was told to pay attention to my dreams and they would provide guidance throughout my life. All my future guidance could come as a result of the information. One week after I was told, by a Native American, I had an interesting dream that provided information to me regarding my actions with two individuals from three years previously. This was not a dream that was complimentary to me but a dream that somehow touched me to find out what was involved with the other two individuals. As a result of making the contact and following through with what the dream was showing me...I activated something within myself that changed my life.

I then found I would have four to seven dreams a night, for two months, showing me many aspects about myself, how I interacted with other people and what would be the 'highest and best manner' to conduct myself in various situation that might confront me during my life. After two months I began receiving telephone numbers as well as the library dream of people that I needed to learn about from past history. Was I lucky, no I don't believe that! As Nike says in their commercial, 'Just Do It!' I decided to pay attention to my dreams, learn from my dreams and understand that they are sacred and a portal for me to reach greater awareness and be in contact with Higher Beings that could assist me.

I have learned that we all have so much love, beauty and helpful spiritual beings surrounding us as provided by God. Through the information that has come through to me I have been told repeatedly that all people have access to the Sacred Portal of dreams to be in direct contact with loving entities and receive messages from God.

Shortly after my contact through dreams I received messages that I was a conduit from spirit to help people with their health difficulties, both mental and physical here on earth. As a result of following the loving guidance and direction I received from spiritual messengers, Jesus and God I have been a party to numerous healings around the world. I know that I would not have undertaken the healing work and I would not have had this ability on my own, without Gifts from the Spirits.

I thank you for taking your time to read about my experiences and I want you to understand that my journey is meant to inspire you to make the commitment to have a better understanding and experience regarding your own Sacred Sleep and dreams. Somehow we have lost the proper reverence that the ancient people held for the mechanism of dreaming. Dream temples and special incubation procedures were established so that individuals would have their direct contact with God. Without causing too much controversy I believe that as people became more dependent upon individuals who claimed that they were the only emissaries and interpreters of sacred writings, individuals gave up their understanding that they could talk with God directly.

In my more than forty years of working with my own personal dreams and hearing experiences of other people sharing their experiences with their dreams I 've come to the conclusion that people would have had more profound waking-time experiences if they had trusted the information that came through in their own personal dreams. There is no question that so many people that I've met had prophetic dreams as well as dreams that would have provided them wonderful and sound guidance if they had followed through with the 'contact' that they had received. The majority of the individuals shared that they just couldn't believe that what they received was possible. This is where the trust issue comes into play. People have a hard time believing that they have this conduit, to higher awareness coming directly through their own self. It seems that the majority of people have fallen into the belief system that someone else is wiser, smarter, more in-tune then they themselves.

So, my message is two-fold. First, that you already have in your possession the capability that places you in contact with everything and everyone that you need to have a happier, more productive life filled with more laughter, excitement, fun and love. Secondly, we are not alone in this journey on earth. Even though many people have partners and friends in life, at times they still feel alone. We are surrounded by loving spiritual entities that are always with us in every moment and every experience that we have here on earth. I know that they are always supporting us with love and guidance. In our journey it is our choice what we choose to accept from this higher guidance.

We receive more support when we open ourselves up and explicitly ask for more guidance. The love from those spirits that surround us is always present and never leaves us. We shut ourselves off from the love and beauty coming from the higher realms as we become short-sighted, egotistical, greedy and self-centered. The activity of the higher beings that surround us is to constantly send positive and loving energy to us. They reinforce our positive moves with their positive loving energy and they still are sending positive and loving energy when we are engaging in activities that are not so positive and this is when we do have an inkling that perhaps there is a way of looking at a situation in a more positive manner. This is where we have our choice.

May your journey be surrounded with laughter, excitement, fund and love and may the highest and best manifest for you in your life.

End Notes

---

[i] Deborah King describes this as "the doorway between your immortal soul and your earth-bound personality… Opening your 8th chakra and stepping through the veil that separates your earthly self from your eternal soul will open your eyes to the vast space beyond physical plane boundaries." From: https://deborahking.com/5-things-you-need-to-know-about-your-8th-chakra/, accessed March 19, 2018.

[ii] Current neurological research has shown the different centers of language processing within the brain. See: *Say What? How the Brain Separates Our Ability to Talk and Write,* John Hopkins University http://releases.jhu.edu/2015/05/05/say-what-how-the-brain-separates-our-ability-to-talk-and-write/ Accessed April 7, 2018.

[iii] See: *Do Dreams Give Voice to the Divine* by Amira Mittermaier, https://www.sapiens.org/culture/dream-interpretation-islam/. Accessed April 1, 2018.

[iv] 1 Kings 3:2-12

[v] Robert Louis Stevenson, *Across the Plains,* (1982) Chapter 8.

[vi] Olu Jenzen, (Editor), Sally R. Munt. (Editor). *The Ashgate Research Companion to Paranormal Cultures (1st Edition).* (London: Routledge, 2016), 330.

[vii] Willis Harman and Howard Rheingold, *Higher Creativity, Liberating the Unconscious for Breakthrough Insights* (Los Angles; J.P. Tarcher, Inc., 1984), 46.

[viii] Alexander Gilchrist, *Life of William Blake: With Selections from His Poems and Other Writings, Volume 2,* (Macmillan and Company, 1880), 185.

[ix] Steven Glazer, *The Heart of Learning: Spirituality in Education,* (Jeremy P. Tarcher/Putnam, 1999), 73.

[x] Jane Piirto, *Creativity for 21st Century Skills,* (Springer Science & Business Media, Oct 23, 2011), 54.

[xi] Op. cit., *Higher Creativity,* 45-47.

[xii] See: https://www.famousscientists.org/dmitri-mendeleev/, accessed April 21, 2018.

xiii Scott E. Page, *The Difference, How the Power of Diversity Creates Better Groups, Firms*, *Schools, and Societies* (Princeton University Press, 2007), 411

xiv Sirach 1:4-10, *New American Bible, revised edition* © 2010, 1991, 1986, 1970 Confraternity of Christian Doctrine, Washington, D.C.

xv Sir. 14:20-21.

xvi This Photo by Unknown Author is licensed under CC BY-NC-ND

xvii Perichoresis is a Greek term (περιχώρησις) used to describe the triune relationship between each person of the Godhead. It can be defined as co-indwelling, co-inhering, and mutual interpenetration. Alister McGrath writes that it "allows the individuality of the persons to be maintained, while insisting that each person shares in the life of the other two. An image often used to express this idea is that of a 'community of being,' in which each person, while maintaining its distinctive identity, penetrates the others and is penetrated by them." From: https://www.theopedia.com/Perichoresis, accessed May 5, 2018.

xviii Charles Mortimer Carty, *Padre Pio, The Stigmatist*, Tan Books, 1994, pg. 69.

xix See: Yale Center for Faith & Culture, *Joy, Human Nature, and Human Destiny*, https://faith.yale.edu/joy/human-nature, accessed June 3, 2018.

xx *The Hidden Power of Kindness*, p.6, Cf. Frederick William Faber, Spiritual Conferences (Baltimore: John Murphy Company, 1859

xxi 1 Kings 19:11-13.

xxii De Divinatione I, Cicero, Loeb Classical Library, 1923 (public domain).

xxiii A Dictionary of Greek and Roman Antiquities, p.415-418, William Smith, D.C.L., LL.D, John Murray, London, 1875. See also: http://penelope.uchicago.edu/Thayer/E/Roman/Texts/secondary/SMIGRA*/Divi natio.html, accessed July 2, 2018.

xxiv Allopathic medical care is the treatment of disease by practice considered to be of "conventional means". This would include, drug therapy in which the prescribed drugs would have opposite effects to the symptoms. Allopathy is often contrasted with homeopathy.

Printed in Great Britain
by Amazon